Mark Obmascik has been a journalist for two decades, most recently at the *Denver Post*, where he was the lead writer for the newspaper's Pulitzer Prize in 2000 and winner of the National Press Club Award for environmental journalism in 2003. His freelance stories have been published in *Outside* and other magazines, and he has aired numerous political stories on public affairs and television news programmes. An obsessed birdwatcher himself, he lives in Denver with his wife and sons.

www.transworldbooks.co.uk

Praise for *The Big Year*:

'Can birding be an extreme sport? You bet it can'
Sunday Times

'Here, at last, is a book that reveals in hard-bitten language just how satisfying the hunt for a lesser spotted whatever can be . . . promises to tell you as much about the men doing it as it does about their objectives, and Obmascik delivers . . . in following his birders you enter an obsessive world where spotting a Black Rosy-Finch at 10,947ft above sea level is akin to finding Liv Tyler in your sleeping bag. Clearly a trip worth taking'
Jack magazine

'The marvel is that he [Obmascik] succeeds in recruiting the reader in the great race to spot a record number of birds, so that by the end of this adrenaline-rush of a book we are willing the three protagonists to climb one last peak or to scout one last icy island in search of an elusive migrant. This is not a book about bird-watching. It is about record-breaking and human endeavour, about an obsession almost as mad as it is magnificent'
Yorkshire Post

'Birders are the Don Giovannis of natural history. Their heads are turned by the merest flicker of coloured plumage . . . Obmascik tells a very American story, grounded in a very human, or possibly very male, obsession. He tells it vividly and with humour'
Sunday Herald

'Think twitcher, think anorak. Well, think again. Mark Obmascik's story of ornithological obsession is an exciting road trip of a story . . . this sense of thrilling liberation, forays into uncharted territories and an understanding of what drives these men is as much part of the story as the quest itself. "In pursuit" is where the characters feel most alive and free. I think I've found a new hobby'
The List

'There are few funnier things to read about than the exploits of the true obsessive. If you don't believe me, take a look at Mark Obmascik's frequently hilarious account . . . endlessly entertaining'
Yorkshire Evening Post

The
Big Year

*A Tale of Man, Nature,
and Fowl Obsession*

MARK OBMASCIK

BANTAM BOOKS

LONDON • TORONTO • SYDNEY • AUCKLAND • JOHANNESBURG

TRANSWORLD PUBLISHERS
61–63 Uxbridge Road, London W5 5SA
A Random House Group Company
www.transworldbooks.co.uk

THE BIG YEAR
A BANTAM BOOK: 9780857500694

First published in Great Britain
in 2004 by Doubleday
an imprint of Transworld Publishers
Bantam edition published 2005
Bantam edition reissued 2011

Addresses for Random House Group Ltd companies outside the UK
can be found at: www.randomhouse.co.uk
The Random House Group Ltd Reg. No. 954009

The Random House Group Limited supports the Forest Stewardship Council
(FSC®), the leading international forest-certification organization. Our books
carrying the FSC label are printed on FSC®-certified paper. FSC is the only forest-
certification scheme endorsed by the leading environmental organizations,
including Greenpeace. Our paper-procurement policy can be found at
www.randomhouse.co.uk/environment.

Typeset in 10.5/13.5pt Goudy by Falcon Oast Graphic Art Ltd.
Printed in the UK by CPI Group (UK) Ltd, Croydon, CR0 4YY.

2 4 6 8 10 9 7 5 3 1

To Merrill

CONTENTS

The first time I met a real birder, I couldn't tell a tit from a tattler.

I was a cub newspaper reporter, stuck on the graveyard shift and scrambling for some way, any way, to get off. If I wasn't chasing some awful car accident, I was hustling to find the relatives of a homeless man slashed in a railyard knife fight. Nobody was happy.

Then one night, an anonymous call came in to the *Denver Post* newsroom.

There's a man right here in Colorado, the caller told me, who is one of the world's foremost experts on birds. He's a law professor and he's old, and you should write something about him before he dies. His name is Thompson Marsh.

A chance to work among the living? I grabbed it. I called Professor Marsh the next day.

Professor Marsh, however, never called back. This really bugged me. In my line of work, even grieving widows returned phone messages. Surely a man who was one of the best in his field would want to talk, even if his field was a bit goofy. I decided to chase the story.

Slowly, from some of his friends, a picture emerged: Thompson Marsh was a birdwatcher possessed. To chase rare birds, he would rise before dawn on weekends. He would take expensive vacations on desolate Alaskan isles and pray for foul weather. He would wait for phone calls in the middle of the night, then rush to the airport for the next red-eye flight. Only five others in history had seen more species of birds in North America.

He managed to do all this while becoming a lawyer so sharp, so demanding, that many of his former students still felt intimidated by him. When Thompson Marsh was hired by the University of Denver in 1927, he was the nation's youngest law professor. Now he was eighty-two and the nation's oldest, having worked the same job for fifty-eight years. Some days he still walked the four miles from his home to class. A few years back, he conquered all fifty-four of Colorado's 14,000-foot mountains.

But the old coot wouldn't pick up a phone to call me.

To hell with him, I decided—until his wife unexpectedly called and arranged a meeting at their home.

I rang the doorbell on time, and his wife sat me down on the couch and poured tea. Behind her, in a room facing the garden, I spotted a tall, thin man with a shock of silver hair—the bird-man himself.

I stood and offered a handshake, but it wasn't accepted. The master legal orator looked down at the floor and said nothing.

His wife apologetically explained there would be no interview.

"He is a bit embarrassed by it all," Susan Marsh told me. "For some reason, he thinks it's a little silly. Why, I don't know."

Actually, she did know. The professor was a proud man who had been thinking about his newspaper obituary, and he didn't want to do anything now to change the story. Or, as his wife eventually confided, "He wants to be known as an attorney, not a birder."

Thompson Marsh, browbeater of future judges, was struck mute by a bird.

I returned to my newsroom and wrote a general story about the quirky world of competitive birdwatching and then moved on to covering murders and politicians and other typically depressing newspaper subjects. But my memory of that famed law professor, fidgeting horribly before a twenty-three-year-old reporter, still nagged me. What was it about birdwatching that gave a man such joy and discomfort?

I couldn't let the question go. Over the years I learned more about birds and their lovers, and I wrote the strange stories with glee. There was a Baikal teal that caused an international stir by wandering from its native lake in Siberia to a creek behind a Baskin-Robbins ice cream shop outside Denver. There was a biologist who implanted microchips in geese so he could track the spring migration from New Mexico to the Arctic by computer from the comfort of his home. There even were twitters about a new species of grouse—North America's first new bird species in a century!—having sex in the sagebrush somewhere in the Utah high country.

Slowly but certainly I realized I wasn't just pursuing stories about birdwatchers. I was pursuing the birds, too. Marsh's obsession was becoming mine. My relentless pursuit of a rare sub-species of law professor had tapped a trait repressed deep in my character.

I needed to see and conquer.

This is not a unique craving. In the course of civilization, others have responded to that same fundamental urge by sailing uncharted oceans, climbing tall mountains, or walking on the moon.

Me, I watch birds.

Today I stroll in the park and I no longer see plain birds. I see gadwalls and buffleheads and, if I'm really on a hot streak, a single old squaw. A road trip finds me watching the sky as much as the pavement. It gets harder to pass a sewage treatment pond, that notorious bird magnet, without pulling out my binoculars. When somebody cries, "Duck!" I look up.

No longer is it accurate to call me a birdwatcher, a term the pros use to dismiss the spinsters and retired British army colonels who wait passively for birds to come to them. I have become an enthusiast, a chaser—a birder.

If Thompson Marsh were still alive—he died in 1992, at the age of eighty-nine, from injuries in a car accident on a birding trip—he might even talk to me. He was, after all, my first truly tough bird.

Today I can say without hesitation that there are seven kinds of tits (Siberian, bridled, bush, juniper, oak, tufted, and wren) and two tattlers (gray-tailed and wandering), but I can't say this knowledge impresses anyone, certainly not my wife.

Why this happened to me, I can't easily explain. It's never been very manly to talk about feelings, especially when these feelings involve birds. But put me on a mountain stream with our two sons and give us a glimpse, a fleeting glimpse, of a bald eagle, and it's hard to tell who's more excited—the four-, seven- or forty-year-old. I watch a hummingbird dive-bomb a feeder outside our kitchen window and marvel at its grace and energy; I pull out a birding field guide and learn that this finger-sized creature probably sipped tropical blossoms a few weeks ago in Guatemala, and I'm awed by the miracle of migration. On the prowl through the pines in the middle of the night, I hoot a few times through my cupped hands and wait. From the trees above, I detect wingbeats, then a returned hoot. It's an owl! Move over, Dr. Dolittle. I'm talking to the animals.

Birding is one of the few activities you can do from the window of a Manhattan skyscraper or the tent flap of an Alaskan bush camp; its easy availability may explain why it can become so consuming. There are one-of-a-kind birds living on the streets of St. Louis, below a dam in Texas, and amid the suburban sprawl of Southern California. One of the earth's greatest avian populations—with 3 million birds passing through each day during spring migration—is in New Jersey, just off the Garden State Parkway.

Birding is hunting without killing, preying without punishing, and collecting without clogging your home. Take a field guide into the woods and you're more than a hiker. You're a detective on a backcountry beat, tracking the latest suspect from Mexico, Antarctica, or even the Bronx. Spend enough time sloshing through swamps or scaling summits or shuffling through beach sand and you inevitably face a tough question: Am I a grown-up birder or just another kid on a treasure hunt?

During certain periods of our lives, the world believes it's perfectly acceptable to collect rocks or seashells or baseball cards.

The truth is that everyone has obsessions.

Most people manage them.

Birders, however, indulge them.

By the time you find yourself compiling lists and downloading software to manage, massage, and count birds, you—well, I—have become a hopeless addict.

As I spend another winter night by the fire, fingering David Sibley's 545-page birding guide and trying to memorize the field marks of thirty-five separate North American sparrow species, I'm jarred from self-absorption to self-doubt: Am I weird? Am I crazy? Am I becoming Thompson Marsh?

There is, I decide, only one way to fully understand my condition. If birding is an obsession that takes root in a wild crag of the soul, I need to learn how strong it can grow. I need to study the most obsessed of the obsessed.

I need to meet the birders of the Big Year.

The Big Year

The Big Year

ONE

January 1, 1998

SANDY KOMITO

Sandy Komito was ready. It was an hour before sunrise, New
Year's Day, and he sat alone at an all-night Denny's in
Nogales, Arizona. He ordered ham and eggs. He stared into
the black outside the window.

At this stage in his life, he knew men who lusted for a new
wife or a Porsche or even a yacht. Komito had no interest.

What he wanted was birds.

For the coming year he would dedicate himself to a singular
goal—spotting more species of birds in North America than
any human in history. He knew it wouldn't be easy. He
expected to be away from home 270 of the next 365 days
chasing winged creatures around the continent. There were
ptarmigans to trail on the frozen spine of the Continental
Divide in Colorado and hummingbirds to hunt in the heat of
the Arizona desert. He would prowl the moonlight for owls in
the North Woods of Minnesota and wade the beaches of
South Florida at dawn for boobies. He planned to race after
birds by boat in Nova Scotia, by bicycle in the Aleutian
Islands, and by helicopter in Nevada. Sleep was not a priority,
but when it came, he would be tossing in the army bunks of

Alaska and turning on the rolling waves of the Dry Tortugas.

This was, after all, a competition, and Komito wanted to win.

He ordered his second thermos of coffee and spread paper-work across his place mat. One sheet was an Internet printout of a North American rare-bird alert from Houston. The other was a regional alert from Tucson. Komito smiled. There were more rare birds spotted last week in southeastern Arizona than anywhere else on the continent.

His gut told him that this chain restaurant was the right place to start. He'd eaten in so many Denny's over the years that he didn't have to waste time with a menu. Besides, other birders reported that the trees around this Denny's were roosts for the great-tailed grackle and black vulture. Either of these fine local birds, Komito decided, would be a wonderful launch for his year.

From his window Komito watched the horizon lighten with the gray promise of dawn. Little moved.

Across from the restaurant, though, a freight train suddenly rammed through the quiet. All the ruckus made something take wing outside and land just beyond his window.

Komito's heart raced: it was his first bird of the competition!

He lurched forward for the identification.

Plump . . . gray . . . head bobbing.

"It's a damn pigeon," he muttered.

Every year on January 1, hundreds of people abandon their day-to-day lives to join one of the world's quirkiest contests. Their goal: spotting the most species of birds in a single year. Most contestants limit themselves to the birds of their home county. Others chase birds only within the borders of their home state. But the grandest birding competition of them all, the most grueling, the most expensive, and occasionally the most vicious, sprawls over an entire continent.

It is called the Big Year.

In a Big Year, there are few rules and no referees. Birders just fly, drive, or boat anytime, anywhere in the continental United States and Canada, to chase a rumor of a rare species. Sometimes birders manage to photograph their prey, but usually they just jot down sightings in notebooks and hope other competitors believe them. At the end of the year, contestants forward their self-reported species totals to the American Birding Association, which publishes the results in a magazine-sized document that generates more gossip than an eighth-grade locker room.

In a good year the contest offers passion and deceit, fear and courage, a fundamental craving to see and conquer mixed with an unstoppable yearning for victory.

In a bad year the contest costs a lot of money and leaves people raw.

This is the story of the greatest—or maybe the worst—birding competition of all time, the 1998 North American Big Year.

Nutting's flycatcher is a small, plain, grayish brown bird, native to Central Mexico. Its cry is distinct. It says, "Wheek." The last time this rarity was confirmed in the wilds north of the border, Harry Truman was president and Jackie Robinson was slugging his first home run in an All-Star game. But in mid-December 1997, a birder hiking along an irrigation reservoir near Nogales, Arizona, saw the flycatcher and reported it to the local Maricopa Audubon chapter in Phoenix.

Maricopa Audubon flagged the news on the Internet; the Tucson Rare Bird Alert posted a message on its twenty-four-hour phone number; the North American Rare Bird Alert in Houston started phoning people on its High Alert subscriber list.

From 2,400 miles away, at his home in Fair Lawn, New Jersey, Sandy Komito answered the call. It was the sighting of the Nutting's flycatcher, above all other birds, that had convinced him to begin his Big Year in Nogales.

He left Denny's and drove through the hills of prickly pear and mesquite until reaching the gates of Patagonia Lake State Park.

A ranger greeted him.

"Five dollars, please," she told Komito.

Komito had already spent hundreds of dollars on airline tickets, car rental, and motel room just to be here. But he had worked years as a New Jersey industrial contractor and he knew how to get things done. So he put a little sweetening in a deep voice that, back home, could startle work crews on the far end of a factory rooftop.

"Oh, I'm just a birder," Komito told the ranger. "I'm here to look for one bird. I'll only be here ten minutes. Do I really have to pay five dollars?" he asked, trying to take advantage of the park's unofficial policy of free entry for people who drive through and stay less than fifteen minutes.

The ranger stared him down. His bargaining routine hardly ever worked, but he still made a game of it.

From the Web, Komito had downloaded precise instructions on how to find the bird: "Turn right at the bottom of the hill and go through the campground. Where the loop turns around, there is a trailhead and about four parking spaces. Park here and walk in about one-third of a mile. On the left is the lake and willows; the bird is usually on the right in mesquite."

Komito found the parking area and felt suddenly, uncharacteristically nervous. His car, for one thing, was all wrong. For years, he had rented a Lincoln Town Car on all out-of-state expeditions. This helped pigeonhole his reputation among birders as the loud wisecracker from New Jersey who barreled around in a giant land barge. For this Big Year, though, Komito had converted to midsize rentals. His thinking was simple: to stretch his travel budget, he would spend money on miles, not comfort, and a less prestigious car was cheaper than a Lincoln. Still, birding was all about classifying creatures—long-eared owls always had long ears, and short-eared owls always had short ears—and now he was abruptly changing his own personal field mark. Was the birding world ready for Sandy Komito, Ford Taurus man?

There was another complication. All four parking spaces were filled; more cars perched along the narrow shoulder of the park road. The other vehicles had telltale stickers: Sacramento Audubon, Tucson Audubon. Komito wondered: Am I late? I hope I'm not too late.

The trail wasn't exactly a trail. It looked more like a hard-packed cattle run—and smelled like it, too. Meadowlarks darted through the brush, but Komito ignored them. He had only one bird on his mind.

Three hundred yards up the path, two men were criss-crossing the mesquite. They looked as if they were searching for something—a lost hat, maybe, or even a flower or a butterfly. Komito guessed otherwise.

"Have you seen the bird?" he called to them.

"No," one replied.

Komito loved it. In the brambles of the Arizona desert, he had found complete strangers who understood, and spoke, his intentionally vague language.

Though Big Years were intensely competitive, Komito preferred to join a gaggle chasing rare species. Sure, working in a
crowd meant that many people would identify and list the
same bird. But to Komito, all these other people were more
than just birders. They were witnesses. Top birders have
closely watched each other for years, and many suspected
some of fraud. In fact, the nastiest, most personal fights in the
history of North American birding had come over disputed
sightings.

Komito had no time during a Big Year to slog through one
of those quagmires, but he did expect at some point to come
face-to-face with questionable characters. In a contest built
on trust, credibility was like virginity—it could be lost only
once. Komito wanted more than a Big Year record. He wanted
a Big Year record that was bulletproof.

Up the trail, other birders worked the scrub. Komito
recognized two.

Dr. Michael Austin was a general practitioner who had
moved a few years ago from his native Ontario to South Texas
to get easier shots at hard birds. His strategy had worked: now
he had seen more species than all but fifteen birders on the
continent. While Komito was watching the sun rise over
breakfast at Denny's, Austin was already out in the field,
searching for the flycatcher.

The other birding acquaintance coursing the brush was Dr.
Craig Roberts, an emergency-room physician from Tillamook,
Oregon. Roberts was an intense man who, in the birding
version of machismo, told others how he had spent hours
memorizing tapes of birdsongs and chip notes. When Komito
told jokes, Roberts rolled his eyes.

Behind a bush Komito saw one member of the search party
pointing a Plexiglas dish; the contraption was supposed to
amplify faraway birdcalls. So far, no luck. Komito tilted back

his head to scan the high mesquite branches. His neck was so accustomed to this exercise that it had bulged in size from fourteen and a half inches to seventeen inches. Among birders, this peculiar condition was known as warbler neck— spending too much time looking up at treetops for darting songbirds.

Suddenly somebody hollered, "I've got the bird!"

Komito ran. His binoculars slapped his chest. What if the bird flew off? His cross-continent hunt closed to its last hundred yards. His stomach knotted. He ran harder.

Bird still there?

Slow down!

Now he was close. The last thing he wanted was to scare it off. Gasping, sweating, heart pounding, he edged ahead on tiptoes.

Twenty feet in front of Komito was Craig Roberts. Twenty feet in front of Roberts was a drab bird perching and darting among the thicket. Komito quickly positioned himself with the sun at his back and raised his binoculars. He knew Roberts, a gifted scout of obscure species, was unlikely to misidentify the bird. Still, the Nutting's flycatcher did look strikingly similar to the ash-throated flycatcher, a far more common bird. Like a cop homing in on a stakeout suspect, Komito hurriedly searched for the distinguishing characteristics—a browner face, rounder head, shorter bill, yellower belly.

Then the bird sang.

"Wheek."

That call clinched it. Komito grabbed the Nikon from his backpack and rattled off a dozen shots on slide film.

The bird was his, with witnesses and photographic proof. He pulled out a palm-size notebook and wrote: *Nutting's. 1/1/98. Patagonia, Arizona.*

He wanted to whoop with joy, but that might scare the bird.

His intensity melted. He stepped back and marveled at the scene around him.

A throbbing, twitching pulse of thirty people had emerged from the mesquite with a collection of the world's finest optics—Leica, Zeiss, Swarovski, and Kowa—and encircled the flycatcher. Cameras cascaded with clicks and flashes and whirs. This bird had paparazzi.

The irony was hard to resist. In Nogales, the INS had assigned one thousand Border Patrol agents to keep Mexicans out of the United States. But put wings on a lone migrant no larger than a Lonsdale cigar and dozens of people across America formed a pilgrimage to greet it.

Many birders remained with the flycatcher, savoring their glimpses of such a rarity and swapping stories with old friends. Though these postdiscovery klatches were one of the main reasons why Komito loved birding, he glanced at his watch.

Even on the first morning of the first day of his Big Year, Sandy Komito knew time was slipping away. He hustled back to his Ford Taurus.

AL LEVANTIN

Al Levantin had waited forty years for this day. When he toiled in the lab, mixing the chemicals that won two patents for the company, he waited. When he flew one hundred thousand miles a year to sell products for the company, he waited. When he moved his family overseas for seven years to run the European division for the company, he waited. He waited during the weeks when he worked sixty hours, and he waited during the weeks he worked eighty. He waited for his two baby boys to grow into men, and he waited for his wife to become a grandmother.

Now the waiting was over.

He had set his alarm for 6 A.M., but he already lay awake. He looked out the bedroom window. Though the moon was barely a sliver, it was bright enough to reveal the outline, just beyond his aspen stand, of Snowmass ski mountain. He didn't want to wake his wife, so he didn't turn on the bedroom light. It was dark, but he knew where he was going.

Today he would set out on his quest to break the North American birdwatching record.

From his closet he grabbed a sweater and headed for the kitchen. Levantin lived in a spectacular home. Built on seven timbered acres along a ridge of the Elk Mountains near Aspen, the house was one of those architectural marvels that appeared to ramble across several county lines while still feeling all warm and intimate on the inside. The hallway and dining-room floors were made of brown flagstone, with hot-water pipes beneath to keep naked toes cozy even in the depths of a Colorado winter. You couldn't move anywhere in this house—the stairway, a hallway, an office area—without passing some vast window with some breathtaking view. Ceilings were high and vaulted, with husky wood beams, and a fireplace gaped large enough to swallow unsplit logs. Levantin walked into his kitchen—floor of cherry planks, Sub-Zero that could ice a Volkswagen—and fired up the coffeemaker. It had taken eighteen months to build this place, six more than planned, but the results were worth it. Sometimes there were perks for waiting.

He picked up his Leica binoculars and Kowa scope and followed the covered outdoor passageway to the garage. No fresh snow last night. From an elevation of nine thousand feet, stars seemed to spill everywhere.

The gate at the end of the road opened automatically when his Audi approached. He goosed the gas. He wanted to be in a certain spot before the sun edged over the Continental Divide.

Levantin had Highway 82 all to himself. Most people in the Roaring Fork Valley did not rise before dawn. Some didn't sleep before dawn. They came here for Aspen, eight miles up the road, where Marla told Ivana that Donald was hers and Kennedys tossed footballs on the slopes and Goldie and Kurt and Don and Melanie and Barbi and Arnold and Jack all pranced for the cameras. Last night, Levantin had been at a small dinner party, with Ethel, his wife of thirty-eight years. At 10 P.M., mountain standard time, they turned on the TV to watch the New Year arrive at Times Square in New York. They were home in bed by 11 P.M.

Where the highway curved, his headlights strayed beyond the road onto the river below. Steam rose. There were other places in North America—the Rio Grande Valley of Texas, the mountains of southeast Arizona, Cape May of New Jersey—where birders were so thick that a flycatcher could barely lift a wing without having its every movement broadcast around the world on the Internet. But Aspen was uncharted territory for a birder. Levantin liked it that way. A self-made man in business, he was determined to be a self-made man in birding. That meant a Big Year on his own terms. Others started a Big Year in some big birding hot spot; Levantin insisted on being with his wife for New Year's. Others hired guides to ease the discovery of rare birds; Levantin wanted to find everything himself. Others depended on the advice of veterans; Levantin relied on his own wits. What was the point of going for a personal record if everyone else was going along, too?

Finally the black of night washed into gray. For the first

time he could see beyond his headlights, the red of the river walls, the snow on the box elder branches. Then he saw: not all that white on the tree was snow. He slowed his Audi and raised his Leicas.

A bald eagle! Levantin beamed. It wasn't exactly a rarity, and there definitely were other birders, the grizzled types, who would shrug off this bird as a commoner, but Levantin was not so world-weary. A bald eagle on a tree above the Roaring Fork River in the snow on New Year's Day—that was magnificent.

Gray gloom in the valley gave way to yellow warmth, and birds moved into the light. It was the magic hour: an American dipper in a river eddy, an evening grosbeak atop a willow, a red-tailed hawk spiraling a thermal—nature was rising. Black-billed magpie. Black-capped chickadee. Dark-eyed junco. Levantin was making his list—birds spotted today wouldn't have to be spotted again for the rest of the year—but he could hardly keep up. American coot, American goldfinch, American kestrel. He looked down to scrawl the names in his notebook. He looked up and saw a merlin, diving, and he wrote that, too. Out flitted a northern flicker. The birds came faster than his fingers could move.

He stopped.

He heard no phones. He wore no tie. He took no meeting.

From the soul of a company man, forty years of repressed obsession was simmering into the dawn mist of the Roaring Fork River.

Al Levantin was free.

In the area around Aspen, there were two kinds of life—up-valley and down-valley. Up-valley was home of the resorts, Snowmass, Ajax, Highlands, and Buttermilk, where the skiing was rivaled only by the shopping, and the air-kisses by day became tabloid headlines at night. They used to say that tourism was king here, but locals knew better. Real estate ruled. In Aspen, the average home cost $3 million, and nearly one of ten city residents had a license to sell it. Real estate offices were so abundant that boutique owners complained they were killing downtown's street ambience; the city council debated whether to slap a quota on the number of brokerages permitted on Main Street. City lots were so expensive that people paid $4 million to buy a house, tear it down, and build a new one in its place.

Of course, few Aspenites had calloused hands from any actual tearing down or building. Those people, the worker bees, were down-valley. In El Jebel, Mexican families lived in shifts in $1,200-a-month trailers; one year of demolition work in Aspen earned them enough to buy their own house south of the border. The store managers and chefs lived in Blue Lake, where three-bedroom, two-bathroom tract homes cost $400,000. The $260,000 town houses at the Ranch at Roaring Fork were filled with framers, electricians, and tilers. Auto mechanics, however, remained a problem. Once a week a garage had to fly in mechanics 160 miles from Denver just to work on Range Rovers.

Up-valley and down-valley were linked by four lanes of Highway 82. This worried Levantin. In a few minutes, the maids, busboys, and dishwashers from down-valley would start funneling onto Highway 82 for the bumper-to-bumper grind to their up-valley jobs. The Roaring Fork rush hour could be so nasty that the Colorado State Patrol installed roadside signs with a simple message—Road Rage: *CSP— that was punched in repeatedly by frustrated commuters. Levantin didn't want to be caught in that mess. So he quickly scoped Blue Lake for ducks and cruised the Missouri Heights for hawks and jays in the piñon and juniper.

He tallied thirty-two species before turning back up-valley.

Just outside the El Jebowl bowling lanes— "The Most Fun You Can Have With Your Shoes On," where a vacationing Diana once picked up spares with Harry and William—traffic congealed. This meant Levantin had to pay more attention to cars than birds. By the time he finally reached Woody Creek, Levantin felt his watch ticking against him. His twenty-five-mile return up-valley seemed to take forever. He knew the best part of his day was supposed to come next, but he hadn't counted on racing the clock to enjoy it.

It was 10:30 A.M. Levantin hustled home and buckled a stiff plastic ski boot onto his left foot while keeping a shoe on his right. This was an old trick. He used his shoe to brake and accelerate his car up the twists and turns of Snowmelt Drive— the whole road was heated with underground coils to ward off icy spots—and parked at the base of the ski mountain. Now he had to squeeze into only one ski boot; doing half the job in the comfort of his house had saved him five minutes of awkward foot-stomping in the parking lot.

At the base of the Fanny Hill lift, the wild life of Snowmass, two-legged variety, strutted in full display. There were Spyder suits on lady-killers and goose down over chicken hearts, with even a few mink and ermine on the side. Though loud colors were the fashion statement this season, Levantin wore plain black pants and a dull blue coat. He sported one unique accessory around his neck—binoculars.

Al Levantin usually bubbled with a Boy Scout's enthusiasm, but skis made him more excited. He did not like to ride ski lifts alone. He loved stories, both telling them and hearing them, and a ride up the mountain with a stranger was a great way to indulge one of his favorite treats. He enjoyed meeting new people so much that, after making vice president of an $8-billion company, he still volunteered to work as a greeter at the base of the ski mountain. He teased. He started conversations with young women by saying, "I'm an old man. I can't flirt." He was sixty-six years old, but often accused of lying about his age. With an outdoorsy pink in his cheeks, slate-blue eyes, and shoulders that still packed some muscle, he looked fifty. He acted thirty. He had charisma.

Skiing and birding were the two things Levantin loved most about Colorado. That's why, when he'd mapped out this day months ago, he'd decided to become the first birder in history to launch a Big Year from skis. To hell with how everyone else said a Big Year should be done. He was having fun.

Halfway up the mountain, as skiers glided off the Fanny Hill lift, ski area greeters passed out free cookies. Levantin took one and waited. He had a plan. Sure enough, something moved in the aspens. A Clark's nutcracker, gray body with distinctive black wings, swooped down into the snow to scoop up cookie crumbs. Levantin smiled. Unless you knew the right places, a Clark's could be a tricky species to find in winter.

Bird bagged, Levantin hopped on the adjoining Coney Glade lift. Just below was the Spider Sabich Ski Racing Arena, named after the Olympic ski racer shot to death by his live-in lover, Claudine Longet. The O.J. of the seventies, Longet had paid for her crime with only thirty days in a specially redecorated Aspen jail cell, then ran off with her married defense lawyer and became the butt of endless *Saturday Night Live* skits.

The two-lift shuttle up Snowmass mountain took ten minutes. Levantin was itching to get off his duff. He cut a quick left from the lift and pointed his skis downhill. Hands up, elbows out, and a grin on his face, Levantin blasted down the Max Park run. He was a ferocious skier, diving straight for the fall line and throwing up a rooster tail of conquered snow with each carved turn. There was no subtlety in his style—he looked like a fullback on ice. He had the strength to streak downhill at forty-five miles per hour but the grace to hold his knees close enough to keep any sunlight from peeking through. Anyone who saw Al Levantin on skis wondered how he ever qualified for an AARP card.

With perfect timing, he hockey-stopped at the Ullrhof mountain cafeteria just as skiers started carrying their trays outside for lunch. The arrival of the day's first french fries on the restaurant deck was exactly what Levantin had come to see. A diner raised a fry up high and a gray jay darted from the trees to sweep it out of his hand. Levantin could have wasted a half day in some wild forest in a long and arduous search for this species, but why bother? Ten thousand feet up the Colorado Rockies, the gray jays of Snowmass behaved as if they were seagulls on a Coney Island boardwalk.

Levantin skied past the decks at Gwyn's High Alpine and Café Suzanne, but saw only Steller's jays and mountain chickadees. Though Levantin needed those common birds, they weren't what he had in mind. Snowmass was home to something better.

He tucked down the Adams Avenue catwalk to his car, which he drove this time with two shoes. Now it was payoff time. For the past two years, whenever he'd met anyone in Snowmass who'd expressed the slightest interest in birds, Levantin had returned with a housewarming present—a bird feeder. This was partly because Levantin hoped others would share his love of birds. But he had an ulterior motive. He wanted rosy-finches. Good birders coveted rosy-finches. Fickle and frustrating, the gray-crowned, brown-capped, and black rosy-finch lived most of the year in extremely hard-to-reach places, the tundra of Alaska or the steepest scree fields of the Rockies. During some winters, though, hundreds and hundreds of rosy-finches converged on the much more accessible and comfortable slopes of Snowmass. Why this happened, Levantin couldn't say. He also couldn't explain why, in other winters, the rosy-finches just didn't show up. But if Levantin could keep salting his neighborhood with bird feeders, then maybe, just maybe, he could have his own secret stash of one of North America's flittiest birds.

Rosy-finch hunting required a certain flair. Whenever Levantin glassed the streets on rosy-finch runs, he tried to go with another local birder, Linda Vidal. A man in the backyard with binoculars was always suspect, but a man with a woman in the backyard was much less likely to be phoned in to police as a pervert. Unfortunately, Vidal was busy today. Levantin was on his own and didn't have much time.

Not far away, Levantin saw something moving. He knew just where to go.

Amid all the manses of Snowmass, 249 Faraway Road stood out for one reason: it was ugly. Battleship gray, built across from the neighborhood's bear-proof garbage Dumpster, the house was a rental that turned over tenants. At some point some years ago, one of those tenants had put up a bird feeder. Whoever lived there now kept it filled.

Today 249 Faraway Road had sunflower seeds, tall, leafless aspens—and a pulsating flock of three hundred rosy-finches. Levantin was awed. In the snow their feathers shimmered with a stunning iridescence, like a summer hummingbird on steroids, dipped in raspberry and cinnamon and dark chocolate. Some birders struggled a lifetime to find the three species of rosy-finches. Levantin nailed them all in his hometown on his first day. Could there be any better way to start a Big Year?

Months ago, Levantin had already pondered and answered that question. He raced home, grabbed his suitcase, and kissed his wife good-bye.

At 4 P.M. his United Airlines flight lifted him from the

winter of Aspen to the shirtsleeves weather of the South Texas coast. In his carry-on was the list of forty-five species he had seen that day. He felt good about his list. He felt good about his year.

GREG MILLER

Greg Miller sat alone in his apartment. It was New Year's Eve, and his television clattered with laughter and the pop, pop, pop of champagne corks. Miller was too sad to celebrate. Earlier that day, on December 31, 1997, his divorce had turned final.

Even though Miller knew many marriages ended in court, he still felt shrouded in shame. He had met his wife in a Bible fellowship class after studying to be a preacher at Oral Roberts University, and he had vowed in front of his God, church, and family to stick with her no matter what. When their cuddling gave way to sniping and snarling, Miller was working two jobs. Thinking that was the problem, he quit his weekend duties as pastor for the Voice of Victory World Outreach, where he preached to four evangelical churches around the Washington, D.C., beltway, and tried limiting his weekday hours as a workaholic software jock for the Federal Home Loan Mortgage Co. He and his wife tried being a couple again and went through three marriage counselors in four years. Finally Miller believed that he had found a source of their problems: he was too fat. He had loaded 220 pounds onto his five-foot-seven-inch frame, and his wife, a personal fitness trainer and aerobics instructor, complained about it—a lot. So Miller decided to save his marriage by running, of all things, the famed Marine Corps Marathon. When he started training, he couldn't finish one of his wife's aerobics classes; a one-mile run was completely out of the question. But he started slow and walked when he got tired and gradually worked himself up to the point where he could do a twenty-mile jog without stopping. His wife had never even tried that. He still weighed a rotund 195—no matter how much he exercised, he couldn't break his McDonald's habit—but he felt ready for the marathon. On race day, it rained. He got soaked. Then the temperature plunged. He got chilled. By mile fourteen, both feet had blistered out, and Miller could barely walk, much less run. He wanted to quit, but told himself that he wasn't a quitter. He had given up a whole summer of weekends training for this run, and he was going to finish the Marine Corps Marathon because it was going to save his marriage. Runners passed him. He suffered. He finished in six hours, three minutes, twice as slow as the winner. Hardly anyone was even left at the finish line besides his wife. He promised never to do a marathon again. He was still fat, and his marriage was still busting up.

His wife didn't even show up for the last court hearing. Miller moved one hundred miles away to Lusby, Maryland, and took another software job with the Calvert Cliffs Nuclear Power Plant. He worked ten, twelve, fourteen hours a day, partly to forget the pending legal action and partly to avoid being home. His apartment was a former two-car garage, with a sliding-glass door where cars once entered. The floor was covered with burnt-orange shag carpeting that wasn't thick enough to keep a dropped plate from shattering. Not that he used plates very often. Because the stove and oven didn't work, Miller lived on microwaved food. His dormitory-sized refrigerator had a freezer section that fit either one personal pan pizza or two Hot Pockets. His weight ballooned again. He had lost all the furniture in the divorce, but one wall of his new bedroom was covered, floor to ceiling, with unpacked boxes. The living room had only a nineteen-inch color television and a beanbag chair. He spent a lot of time in the beanbag chair.

Now it was New Year's Eve, and the paperwork said his ten-year marriage had officially ended that very day. Forty years old and alone and no children—he hadn't pictured life this way. He couldn't stop thinking about it. He wondered whether he should call someone, but his wife was gone, his friends were out, and his parents . . . well, his father was a devout Christian in the Amish town in Ohio where Miller had grown up. Miller wanted to feel better. He wasn't sure that calling his father would make anybody feel better.

The television kept showing partyers in Times Square. Miller had no champagne in the fridge. He turned off Dick Clark and those happy, loving couples and fell asleep by 11 P.M.

At work in the nuclear power plant, Miller was known as the Jolt Guy.

On the rim of his office cubicle he had lined a row of empty twenty-ounce bottles of his favorite drink, Jolt Cola. Every bottle boasted that it was loaded with "all the sugar and twice the caffeine" of Coke or Pepsi. Miller downed at least one Jolt a day— three on really bad days—and his workspace had become a castle ringed with sixty red-and-gold turrets. As a new employee in an office with a Dilbert-like maze of identical gray cubicles, Miller enjoyed working inside an instant conversation starter. It was hard to ignore the irony of a Jolt tower in a nuke plant. Occasionally, though, someone reminded him that each Jolt packed the caffeine of three cups of coffee and probably wasn't very good for his health. Miller didn't like to be reminded about his health.

The truth was, Miller was prone to binges. He ate feasts, he ran marathons. And now he was spelunking into the darkest depths of a work binge.

Miller's job was to make sure that millions of lines of software code were ready for Y2K. Years ago, when programmers wanted some procedure or test to be run forever, they entered a simple 00 in computer code. Today, however, 00, or the year 2000, was less than two years away. Miller was in a race to hunt down the 00s and all other Y2K bugs before the new millennium. So he tested a few thousand lines of code, he swilled a few Jolts. It was tedious work with no room for error: there was a good reason why nuclear power plants had become the poster child for the news media's Y2K scare stories. Though Miller often joked that he had no life, he saw less and less humor in his wisecrack.

What kept him sane through all this was birds, or at least the thought of them. Ever since he had identified his first bird at the age of three—female American goldeneye; his father, a birder, had taught him well—Miller had loved to chase birds. Birding time was free time, playtime, the time when he and his father could prowl the woods and talk and come home tired but exhilarated. These days Miller was mostly just tired. But he always kept his binoculars and spotting scope in the back of his Ford Explorer, just in case he drove by a bird that was worth looking at. Of course, when he arrived at his windowless office before sunrise and left after sunset, he never quite knew when, or how, he might actually see a bird. Maybe an owl would swoop by.

Miller stared at his computer screen. More code, more scans, more tests. He had already worked fourteen days straight, seventy-nine hours this week alone, and now it was Sunday. Numbers blurred into each other. He needed at least six more hours of code-crunching today, but he could hardly think.

Actually, he could think.

He stood up, rolled back his chair, and whipped on his coat. He didn't have enough time to walk, but if he drove fast enough he might make it. His urge felt so powerful that he nearly forgot his Cleveland Indians hat.

He raced a half mile from his office to an overlook of the nuclear plant's outflow into Chesapeake Bay. The cooling-tower water was ten degrees warmer than the bay, and baitfish basked here. Above the baitfish, seabirds circled. They were hungry.

The cooling pond of a nuclear power plant wasn't exactly on the National Audubon Society list of birding hot spots, but Miller would take what he could get. Gulls shrieked. He squinted into his spotting scope. It wasn't easy pressing his face close enough for a clear view, but far enough to prevent body heat from fogging the optics.

Through the scope was a circus of bird activity. There were herring gulls and laughing gulls and great black-backed gulls and— whoa!—what was that bird? It was a gull, definitely, with gray wings and dark tips, but wasn't that a dark ear spot? Laughing gull—a nonbreeder, maybe? No, this one was too small, and with a patch on the head, not streaking. Little gull? No, too big. Black-headed gull? Nah, those legs were pink, not orange.

No question: it was a Bonaparte's gull, named after the nephew of the great conqueror himself. Nice bird, dependable visitor to the mid-Atlantic, but a good identification challenge nonetheless.

Miller stopped himself. He was breathing, really breathing. His face flushed. He opened his winter coat.

He remembered this feeling: he was back in the hunt.

On Christmas, his brother had given him a birding book, but Miller had stuffed it in a box without cracking the spine.

He feared that book. He was already on a work binge. He didn't have time for any other kind.

He returned to his desk and called up some more code, but his mind wandered. Tonight, he told himself, I'm going to find that book and I'm going to read it.

TWO

A Birder Is Hatched

A few minutes after I first met Sandy Komito, he was looking for an angle.

He was driving me in his beloved Lincoln Town Car to his favorite steak house, a stand-alone joint in the New Jersey suburbs, when he saw there was a line for valet parking. The line offended two of his sensibilities. He didn't like to wait, and he didn't like to turn over his car to a stranger.

So he cleared his throat, reached in the glove compartment, and pulled out a handicapped placard. There was no way Komito was hurt; in fact, after hours of phone interviews I had concluded that he was probably a lot tougher than me. But he hung the blue-and-white wheelchair logo on his rearview mirror and parked in the free space right next to the front door of the restaurant.

I was too shocked to say anything. As I watched him walk straight past all those cars still idling in line for valet parking, I tried to feign a limp. Komito greeted the maître d' with a smile. I grasped one essential truth:

Sandy Komito didn't give a hoot what anybody thought.

His wife, it turned out, had been given the handicapped card years ago because she suffered from horrible back pain. But now she was out of town with friends. In Komito's mind, it was ridiculous for a place with valet parking to offer a handicapped spot at all. Why should the ticket to a primo parking spot lie wasted in the darkness of a glove box just because his wife was on vacation?

It's embarrassing to admit, but Komito nearly had me convinced that it was okay to take advantage of the system. His power of persuasion was that strong. He looked me in the face with those sky-blue eyes and soothed my guilt with that assuring deep voice, and the next thing I knew, he had me feeling like the most important person in the universe.

Then the waiter came—and Komito ordered his salad chopped. Mine came that way too.

I don't eat my salad chopped into one-inch squares. I don't know anybody else who does. But Komito has his own tastes, and I found being with him was like riding the Tilt-A-Whirl at the amusement park—it's fun if you don't get too queasy. When Komito was at the table, waiters seemed to linger longer, just to overhear his stories. He was a ham and proud of it. He was as brash as Oscar Madison and as fussy as Felix Unger.

He also was fun in the field. For our first birding trip, he took me a few miles from his house to the Hackensack Meadowlands, the notorious swamp that had been filled in, dumped on, and raked over ever since New York City gazed west and saw unclaimed industrial profit. The Meadowlands were an amazing place. Birds moved everywhere—terns soaring, egrets wading, wrens burbling, swallows diving. Komito, however, was hacked off. A few years back the government had built a posh glass room above the swamp for weddings, and now the engineers kept water levels in these tidal wetlands artificially high. For happy brides, that meant lots of graceful mute swans in the background for wedding pictures. For Komito, however, it was a man-made travesty. Mute swans were not native birds. He wanted the swamp as nature intended—with skittery shorebirds teeming on miles of stinking mudflats.

When I told Komito that the Hackensack Meadowlands certainly offended my sense of smell, he huffed. That wasn't swamp gas, he said. It was the landfill over the hill. Or maybe Jimmy Hoffa.

We walked a few twists and turns on the dikes above the swamp and found a wonderful surprise—a big containment basin that the engineers hadn't flooded. There were hundreds of shorebirds—dowitchers drilling the mud like two-legged sewing machines, sandpipers scrambling for snails, herons prowling for baitfish. Just as Komito tried to teach me the difference between greater and lesser yellowlegs—the longer bill curls up slightly on a greater—something startling happened. All those shorebirds suddenly took flight.

I stood slack-jawed, watching hundreds, no thousands, of birds fly up from places that I couldn't even see. Komito set me straight.

There's only one creature that can scare the hell out of that many shorebirds, Komito said, and it's a peregrine falcon.

Sure enough, ten seconds later, a big, dark bully muscled in from up high. It was Mr. Peregrine himself, swooping down for a late lunch.

Now Komito stood as gape-mouthed as I. He had witnessed this same natural phenomenon hundreds of times before, but still couldn't contain his awe. He had the zest of a ten-year-old boy.

So did Greg Miller. But Miller didn't wait for me to learn that same fact about him. He told me first.

When I met him in his apartment, boxes were everywhere. Some were being used for storage. Others served as tables and coat hangers. I knew he hadn't changed apartments for months. Miller must have seen the puzzled look on my face, because he offered an explanation:

"A long time ago I decided that the people with their priorities straight are ten-year-olds. When you're ten, you want to spend the whole day playing. You know everyone has some obligations and some work to do and that's okay. But play comes first and work comes second."

In Miller's mind, unpacking was work. He grabbed his scope and tripod from the top of a box.

"Let's go play."

Miller's car had been conking out lately, so we took my rental. We drove to a field near his home with some woods and parked. I slammed the driver's side door and Miller said, "Dickcissel."

Huh? Where?

"There, about fifty feet in the field, by that tall thistle."

Just as I raised my binoculars, Miller blurted again.

"House wren, over there. Northern cardinal, in those oaks. Indigo bunting, across the way. Song sparrow right next to it."

Something seemed fishy here. Miller hadn't even raised his binoculars.

He was birding by ear.

At first I suspected he was pulling one over on me. But he stood with me patiently until I klutzed my way with my binoculars and finally focused on the dickcissel, wren, cardinal, and song sparrow that he had first heard. (The indigo bunting, brilliant blue in the afternoon sun, I found by myself, thank you.)

What sounded like a plain old chip note to me was clearly a chipping sparrow to him. He called out warbler species that were too far away for me even to find field marks. I put down my binoculars and started watching Miller. His ear was incredible. He picked off calls one by one and paused only at the ones overwhelmed by car or jet noise. I wanted to take him to the symphony, just to see him figure out the manufacturing date of the Stradivarius being played in the third-violin seat.

Miller thrived off others' enthusiasm. When he saw my astonishment over his aural birding, he got even more excited and insisted that we drop everything to teach me to separate the grinding buzz of a marsh wren from the chatter of a sedge wren. He was patient. He was playful. There was nothing threatening or intimidating about him. He was the kind of guy who got a lot of hugs without trying.

His goal was to wring every possible ounce of joy from life. We stopped birding one day to go to an Indian restaurant, where he ordered the spiciest dish on the menu, chicken vindaloo. The waiter asked Miller if he was sure he wanted something so hot. Yes, he did. Miller told me he had grown up eating a lot of bland food, and now he loved to make up for lost time. Sure enough, when the food came, it was a scorcher. His eyes teared. His nose dripped. He coughed. Sweat beaded on his bald forehead, and his cheeks flushed. Frankly, I got worried about him.

You okay? I asked.

He could hardly talk. He nodded his head. He took another bite.

I got the feeling that when Greg Miller started something, he finished it.

With Al Levantin, the challenge was keeping up with him.

Out the door of his house and up his private road, Levantin was at nine thousand feet and climbing fast. At the first switchback he marked a wren's nest. At the second was a swallow in a woodpecker hole. Higher still darted a mountain bluebird.

If Levantin was trying to bird by ear, I couldn't tell. My heart was pounding too loudly to hear. He had biked thirty miles the day before and hiked up a mountain the day before that. He was older than my father. He was turning my legs into marshmallows.

We finally reached the ridgetop. Far below our feet snowmelt rushed down the Roaring Fork River. Behind us was the knife-edge of 14,000-foot Capitol Peak. To our right in the distance was the city of Aspen; to our left rose the snow cone of majestic Mount Sopris. Levantin had hiked to this spot a million times before. He grinned as if this time were his first.

That was the thing with Levantin: he loved the birds, but he really loved the places they brought him. When you spend your career in the confines of a gray suit, the pipits at dawn above timberline are even more wondrous. He lived to be in the field. He may not have been the world's most expert birder—he could hardly identify the song of anything—but he clearly was one of the most spirited. Through the sage of a dry meadow we chased some kind of sparrow. We drew closer; it took off. Closer, off. We followed the creature thirty feet at a time this way for at least a quarter mile. We never did get a close enough look to clearly identify that bird. But halfway through our chase, Levantin chortled. I reminded myself: this man ran one of the biggest divisions of one of the biggest corporations in the world. A bird made him giggle.

Levantin could talk and laugh at the same time. At the end of a good story, a sentence became a blurt, as if his tongue had lost a race with his funny bone. He bubbled. He teased. He was the guy you wanted at your cocktail party.

He even had some true grit. While we were being out-smarted by that sparrow in the sage, I saw Levantin doing something odd with his binoculars. He wore the strap on his shoulder, like a purse. How come? Let me tell you a story, Levantin said, which is what he always said when he was about to poke fun at himself. One day Levantin had woken up and felt something terribly wrong with his right hand. He could barely move it. He couldn't make a fist, he couldn't write his name, he couldn't even shake hands. He went straight to the doctor, who suspected a stroke. But tests said no. He feared a neuromuscular disorder. No evidence of that, though. So Levantin submitted to an MRI, which found damage to his C-7 neck vertebra. The doctors were mystified. Had the patient suffered some kind of spinal trauma? Then Levantin remembered: he had just driven from Philadelphia to Colorado and, like any good birder traveling beneath three different flyways, had looped his binoculars around his neck the whole way. Levantin even found a story in a birder's magazine identifying the malady—binocular neck.

"See!" Levantin blurted. "I risked paralysis to be a bird-watcher!"

In the heart of an aspen grove, on a bluebird day of summer, there was no risk in sight. Levantin lived in Snowmass with some pinnacles of the business world—turn left at the gate on his road and you arrive at the magic kingdom of Michael Eisner; go straight and it's the mansion of the widow of the *National Enquirer* publisher—but Levantin still wasn't beyond rubbernecking. At lunch in a slopeside restaurant, Levantin and I watched a dozen or so people grab a table across from us. Levantin kept eyeballing them, eyeballing them, until something finally registered. He grabbed my pen and reporter's notepad from across the table and wrote: *Jerry Jones, Dallas Cowboys owner.*

Levantin was so excited that I thought he would go over for a handshake. But I had misread him. Levantin was a Philadelphia Eagles fan. He wanted to jeer Jones.

But he didn't. Levantin may have been a fervent fan, but he believed in social niceties, too. Of course, if Sandy Komito had been at the next table, the Cowboys owner would have been in big trouble. Greg Miller, I suspected, might have asked for an autograph.

I wondered if there was an unlikelier group of competitors than these three Big Year men—Sandy Komito, Greg Miller, Al Levantin. Sure, they all had the same wonderful, boyish sense of enthusiasm. But I couldn't imagine what else a New Jersey industrial contractor, a nuclear power worker, and a corporate chief executive could hold in common.

If you had a year of your life to do anything you wanted, and you could do only that thing for a year, what would you do? These three guys all chose to chase birds. Something deep in their backgrounds must have made them so susceptible to an ornithological takeover.

For Sandy Komito, it began over the breakfast table in the Bronx during the Great Depression. His father, an $8-a-week printer, was out of work. His mother raised food money by making ladies' hats. Komito wore knickers to school because the relief office was out of long pants. His younger brother would get the knickers when Komito outgrew them. For the past six months they had lived in this first-floor "concession" apartment—a home no one would lease unless they got the concession of six months' free rent. If the father didn't find a job soon, the family would move out in the middle of the night for the next concession. The Komitos had gone concession-hunting before. They didn't want to do it again.

The father worried about shame. A native of Austria, he had been a prisoner of war during World War I—he fought for the losers—and had moved to America hoping for a fresh start. Now he couldn't even afford sausages. It was bad enough for a man to feel humiliation, but his sons, his two young sons—they deserved better. Though the boys might never have enough money to see the world, they could at least learn something about it.

So everyone gathered over morning cereal to play a little game. The father started it by naming a bird. Then Komito named a different one. Next came his mother's turn. (Komito's brother was too young to play.) And so it went around the table until someone finally failed to come up with a new bird. That person was forced to drop out. The winner named the most species.

Why this game required a bird's name, Komito couldn't say. His father never seemed more interested in birds than mammals or fish. He wasn't even an outdoorsman. But in the concrete depths of the Bronx, the Komitos ate breakfast each morning with a spirited game of Name the Bird. His parents occasionally let him win.

That wasn't good enough for Komito. One day at home, he thumbed through the family's biggest book, the dictionary, and found a word accompanied by an inked picture of a new bird. When the family game began the next morning, he let it progress in the usual fashion—"sparrow," "pigeon," "seagull," "robin," "hawk," and so on—until the easy names were exhausted. Then Komito played out his prize.

"Jackdaw."

"What?" asked his mother.

"Jackdaw," the boy repeated.

"That's not a bird," chided his father. "You're making that up."

Komito proudly whipped out the dictionary. The jackdaw was *too* a real bird, a crow that lived in Europe. It said so right there in the book. Nobody in his family had ever heard of it, but now nobody could ever dispute it.

Even at age six, Komito couldn't stand to lose a game about birds.

The family moved in and out of three more Bronx apartments. When his father found work, he did it six and even seven days a week. But the jobs kept running out, and the boys had to help. In the winter, Komito prayed for snow days, when he could earn twenty-five cents shoveling storefront sidewalks. That was easy money. The rest of the year he struggled to elbow his way past other neighborhood kids for the prime spot in front of the subway elevated station, where he shined shoes for a nickel and hoped for a nickel tip. On a good Saturday, he could make $10, but $7.50 of that went straight into his parents' pockets. He owned only one shirt, a white one, which he washed every night by himself. When he tired of wrestling for the prime shoe-shining position at the subway stop, he hired on as a delivery boy for local markets. Hauling groceries to the fifth floor of a walk-up was supposed to earn him a nickel tip, but times were so hard that mothers sometimes pretended they weren't home. Komito learned to drop the groceries at the apartment door and then bang his feet on the stairs, as if he were walking away. Almost always, the door opened. Almost always, Komito embarrassed the mother into forking over his nickel. Once, a newcomer to the neighborhood made the mistake of asking Komito about the size of his average tip. It's a dime, he told her, and she gave it to him. As far as Komito knew, she was the first mother in the history of the Bronx to pay a dime to a market delivery boy. He quit right there. On that day, his average tip truly was a dime.

By the time he was twelve, Komito knew how to hustle business. He also knew he wanted something different.

The same cereal, the same shirt, the same streets, the same tension—did it always have to be that way? He found himself spending more and more time in that green island of the Bronx, Van Cortlandt Park. There, he found the creatures that were free to leave the city whenever they wished.

They weren't the sparrows or pigeons of the streets. These birds were wild.

On February 19, 1944, Sandy Komito made his first list. (He still has it today.) In the block-letter scrawl of a boy, he wrote: CANADA GOOSE. MALLARD DUCK. BLACK DUCK.

One day Komito was poking around the park when he saw a boy gaping up at the clouds.

"There's a red-tailed hawk,".the boy told him matter-of-factly.

Komito saw nothing. But the other boy, only a few years older than Komito, held in his hands a powerful black magic—binoculars. The boy offered his prized possession to Komito, who took a breath, pointed the glass at the sky, and saw a regal bird soaring on a distinctive roan fantail. It was Komito's first glimpse at a new world.

The boy with the binoculars was Harold Feinberg, who turned out to be a leader of a Bronx Boy Scout troop. Komito took the hint. He joined and found a troop full of other boys who also were interested in life, wildlife, outside the Bronx. The Boy Scouts offered a merit badge for anyone who could learn and identify forty birds. Komito learned one hundred. He was off to the races.

He visited the public library often enough to memorize Roger Tory Peterson's *A Field Guide to the Birds*. (When he wrote a long book report on it for school, his teacher was impressed—until she found out that half the *Field Guide* was pictures.) Komito saved his shoe-shine money and bought a pair of used binoculars for $30. He took the trolley to Pelham Bay for his first greater scaup, the train and a bus to Jones Beach for his first American avocet, and the bus to the

Palisades over the Hudson River for his first peregrine falcon. On one winter subway trip to Atlantic Beach, he found a great black-backed gull dead in the flotsam. He couldn't just walk away from it. He brought it home, gutted it, and suspended the five-foot skin above his bed. People walking outside on Davidson Avenue would stop and stare through the window at that dead seagull skin. Komito didn't care. He fell asleep every night looking up at proof that something could soar above those streets.

If his parents worried about this sudden change in their oldest boy, they didn't say anything. That Name the Bird game was turning into a Find the Son challenge. Komito was out chasing birds all the time. But his grades were good and he still brought home work money, so the parents let the boy indulge his obsession.

His mother, however, drew the line when the gull carcass in the bedroom finally was claimed by maggots.

Soon Komito began to feel his birding being cramped by the New York subway system. One summer day, when he was sixteen, he read in a magazine about some islands off the coast of Maine. He and a friend, a fisherman, started hitchhiking north. They made it in three days to Rockland, Maine, where it was 2 A.M. Too broke for a hotel room and too tired to roll out their sleeping bags, the teens walked in the open door of a lobster cannery and huddled for warmth. Within minutes, the night watchman turned them in to the night patrol cop. He let the teens sleep in jail, with the cell door open, until 6:30 A.M. The boys walked out with empty stomachs and hitched thirty miles with a lobsterman—the old salt understood the kid who wanted to catch pollack, but wasn't too sure about the one who wanted to see birds—on the waves of the North Atlantic to the Coast Guard station at Matinicus Rock. Komito may as well have landed in heaven. Every rock crevice on Matinicus Rock was filled with an Atlantic puffin, the penguinlike seabird with the massive orange bill that came to land only once a year to breed. Komito was thrilled: his first offshore species. The Coast Guard was so enamored of the visiting Huck Finn and Tom Sawyer from the Bronx that the teens were allowed to sleep in an old light-house barracks. During his first night, though, Komito kept hearing an eerie whoosh. He walked outside to investigate— and was struck upside the head by a Leach's storm-petrel. The bird fell unconscious at his feet. Komito's head had a bump, but he felt knighted. He knelt down and memorized the look and location of every feather on that black storm-petrel, eight inches long with a twenty-inch wingspan, before it flew off again into the night.

From the Maine trip Komito learned that the best adventures were unscheduled. He loved to go places on the spur of the moment. He prided himself on his ability to stay unfrazzled.

Drafted by the army during the Korean War, he spent a year and a half training in Texas. The birds were amazing—the fields were full of the orioles, buntings, and jays that he could only read about in New York—but the birding was brutal. Other soldiers mocked him. Birdwatching was for sissies and little old ladies in big, floppy hats and the bachelor dandies who still lived with their mothers. Komito was distressed. South Texas was supposed to be the promised land for birders. Who'd have thought that it would be easier to watch warblers in the Bronx? He survived the army by hiding his binoculars in the legs of his five-pocket fatigues.

In January 1957, he was at a buddy's wedding in the Bronx when he spied the maid of honor across the ballroom. He told her stories. He made her laugh. He invited her to another friend's wedding the next Saturday in Manhattan. But when they arrived, they learned that the wedding actually was the following day, Sunday. So there they were, downtown on a Saturday night, and Komito had no money for a real date. He took her to the courthouse to watch criminal arraignments as entertainment, then walked her to Chinatown for fried rice. She thought he was funny, honest, and hardworking. Her friends, however, weren't too sure. Komito always spoke his mind, which wasn't always pretty. One friend told her, if Dale Carnegie had ever met Sandy Komito, he would simply have given up. But a man who thrived on the blunt truth would never be boring. They were in love. Eleven months after they met, Sandy and Bobbye Komito married.

He tried night school at the City College of New York, but it wasn't for him. Too slow, not practical enough. He hired on with an industrial supplies company and became the number one salesman, in a sales force of 150, in just three years. He demanded to start being paid on commission, but the boss told him to go jump. So he did. In the garage of his home in suburban New Jersey, Komito began mixing his own epoxies and sealants. He ordered ten tons of sand for flooring material and had it dumped on his driveway. When the neighbors started nosing around, Komito painted his garage windows black. He was in the garage by 6 A.M., and many days he stayed there until 11 P.M. Industrial Resurfacing Co. was born.

He had a partner for the first three months, but they busted up because Komito kept calling all the shots. Komito did the purchasing and the mixing and the cold-calling factories and warehouses across New York, New Jersey, and Connecticut. Komito refused to go union; too many rules. Komito refused to work Manhattan; too much hassle. Komito refused to ply clients with sports tickets or dinners; too expensive. In New Jersey, especially, the Mob and corrupt politicians wanted their palms greased, but Komito refused to pay bribes. When a businessman told Komito that no one could work industrial roofing without payoffs, Komito snapped, "The only people who believe that have no faith in themselves." He took no guff. When one customer refused to pay a $2,400 bill, Komito spent $13,000 on lawyers to stick it to the bastard. He liked being thought of as a maniac. Industrial Resurfacing Co. was the Sandy show, and you could take it or you could leave it. He wrote so many client letters that he learned to type eighty words per minute. His wife tried to help by addressing sales-pitch letters to prospective clients, but Komito ripped up dozens of her envelopes. Bobbye's mistake: she had failed to center the stamps perfectly with an exact eighth-inch border to the edge of the envelope. You can never make another first impression, Komito scolded, and the front of an envelope is the first thing a customer sees.

He was a perfectionist's perfectionist. It drove his family nuts, but it also made them rich.

Though he had not grown up dreaming of becoming an industrial contractor, he learned to enjoy it. He wanted to be a success, but he believed the easy businesses already were taken. Roofing, flooring, and waterproofing were some of the hardest. Spend a day on the roof of a chemical factory near the swamps of the Meadowlands in August and nobody called you a sissy. Once a six-foot-nine college football lineman ducked into Komito's doorway and asked for a roofing job to keep him in shape during the offseason. He lasted one day. At first Komito tried hiring the traditional roofers—the felons, the Hell's Angels—but grew frustrated with all the unexplained absences. He needed more dependable people, but only the desperate would accept such hot, dirty, backbreaking work. He started hiring Latinos. Soon almost everyone on a Komito crew spoke Spanish; Komito spoke Spanglish with a Bronx accent. He gave them twelve months of work and all the overtime they could handle.

During certain times of the year he'd go on a nearby factory roof with binoculars. Sometimes he'd look for signs that his crews were dogging it. Sometimes he'd look for shorebirds on migration.

Usually, though, he was hustling sales. Komito loved to sell. He was one man, focused like a laser, piercing the corporate flab of secretaries and engineers and middle managers until he finally found the one person with the power to hire him. Nobody was more dogged than Komito, and nobody had a thicker skin. His motto: Your sale starts with the first no. He sent out a thousand letters a month with hopes of getting twenty back. Komito may have been selling the same service as dozens of competitors, but he could soften even the toughest factory man with his own secret weapon—slapstick humor.

On one of Komito's early sales calls, the manager of a small plant wouldn't even answer the bell. But Komito kept ringing and ringing until the man finally poked his head out a second-story window.

"What do you want?" he snapped.

"You got a problem with your roof and you don't even know it yet," Komito shouted up at him. "Let me show you."

"I ain't buying nothing."

"You know, I wish I had a hundred customers like you."

The manager's glare melted. "Why do you wish you had a hundred customers like me?"

"Because I have a thousand!"

The manager let Komito inside—and eventually gave him the job.

If Komito walked in a manager's office and saw a golfing picture on the desk, Komito said, "Oh, you play tennis." A man with a fish on the wall was asked about hunting. To a sailor: "How's the golf?"

Komito always wanted a reaction. A bad joke kept them off-balance. The greater the groan, the more he liked it. He was trying to make an impression. Maybe next time they would remember him.

He was a type-A workaholic from the Bronx who scored big in business with the tough guys. And he still loved his birds. In the early 1980s, Komito set out to find them.

From his weekend trips to the Jersey shore and Jamaica Bay and Cape May, Komito was an expert on the species of the Northeast. And he had lugged Bobbye and their three kids on enough "vacations" to Florida, Texas, and Arizona to become familiar with the local birds there. All that knowledge and experience gave him a life list that put him in the top 10 percent of birders.

But Komito was Komito. He didn't want to be the top 10 percent. He wanted to see all the birds, period. That wouldn't be easy. All the best birders seemed to belong to their own little elite fraternity, and Komito wasn't a member. It grated him that when a western reef-heron, an elusive Eurasian species, turned up in Massachusetts, he didn't learn about the sighting until the *New York Times* published a story months after the bird had left.

He had the money. He just needed the know-how.

He got lucky. Just as birds eclipsed business on the Komito list of personal obsessions, an enterprising birder, Bob Odear, found a new use for Komito's restless bank account. Odear launched the first North American Rare Bird Alert. For the first time, birders could pay a fee and get the inside dope on rarity sightings—identifications, locations, directions—as soon as they happened. The new service revolutionized birding. Before NARBA, elite birders spent decades cultivating networks of informants who would call whenever a weird species turned up. That took work. With NARBA, however, the information, the crucial inside dope on the whereabouts of the continent's hottest birds, was sold just like any other commodity. For Komito, who had cash in pocket but not an ounce of schmooze in his bones, this was a godsend. To get his birds he wouldn't have to suck up to anyone. For a long, long time in business, Komito had always done things his own way. NARBA meant he had no need to change just for birding.

With hot-line information in hand, Komito birded the same way he did business: he was relentless. A bananaquit slipped into some gardens in Kendall, Florida, and Komito was there. A northern hawk owl roosted in Minneapolis and Komito traveled through the snow to get it. He even picked up a jackdaw, his old Name the Bird species, after a red-eye to Nantucket.

The kids were grown. The business was established. The wife was happy.

The contractor had become a chaser.

Greg Miller grew up in the Land of No. In Holmes County, Ohio, home of the world's largest population of Amish, people believed in a literal interpretation of John 2:15—*Love not the world, neither the things that are in the world*—and they lived their lives accordingly. For fifteen thousand of Miller's neighbors, that meant no driving on roads, no electricity at home, and no doing anything else that might make anyone appear to be an individual. Amish girls in Miller's school had no jewelry, no makeup, and no haircuts; their hair stayed wrapped in buns or braids, and their knees stayed hidden above the hem of their plain pastel dresses. Boys wore no sneakers, no jeans, and no T-shirts; they answered "Yes, sir,"

"No, sir," and gave the teachers no lip. Because of the instruction in Exodus 20:4—*Thou shalt not make unto thee any graven image*— there were no class pictures.

Thanks to the prevailing religion, Holmes County had no movie theaters, no bowling alleys, and no businesses open on Sunday. The high school had no football team. The restaurants had no liquor. The teenagers had no hand-holding.

Though half the population of Holmes County was Amish, the Miller family was not. They belonged to a sister religion, the Mennonites, who shared almost all the same religious convictions, but believed a family could accept modern technology without disobeying the Bible. Mennonites drove cars, not horses-and-buggies. They wore Levi's. They used computers. But they also remained staunch social conservatives. Miller was in his junior year of high school before a classmate, non-Protestant, offered him his first cigarette. He declined it. He never saw drugs. Dancing was banned at Hiland High School, which posed challenges for the organizers of the senior prom. Students celebrated with progressive dinner parties—in the house of one classmate the mother would serve appetizers, the next made soups, another prepared the main course, and someone else, a very special someone else, was awarded the honor of dishing up dessert. The Land of No said an emphatic yes to pies. There were pecan pies and apple pies and pumpkin pies and rhubarb pies and cherry pies and pies made of anything else that could be sealed deliciously beneath two layers of butter-laden crust. Holmes County residents rarely boasted, but they did talk about the joys of living in the Pie Capital of the World. No one accused them of bragging; their pies made it a simple fact. If a family celebrated a new baby, neighbors gave them a pie. Tough night calving a Hereford? Give that family a pie. Mourning the sudden loss of a dog? A pie eased the pain. All these pies certainly helped build community, but they also gave local doctors considerable heartburn. The one vice that Holmes County embraced was eating. It was a fat community. Sunday dinner after church was a bountiful affair, with noodles and mashed potatoes and gravy and homemade breads and roast beef and the inevitable pies. Greg Miller was bred to eat.

Waistlines were about the only thing that changed in Holmes County. In fact, residents prided themselves on being an oasis free from change. The biggest upheaval people still talked about came in World War I. When the kaiser made all things German unpatriotic, the town closest to Miller's home, Berlin, Ohio, summarily switched pronunciation of its name from Ber*lin* to *Ber*lin. Even in the 1960s, Holmes County remained the eye in the nation's cultural hurricane, the one place where nobody embraced sex or drugs or rock and roll. Sixty miles away, at Kent State University, the Ohio National Guard gunned down four Vietnam War protesters, but the major debate at Miller's home church, Berlin Mennonite, was over the proper disposition of a donated organ. Church rules said no instruments were allowed during Sunday services. Church elders, however, didn't want to offend the contributor. A compromise finally resulted: the organ was played while worshipers filed into the yellow-brick church, but was silenced during the service.

Outsiders might think this was a restrictive life, but Miller never viewed it that way. Yes, as a boy, he lamented that his town had no McDonald's. But it also had no crime, no violence, and no corruption. Children played outside whenever they wanted. Nobody thought twice about a boy trekking across town by himself to find the best sledding hill. He knew people made fun of the Amish because they all wore the same clothes. But when Miller drove somewhere outside the county, he saw teenagers all wearing bellbottoms, bare feet, and long hair. Who really was trapped in a uniform? he wondered.

If there was one thing Miller had patience for, it was someone who was different. His younger brother Brent, born eleven months after him, was profoundly mentally retarded and autistic. He couldn't talk. He couldn't dress, feed, or bathe himself. His family never really knew how much he understood. Some experts recommended that Brent be institutionalized, but the Millers would never allow it. The family brought him everywhere. And everywhere they went, people stared. For many years, the Millers just ignored it. But when Greg and his younger brother Ned, and his younger sister, Ann, grew into teenagers, they turned more defiant. When a stranger started gawking at Brent in a restaurant, the Miller children would join together in a huddle. On the count of three, they would all turn around and gawk straight back at the stranger.

A profoundly mentally retarded child would rip apart some families, but Brent helped bond the Millers. They lived in a three-bedroom house on County Road 201 with a station wagon in the garage and all the kids in one room with two bunk beds.

The combination of their religious beliefs and Brent meant that the Millers were a family of few luxuries. But they did set aside time for one diversion.

Greg Miller was a birder before he could remember being a birder.

It was one of his family's favorite stories: At age three, Miller was toted to a farm a few miles from home. His mother and father enjoyed the peaceful natural setting; Miller chased ducks around the farm pond. On the way back home, they stopped at a neighbor's house. Miller ambled out of the family station wagon with 7×50 Binolux binoculars strapped around his neck. "See anything with those binoculars?" the neighbor asked. Miller beamed. "American goldeneye—female," the preschooler replied. The startlingly specific answer took everyone aback except his mother. A career kindergarten teacher, she knew her son was different. He was the only little boy she had ever seen who never, ever splashed in a mud puddle.

Miller's father had caught the birding bug while growing up on a farm a few miles away. He worked during the week as an Ohio state large-animal veterinarian, inspecting the cattle, horses, and sheep of the Amish, but he saved his off-duty time for the birds. Miller's father also had a remarkable ear. On one family trip, he had hoped to find the elusive Kirtland's warbler, a federally protected endangered species that lived most of the year in the Bahamas but nested briefly in the jack pines of northern Michigan. In early summer, the forests of the Upper Midwest trilled with the songs of at least thirty-five species of wood-warblers. Some species, such as the ovenbird, had two-note calls so distinctive that even neophytes could pick it out. Most other calls were extremely subtle; telling one from the other was like identifying the model of a car solely by engine rumble. In the woods that day, however, Miller's father somehow heard one warbler song he didn't recognize. Sure enough, on a pine bough not far from the road was perched a nondescript yellow-and-gray songbird, the Kirtland's warbler. What kind of birder could pick out a species only because it didn't sound like thirty-five others? Miller was awed.

Rare was the time when the father could go afield without his oldest son. By the time he reached high school, Miller, too, had learned to bird by ear. Some teenagers could identify every Beatles song by the first three chords; Miller could identify the songs of all thirty-five wood-warblers that frequented the Midwest. Occasionally Miller pushed further than his teacher. While his father tried to watch college football on television, Miller would pull out the Golden Guide *Birds of North America* and ask for an impromptu test. His father, after rolling his eyes, would pick a species at random and read aloud its text description. Without seeing any illustration, Miller had to guess the bird. When that became too easy, Miller told his father to read only a few words at a time. The challenge: naming the bird in the fewest number of words. When that became too easy, Miller upped the stakes even further. His father would name one bird, and Miller had to identify all the other species listed on the same page. Though his father hardly ever admitted it—he did, after all, really want to watch the game—the boy's exploding knowledge of birds was a lot more surprising than Woody Hayes and his three-yards-and-a-cloud-of-dust Ohio State Buckeyes.

As a state employee, Miller's father got three weeks of vacation a year. In the 1970s, he started saving up all his time off in the odd years so he could take off six weeks in the even years. Then it was time for the big trip: The parents piled their four kids into a green '69 Pontiac station wagon and pop-up tent trailer and drove West. The idea was to see the country—the Grand Canyon, Old Faithful, the kids' first drive-in movie—but they saw a lot of birds, too. At one point, the car broke an axle at Milepost 101 of the Alaskan Highway and the family was stranded twelve days at a wide spot in the road waiting for a replacement. One morning a hungry adult bear popped its head into the family camper, but Miller's father, the large-animal veterinarian, scared it away with a hard punch to the nose. Miller was astounded. He preferred to amuse himself with three-toed woodpeckers.

Back home in Ohio, he brought his binoculars to school so he could hop off the bus at the end of the day and scan the woods across the street for chickadees and warblers. Other teens teased by calling him Bird Brain, Bird Nose, and worst of all, Miss Jane Hathaway, that eccentric birdwatching spinster from the *Beverly Hillbillies*. Miller didn't like the ribbing, but he didn't spend much time worrying about it. When your fifteen-year-old brother has a diaper that needs changing, you focus on what's important.

His family concentrated more and more on the Bible. On their camping trips out West the Millers met different kinds of Christians, charismatic Christians, who believed, unlike Mennonites, that they could be baptized in the Holy Spirit. The Miller family embraced the personal nature of charismatic Christianity and began hosting Bible study classes with fifteen or twenty worshipers in their living room every Thursday. Some charismatics prophesied; others professed wisdom. Miller himself spoke in tongues. The family started driving thirty miles past Berlin Mennonite every Sunday to attend an evangelical church in Canton.

When it came time for college, Miller enrolled in Oral Roberts University in Oklahoma. It was far from home but devoutly Christian, and it scored well in the *U.S. News and World Report* annual rankings of universities. Though the Bible and preaching classes were terrific—Miller learned to read Greek—Oral Roberts wasn't all that Miller expected. Many parents, it turned out, sent their teens to the religious school for the same reason that others used military schools—to tame their wild children. Living away from home for the first time, Miller had peers who dabbled in drugs and alcohol and premarital sex. Miller kept his eyes open, but stayed away. During Miller's senior year, though, Roberts told the world about his vision of a nine-hundred-foot Jesus, which he said towered over Tulsa and told him to raise money for a hospital complex. In the Pentecostal world, Roberts had long been famous for his faith healing. But his nine-hundred-foot

Jesus—bigger than Noah's Ark, taller than the Washington Monument—made Roberts infamous to a larger world audience. In the dormitories of Oral Roberts University, many students gave thanks for the nine-hundred-foot Jesus and prayed for the donations to start rolling in. Miller, however, was embarrassed. Building a hospital was a worthy goal, Miller believed, but what did that have to do with a nine-hundred-foot Jesus? Roberts got his money and built his hospital. Miller graduated from Oral Roberts University with a degree in biblical literature and a strong dose of skepticism.

Even his hometown was changing. In Holmes County, tourists had discovered the Amish. Main Street filled with bakeries and oh-so-quaint crafts shops, and Berlin had to put up its first stoplight. Some locals resented being gaped at like animals in a zoo. After his years with Brent, though, Miller was used to that kind of attention. Besides, he had college loans to pay off. Miller worked two summers at a new tourist attraction, The Amish Farm, where he took families from Cleveland on $5 buggy rides around a green meadow. While the draft horse pulled, Miller reminded the big-city folks that their hamburgers came from Herefords; more than one child swore off Happy Meals.

Miller started teaching math at an Ohio community college partly to pay his bills, but partly to take classes in computer programming. Software writing was a little like birding: it required both precise instructions and creative solutions. Miller liked the challenge, and when he moved back to Oklahoma for his first computer job, he also liked the money. To stay grounded in faith, he took up with a regular Bible study class, where he met a hardbodied woman who was as passionate about exercise as Miller was about birds. She showed him how to get in shape; he found it daunting. He showed her how to chase birds; she found it boring. But they were in love, deeply so, and married, with a wedding reception that had no alcohol and no dancing. They moved to Washington, D.C., because computer jocks and aerobics instructors both were in high demand there. He was proud of his weekend work as an evangelical preacher, but later it reinforced the pain of his divorce. It was hard to deliver Sunday sermons about failed marriages. It was even worse to live through one.

One night afterward, he was eating Buffalo hot wings at a restaurant with his younger brother Ned and talking about the bust-up of his marriage. His brother offered him a cigarette. Miller sucked in a drag—and convulsed in an uncontrollable coughing fit. His eyes bulged. His nose ran. He barely kept himself from throwing up. It was the first time he had ever smoked anything.

He was thirty-nine years old. He was ready to try something new. First, though, he snuffed out that stinking cigarette.

Al Levantin started out with little, which soon became even less. When he was two, his father, a traveling lamp salesman, walked out on the family. Levantin and his mother were left in a one-bedroom apartment. The father promised to pay child support, but never did. Nobody could find him. Al's mother was alone in the Great Depression with a toddler and no money when the landlord came knocking. So she took a full-time bookkeeping job with a lingerie manufacturer in the Garment District of Manhattan and moved in with her parents in the Bronx. They cared for their grandchild during the workday. But when Levantin was four, his grandmother died. His grandfather died a few months later. Levantin's mother had to keep her job. She had no choice. She had to catch the D train. She left her son each morning with a sack lunch in his hand and the apartment key in his pocket. The boy walked to school by himself. Before he learned how to read, Al Levantin learned to be by himself.

For a five-year-old, temptations were everywhere. Every morning by nine, Levantin had to walk down three floors of tenement stairs and along Eastburn Avenue to P.S. 70. On the corner was the market. The market was a problem. Through the window at the market he could see the box of Chunky candy bars, chocolate and raisins and nuts, positioned in that same prominent spot on the counter. Every day he passed that window, and every day he looked inside. Levantin's buddies got to go in for a Chunky.

When the afternoon school bell rang, Levantin faced a choice: he could go home to an empty apartment and work on the pluses and minuses of single-digit arithmetic, or he could play outside. Levantin usually played. He was bigger than most other neighborhood kids, and he learned to use his bulk in basketball to box out for rebounds and put-backs. There was one problem: he didn't own a basketball. For a family that couldn't afford a Chunky bar, a ball was out of the question. If Levantin wanted to play basketball, he had to learn to be nice to the boys who owned the basketball. Levantin became a good basketball player.

He also excelled at the ultimate New York street game, stickball. In the blocks around 175th and the Grand Concourse, Levantin was known as a two-sewer guy—standing in the street with a broomstick, he could belt a pink rubber ball beyond the second manhole cover. A few other players were three-sewer guys, but those bombers weren't as skilled at place-hitting the Spalding between cars and off the fire escapes.

By 6:30 P.M., the D train brought his mother home. Mother and son ate dinner together and fell asleep in separate beds in the same bedroom. In Levantin's world, a man was something that existed elsewhere. His mother hardly ever dated, and all signs of his deadbeat father were banished from the apartment. Levantin had no idea what his father even looked like.

One day Levantin came home talking about the Boy Scouts. His mother was thrilled. In the Scouts, her only child might find a man to look up to. Besides, the Scouts met at his local Mount Eden Synagogue—and joining hardly cost anything.

The Boy Scouts changed Al Levantin. For the first time, he learned about camping and hiking, fishing and swimming, finding stars in the sky and minerals in the ground. All these things happened someplace outside the Bronx. In his whole life, he had been outside the Bronx only on day trips to visit relatives in New Jersey. But Levantin could read about life outside the Bronx in his Boy Scouts handbook. So he read. And he dreamed.

One day the impossible became possible: Levantin was going away to summer Boy Scout camp. How this happened, he never knew. He had no connections, and his mother had no money. Levantin was afraid to ask for an explanation. But for eight weeks in the summer of 1945, he lived at Camp Ranachqua. It was only a three-hour trip by bus, but it may as well have been on a different planet. Camp Ranachqua was where the Boy Scouts handbook became more than a book. It was the first time Levantin ever spent the night outside the Bronx. He slept under the stars and swam in the lake and hiked through the Catskills. There were no sirens. There was no yelling. He could shoot an arrow at Ranachqua farther than he could slug a Spalding on Eastburn Avenue. He learned enough about birds to earn the birdwatching merit badge. At the beginning of camp, he knew nobody.

At the end, he had dozens of friends. He didn't want to leave.

When he did finally return home, he was a birdwatcher possessed. With his mother still balancing books at the lingerie factory, Levantin had afternoons to himself and occupied his time chasing sparrows and warblers through the Bronx Botanical Garden and Van Cortlandt Park. While at DeWitt Clinton High School, Levantin joined his first Audubon Christmas Bird Count and learned there were lots of other people who chased birds not for a Boy Scout medal, but just because they loved it. He tooled around the city with guys named Marshall and Arnold—the same people Sandy Komito joined in the field. Komito lived only a mile from Levantin and was in the class of 1949, one year ahead of Levantin, at DeWitt Clinton. The two now believe they must have birded together as boys, though neither can remember the other. It may have been the first and only time Komito on a birding expedition failed to make a lasting impression.

Levantin's grades and test scores were good enough to win admission to the tuition-free City College of New York; he studied chemistry because the campus offering that was closest to his home. Within weeks after graduation, he was drafted into the army. He served sixteen months as a weatherman in Alaska and became preoccupied with life outside New York. He enrolled at the University of Kansas for a doctorate in chemistry, but the theoreticals and philosophicals of academic life drove him crazy. He quit his doctoral studies after one year, but succeeded in riding a bicycle for the first time. He was twenty-four.

For his third date with a Queens woman named Ethel, he suggested they go to Jones Beach. She thought he wanted to see her in a swimsuit; he brought along his binoculars and tried to teach her birding. She cared about him, not birds. They married in 1959.

He took a job in Philadelphia as a laboratory chemist for Rohm and Haas, the international chemical giant with the slogan: *While few consumers know us, few industries don't.* In his first two years he won two patents for coatings that prevent paint from chipping on cars. He was enthusiastic about his work, but the lab chemicals soon took a toll. Levantin lost his sense of smell. Luckily, his bosses learned that Levantin had a rare skill: he was good with chemicals, but even better with people. They started sending him on the road to meet customers. He was pulling in good money, but had to travel fifty thousand, sixty thousand, seventy thousand miles a year, leaving his wife alone with their two sons. All that weekday travel made him feel too guilty to take off again on weekends to go birding. He tried to teach his sons about shorebirds in the marshes at the Brigantine National Wildlife Refuge in New Jersey, but the boys only wanted to play in the watchtower. He tried to show them hawks in fall migration at the Bake Oven Knob area near Allentown, but the boys amused themselves climbing rocks. When the family went to the beach, he could only spend so much time under the umbrella with binoculars.

Little by little, Levantin stopped birding. He had no time to do it and no one to do it with. His one contact with his boyhood passion remained a subscription to *Birding* magazine, which he read on planes or at home after the boys were asleep. He also hoarded thirty years of Christmas Bird Count reports from around the country. Though these six-hundred-page documents offered just the basics—*13 common redpoll, 12/29, Minot, North Dakota*—they did tell him the best places to find many species in the dead of winter. Maybe someday he would have time to go there. His book knowledge was growing. His life list was not.

In the meantime, he climbed the Rohm and Haas ladder.

His time in product development turned him into the head of the development group, then manager of Polymers, Resins, and Monomers. The company offered him a chance to run the European division—eight major chemical factories, plus sales forces from the United Kingdom to the USSR, Sweden to South Africa. Levantin moved the family to London, where he worked longer and traveled farther. To strengthen parental bonds, he brought his oldest son on a business trip to a Spanish manufacturing plant, but the teenager came away convinced that his father worked for a polluter.

When the family returned to Philadelphia in 1985, Levantin's overseas business experience was a sought-after skill. He was recruited to join the board of another Philadelphia company, CDI, a head-hunting and temporary-staffing corporation anxious to expand in Europe. Levantin, who had never served on a board of directors, was interested in the new experience.

A few years later, though, Levantin's existing employer began cutting back. After thirty-three years at Rohm and Haas, Levantin was offered three years' salary for his early retirement. At age fifty-nine, Al Levantin stopped working.

His retirement lasted six months. CDI persuaded him to take over a money-losing company division that hired out clerical workers as temps. It was Levantin's first and only work outside the chemical business. He wore a suit and tie again. He logged long hours again. He acquired a competitor and joined the operations and made his $175-million-a-year division turn its first profit—all in eighteen months. He was proud. He stopped working again.

His second retirement lasted less than three years. Levantin had moved to Colorado when he got another call from CDI. This time, the subsidiary he had turned around, Today's Staffing, needed a chief executive to mentor a replacement.

This time, Levantin had to live two days a week in Dallas. This time, he worked another two years.

In October 1997, Levantin retired one more time. The dream house had been built and Ethel was ready to enjoy it. At one point, she pulled out some travel records and did some math and came up with a remarkable conclusion: though Al and Ethel had been married thirty-seven years, they had never—not once—lived together thirty days in a row. While Al was spending all those days on the road, Ethel returned to school, earned her master's degree, and opened shop as a marriage counselor. In her business, she had seen her share of workaholics.

Now Al was retired for the third time. All the nights when the kids were running around and Ethel was tired and Al was on the road again—she had been waiting for this time, for just the two of them. But Al had been waiting for something, too.

When Levantin told his wife that he wanted to take off again and spend a year chasing birds, she wasn't quite sure what to say. But she knew they had managed to stay married thirty-seven years. Plenty of friends hadn't. Maybe the key to a marriage, she thought, was keeping it fresh, to let one go off and follow a dream and bring it back home for both of them to celebrate.

Go for it, Ethel told Al.

He didn't need to be told twice.

THREE

The Early Birds

The concept of a Big Year was more than a century in the making. In fact, the urge to see and conquer the birds of North America grew out of a Napoleon complex.

While the diminutive general was marching his triumphant armies across Europe and the Middle East, a young man named Jean-Jacques Audubon dodged Napoleon's draft by fleeing France for America.

The bastard child of a French sea captain and his chambermaid mistress, Audubon was ashamed of his past. He changed his name to John James Audubon soon after arriving in the New World, but then failed at every venture that was supposed to give him a fresh start. He botched the management of his father's estate in Pennsylvania and was forced to sell it. He opened trading posts in Kentucky and Missouri, but they failed, as did an import business in New Orleans. He built a sawmill on the Ohio River where there was little demand for lumber, and the inevitable shutdown shoved him into personal bankruptcy. He emerged from debtors' prison in 1819 with only his clothes, his gun—and his watercolor brushes.

The one thing Audubon excelled at was drawing and painting. As a boy in France, when his father forced him to attend military school, Audubon comforted himself by slipping into the woods with his pastels and drawing paper. Ever the romantic, he reveled in nature. And the most beautiful facet of nature, he concluded, was birds.

Audubon was obsessed with birds. He painted them when his businesses started and he painted them when his businesses failed. Many suspected that his preoccupation with avian life was the true cause of his financial ruin. At one point, Audubon's wife, Lucy, lamented in a letter to her sister, "I have a rival in every bird." Audubon's fifth business failed. In all his wilderness wanderings, he had discovered dozens of birds, but not a single goose with golden eggs.

From desperation rose inspiration. On October 12, 1820, Audubon boarded a boat on the Ohio River in Cincinnati and set out on a great birding adventure. His quest: to paint a life-size portrait of every bird in the New World. His journeys ultimately led him down the Mississippi River to New Orleans across the South to the Dry Tortugas of Florida, through the Atlantic coast to the rocky shores of Labrador, and up the Missouri River to the Great Plains of the Dakotas.

His art became a landmark book. His travels became the basis for a Big Year.

The Birds of America was an international sensation. With 450 magnificent watercolors of the creatures of the untamed New World, Audubon revolutionized wildlife art. His paintings were big, bold, and remarkably animated. Though Audubon's gift for depicting birds in natural settings set him apart from other artists, his work required heavy sacrifice. To complete a single drawing, Audubon would shoot and kill whole flocks of birds—dozens of brown pelicans, bags of warblers—just to select the one or two specimens in freshest plumage. He then threaded wire into the carcasses and posed them as if they were still alive, flitting on branches and regurgitating food for mates.

Audubon, the man, won fame that rivaled Audubon, the artist. In England, where new industrialists were devouring James Fenimore Cooper's latest book, *The Pioneers*, Audubon seemed the living embodiment of wild America. A cocky frontiersman with buckskin coat, sharpshooter's eye, and hair preened with bear grease, he regaled European audiences with his woolly tall tales, many of which were serialized in London newspapers. There were knife fights with Indians, an overnight in a backwoods hunting cabin with Daniel Boone, and most of all, birds, strange and beautiful, tiny and tall, creatures that proved to European industrialists that America was home to more than just cotton, tobacco, and merchant profits. After so many years of poverty, Audubon, now a swashbuckling dandy, was finally able to pay back his supporters. He named the Harris's hawk and Harris's sparrow after a New Jersey farmer, Edward Harris, one of Audubon's earliest patrons. The highest powers of the land also took note. An 1826 portrait of Audubon, with heroic gaze, shoulder-length mane, and long gun at the ready, still hangs in the Red Room of the White House.

Sadly, several of the birds originally painted by Audubon—the great auk, passenger pigeon, Carolina parakeet, Bachman's warbler, Labrador duck, and ivory-billed woodpecker—are extinct today, the victims of habitat destruction and slaughter for food and for fun. Audubon himself was a sharpshooting hunter who enjoyed blood sports, but extirpations horrified him. After a grueling trip through the Great Plains, where men shot animals only because they could, Audubon warned that the buffalo, like the great auk, was on the verge of disappearing forever.

Audubon died in 1851. But his wife, who had paid the family bills for years by working as a schoolteacher, had a former student ready to pick up the conservationist banner.

Editor of *Forest and Stream* magazine, George Bird Grinnell was aghast at senseless wildlife slayings. In 1886, he urged readers to join him in the nation's first bird preservation group, which, in honor of his hero, he called the Audubon Society. In just three months, more than thirty-eight thousand people signed up; Grinnell was so overwhelmed that he disbanded the society. But the naturalist spirit lived on, and the group was eventually reconstituted by Massachusetts women disgusted at the slaughter of birds, especially egrets, for hat decorations. The National Audubon Society today is one of the world's foremost environmental organizations, with 550,000 members and more than a hundred sanctuaries across the United States.

Though the frontier was long gone by the turn of the twentieth century, one old sport was not: many Americans still celebrated Christmas with contests to kill the most birds in a single day. Sometimes these "side hunt" competitions were between individual men; other times they involved teams of men. But they all ended the same way—with a mound of feathers and carcasses piled at their feet.

On Christmas Day, 1900, an Audubon Society ornithologist named Frank Chapman came up with a better idea. Instead of killing birds, Chapman said, outdoorsmen should count them. On December 25 of that year, twenty-seven bird lovers from New Brunswick, Canada, to Monterey County, California—a total of thirteen states and two provinces were represented—went afield. They found 90 species and 18,500 individual birds, but most importantly, these bird lovers discovered each other. The first continental birdwatching network was born.

Audubon's Christmas Bird Count began as a way for birders to meet and greet others with the same quirky obsession. With their annual state-of-the-union census of bird populations across North America, Christmas counters told themselves that serious ornithology was being conducted here. Though this technically was true—university biologists did occasionally rely on Audubon-reported counts to analyze trends among avian species—the Christmas Bird Count also served as a hotbox for birders with competitive blood. Soon some Christmas teams began to compete with other teams to report the biggest list, and some birders began to compete with other birders on their own team to report the most species. Today the Christmas Bird Count has become a birding tradition nearly as strong as spring migration, with more than 52,000 people joining 1,800 different counts across North America.

Inevitably, some birders stopped waiting for Christmas to compete. The result was a Big Day. By rising at midnight to shine lanterns on owls, working the brush at dawn for songbirds, scoping the lakes at noon for waterfowl, and then scrambling through new habitat as the sun set, Big Day participants combined strategy and endurance in a race to see the most species in a single twenty-four-hour period. By the end of World War I, a Big Day with one hundred species, a Century Run, was something to brag about.

Then came Roger Tory Peterson. In 1934, at the age of twenty-five, he converted birding from a pastime of the peculiar to a sport for the masses.

Peterson's pocket-size book, *A Field Guide to the Birds*, summed up the species of eastern North America in 167 pages and revolutionized the way Americans viewed the outdoors. Before Peterson's book was published, bird chasers still sighted their quarry from the barrel of a shotgun; a carcass in the hand was the only proper way to identify many species. But Peterson moved identifications out of the taxonomist's laboratory and into the hands of everyday Americans by showing them how to distinguish live birds by sight and call.

His book grouped similar-looking species together on the same page and then highlighted their field marks—the visual characteristics that made one bird species different from another. Four pages of color plates were reserved for the most brilliant birds—warblers, blue jays, and scarlet tanagers—but most species were illustrated in black and white, with an arrow highlighting each bird's defining physical feature. Until Peterson, many unarmed bird lovers had little choice but to assume that a sparrow was simply a sparrow. Then the *Field Guide* offered indispensable advice: white outer tail feathers signified a Vesper sparrow, large central breast spot meant a song sparrow, unstreaked underparts distinguished a grass-hopper sparrow. The natural history museum's lock on bird identification was broken.

In the depths of the Great Depression, Peterson's book, with its forest-green cover and bufflehead flying below the title, sold out in one week. So did the next press run. And the next. Eventually more than 2 million copies of his field guide were sold. Peterson was so rich he never had to work again.

But he did—he worked and worked and worked. His original idea of using field marks to identify a species spread from birds to wildflowers to butterflies to reptiles to seashells to rocks—more than four dozen guides in all. The Peterson *Field Guide* series became some of the greatest-selling nonfiction titles of all time. Birders soon stopped talking about taking their field guide into the field; they simply carried their Peterson.

Of course, Peterson did more than just paint and write. He evangelized. He preached the gospel of birding in Omaha, and twelve hundred filled an auditorium. Another sixteen hundred heard the good word in Kansas City. In Detroit, officials feared an overcrowded hall, so they tried to limit his audience by giving only one day's public notice for his lecture.

More than a thousand showed up anyway. With their Petersons in their pockets and binoculars around their necks, these birders looked around the packed meeting halls and realized: Hey, there are a lot of people just like me.

In Peterson, many birders also saw themselves.

Son of an immigrant Swede, Peterson was mocked as a boy for his "nuttiness" about nature. He even began one of his books, *Birds Over America*, with a confrontation at home:

"So, you've been out after birds again!" my father snorted. "Haven't you seen them all before? And look at your clothes— nobody with any sense would stay out in the rain." Puzzled, he shook his head. "I swear, I don't understand you," he added reproachfully.

I never could explain to him why I did these things; I never quite knew myself.

Peterson's father, Charles, was a cabinetmaker; Peterson couldn't build a birdhouse. His father drank too much, called his nature boy a "damn fool," and whupped him with a razor strop; Peterson was so afraid he'd look like his father that, as a teen, he tried to ward off baldness by rubbing his scalp with Grover's Mange Cure. (His hair survived.)

He grew up in the furniture-making town of Jamestown, New York, as a "Green Swede"—an immigrant supposedly so dumb that he would eat green bananas—often pitted in gang fights against immigrant Italians. He had few friends. He was so quirky that he missed the historic landing of the first airplane in his hometown because he was watching two grasshoppers copulating. But thanks to Jamestown's Junior Audubon Society, led by his beloved seventh-grade teacher, Miss Blanche Hornbeck, Peterson found solace in birds.

When Peterson told these stories, audience faces beamed back with smiles of recognition. Yes, these were tales of an outcast. But could all these people, in all these auditoriums, with all these similar life experiences, all be outcasts, too?

If anything, Peterson romanticized the outcast path. In 1953, he joined with Britain's most famed naturalist, James Fisher, for a thirty-thousand-mile trek across the New World. Launching their hundred-day adventure amid a kittiwake colony in northern Newfoundland, the two loaded a station wagon with duffels, a portable blind, and a giant rooftop parabolic reflector that amplified birdcalls.

And then the buddies drove.

They marveled at wood-warblers pouring through the Blue Ridge Mountains on migration. They retraced Audubon's footsteps through the sooty tern rookery on the Dry Tortugas. They reveled in the wondrous comeback of egrets—once on the brink of extinction—to the Flying Gardens of Avery Island, Louisiana. Along the way, they swilled an addicting Southern concoction called Coca-Cola. Though the two ornithological icons enjoyed unprecedented behind-the-scenes access to the continent's greatest museums and endangered-species habitats, Peterson and Fisher never became grizzled enough to lose their schoolboy enthusiasm; both men stood speechless for ten minutes after their first view of the Grand Canyon. When Fisher saw his first California condor, soaring magnificently on ten-foot wings above the desert, he turned to Peterson and exclaimed, "Tally—most incredibly—ho!" In their three months of day-after-day travels, the men claimed to argue only once, when Peterson nearly slammed into another driver on a hairpin turn somewhere on a lonely mountain road in Arizona. When the trek finally ended with 2 million murres on Walrus Island off Alaska, they told their story in a book, and documentary film, called *Wild America*.

One footnote in *Wild America* was devoured by a certain kind of birder. "Incidental information," Peterson wrote in small type after an asterisk at the bottom of a page. "My year's list at the end of 1953 was 572 species."

It was the line that launched an exodus from the reading chairs, movie theaters, and auditoriums of the birding nation. Soon hundreds wanted to follow in Peterson's bootprints. They wanted to take the brakes off their obsession. They wanted to bird North America.

They wanted to do a Big Year.

Wild America was published in 1955. The next year, a twenty-five-year-old Englishman named Stuart Keith, fresh out of Oxford, was so enthralled with the travelogue that he decided to repeat it himself. With his Peterson in one hand and *Wild America* in the other, Keith took off in his '53 Ford station wagon. Looking for longspurs on the side of the road in Texas, he was hooted at by cowboys. One of his most pleasant memories was driving sixty miles from San Bernardino to Pasadena—the heart of today's Southern California sprawlurbia—and smelling nothing but sweet orange blossoms the entire way. Keith fell so in love with America during his Big Year that he moved permanently to this side of the Atlantic. His decision was helped by the fact that, with a Bohemian waxwing over Christmas vacation in Edmonton, Alberta, he scored 598 birds that year—twenty-six more than Peterson.

The Big Year ante was upped.

For Keith, it felt lonely at the top. In an *Audubon* magazine story describing his new record, Keith noted that his life list of North American birds, 625 species, was second only to that of the great Roger Tory Peterson, who reported 633. "I know of no other birders who have seen more than six hundred North American species and only three who have seen more than five hundred," he wrote.

Oops! Within weeks of his 1961 article, Keith was

bombarded with dozens of letters from birders reporting that they, too, were proud owners of life lists with more than five hundred species. Nineteen people, in fact, reported at least six hundred species. Keith fared no better than No. 10 among overall life listers, and a previously anonymous birder, Ira Gabrielson of Washington, D.C., turned in a list with 669 life birds—more than even Peterson himself. In a 1963 *Audubon* article headlined, "The 600 Club: America's Top-Ranking Birders," Keith confirmed that a student had indeed surpassed the teacher. But he also felt obligated to defend listing from serious ornithologists who believed that racing to tick birds off scorecards was silly, wasteful, and demeaning.

"Bird listing is a sport," Keith wrote, "and as such, it needs no defense, any more than baseball or bowling. Nobody feels guilty about spending a day at the World Series, nor is an evening bowling considered to be wasted. Why, then, should people worry that their day's listing hasn't contributed anything to ornithological knowledge?"

For the first time, the nation's premier conservationist magazine had published a defense of listing—while reporting the names of its leading practitioners. Meanwhile, other news about the sport advanced. A zoology professor, Olin Pettingill of Carleton College in Minnesota, began publishing how-to guides about the best places on the continent to track down birds. With 659 pages on bird-finding east of the Mississippi and 709 pages about the West, Pettingill promised that his "thorough coverage of bird haunts will bring bird students to think of this book as the ornithologist's Duncan Hines." At the time, Hines was famed as the traveling salesman who reviewed and endorsed restaurants with his personal seal of approval. But Pettingill's own comparison to Hines, who eventually sold out his name to grocery cake-mix makers, turned out to be prescient: competitive birders followed

Pettingill's birding instructions as if they were precise recipes. Want to see a smooth-billed ani? Go to the Loxahatchee National Wildlife Refuge in Florida. Elegant trogon? Cave Creek Canyon, Arizona. Great gray owl? Stop at Sax-Zim Bog, Minnesota—in the winter.

When Pettingill started feeding tidbits of information to hungry birders, they only cried out for more—more detail, more directions, more local contacts. Jim Lane filled the niche with a series of two-hundred-page books, each for a particular state or even just a particular section of a state. Where the Pettingill guides merely stated that the Great Plains intersection of Colorado, Kansas, and Oklahoma was a good place to look for lesser prairie chickens, the Lane guides instructed birders to go "east from Campo on a gravel road for eight miles. Turn right or south for two miles, then left or east again. After nearly three miles, you will see a TV tower on the right. Continue past that for 1.3 miles to a small bridge. Just before crossing it, turn right down a dirt trail along the west side of the gully and go 1.3 miles. The strutting grounds are about one hundred yards ahead on your right. Stay in your car. Repeat, stay in your car or the birds will fly away."

Birding was no longer solely for ornithologists and over-the-top hobbyists; now vacationers could do it, too. But if much of the mystery was stripped from the rare-bird hunt, so, too, was the adventure. The Pettingill and Lane guides made it possible to build a big list of birds without much stumbling, bumbling, or even basic knowledge about birds. Though these species could be found in many places, the guides promoted a paint-by-numbers approach to birding, and many people rarely saw the need to look for birds outside the predrawn lines.

The information revolution was born. So was a debate: Was this birding, or a game?

Hundreds, then thousands, were having too much fun to care. Realizing that the National Audubon Society was more interested in promoting environmental causes than big birding lists, the hardest of the hard core in 1969 formed the American Birding Association. Meetings were reminiscent of an Alcoholics Anonymous session, except that everybody here was proud of their addiction—and looking for more.

Tales were swapped. Road trips were shared. Competitors were eyed.

The American Birding Association soon set ethical standards—a bird "must have been alive, wild, and unrestrained when encountered" to count on a list—and also established geographic boundaries for listing. For Big Year counts, the area was the United States north of Mexico, plus Canada and ocean waters up to two hundred miles offshore. The Bahamas, Hawaii, and Greenland were excluded.

Roger Tory Peterson was still the patron saint of birders. Less than two decades after his landmark drive through wild America, though, his Big Year record had become little more than a speck in the rearview mirror of birders speeding across the continent.

No one raced faster than Ted Parker. By the time he had earned his driver's license, Parker's peers in the underground world of teenage birders already recognized him as a superior being: not only had he memorized the field marks of most North American birds, he could play basketball, too. By 1971, his final semester at McCaskey High School in southeastern Pennsylvania, Parker decided that his best remaining lesson would be to master the continent's birds. He played hooky for a series of three-day weekends and saw all waterfowl that regularly wintered within three hundred miles of his home; he launched other extended field trips to Ontario, Illinois, and South Carolina and found great gray owls, greater prairie chickens, and red-cockaded woodpeckers. Luckily, the mop-headed eighteen-year-old also found a supervising grown-up, Harold Morrin, forty-eight, a local finance executive, to accompany him on these long trips away from his parents. (Parker's father, who was as fanatical about golf as his son was about birds, stayed home on the links.) Morrin and Parker shared a love of birds and road trips, but the older teacher soon became in awe of his young friend, whose amazing ear allowed him to identify virtually every North American song-bird by its call—or just a mere chip note. Serious, intense, and driven, Parker enrolled at the University of Arizona at Tucson in September and vacuumed up dozens of Southwestern and Pacific Coast specialties. He ended 1971 with 626 species, shattering Stuart Keith's fifteen-year-old record by 28 birds. A Big Year had become a young man's game.

When the birding world learned that the new continental record had been set by a mere teenager, many had the same reaction: Hey, I can do that!

Floyd Murdoch was a university doctoral student who wanted to visit dozens of national wildlife refuges for his dissertation on the history of bird protection. Kenn Kaufman was a high school dropout who wanted to hitchhike his way across America. In 1973, both decided to do a Big Year.

When they first met on a January boat trip twenty-five miles off the New Hampshire coast, neither was pleased to see the other. Still raw from a recent divorce, Murdoch, thirty-one, was strapped for cash and forced to rely on his '64 Buick Century, the Blue Goose, to carry him around the country. Just as he started to feel sorry for himself as a suffering under-dog, along came Kaufman, an eighteen-year-old from Wichita with an unemployed father and a habit of pouring Little Friskies braised-liver cat food into a cold can of vegetable soup and calling it dinner. Murdoch was cleancut and neatly dressed with wire-rim professor's glasses; Kaufman had brambles for a beard and looked and sometimes smelled as if he had slept in a Dumpster. Though he originally believed his Big Year could be a David-and-Goliath battle, Murdoch suddenly found himself cast in the wrong role. He didn't like it. At one point, on a rough boat ride back from the Dry Tortugas, Murdoch found himself standing next to an extremely seasick Kaufman—and wistfully entertaining a dark way of ending the competition. "To show my good birdsmanship," Murdoch later wrote in *Birding* magazine, "I held on to Kenn's belt as he hung over the rail. Just a gentle shove and then there was one?"

Kaufman's wanderlust quickly captured the imagination of the birding world. Thumbing rides 69,200 miles back and forth and back again across North America, Kaufman was jailed two days in Virginia on hitchhiking charges; menaced with a shotgun by an Oklahoma rancher who hated longhairs; slugged by a drunken gold miner on the streets of Nome; and swept by a rogue wave from a Texas jetty into the Gulf of Mexico. He didn't have a driver's license—gas was too expensive, anyway, during the 1973 Arab oil embargo—but tired travelers still let the scraggly hitchhiker steer their vehicles through twelve states and two provinces. (Kaufman crashed a new Torino GT in Louisiana and skidded a VW bus into a ditch in the Yukon). He was so desperate for cash that he sold his blood and cashed in his life insurance. He slept under highway bridges. He ate cat food often enough on the docks of offshore boat trips that birders suspected his real goal was for a wealthy birder to take pity and buy him an expensive tour ticket. Incredibly, Kaufman spent less than $1,000 on his Big Year.

It wasn't enough. In the end, Murdoch won the contest with a new record of 669 North American species—three more than Kaufman. (Kaufman actually saw the most birds that year, but the extras came during a cross-the-border detour to Baja, Mexico.) In a postmortem for *Birding* magazine, Murdoch regretted that he wasn't more selfish. "I had a plan, but let others' interests change it too often," he wrote. "As a result, at least five birds were missed because I spent time helping other people get birds instead of working on my own list. Moral of the story: BE GREEDY! You will lose a lot of friends and make a lot of enemies, but you will get a bigger list."

Kaufman was more sanguine. During his Big Year, he met his wife-to-be in Kenmare, North Dakota, at the first American Birding Association convention—"where birding heroes outranked rock-and-roll idols, football stars, and politicians"—and established himself as one of the continent's foremost field birders. Kaufman's memoir of his Big Year, *Kingbird Highway*, turned him into the mythical hero who got mobbed at birding conventions.

Some were impressed by Kaufman; others were inspired. In 1976, during his junior year at Dartmouth College, Scott Robinson watched his classmates taking off a year to travel through Europe or live as a Rocky Mountain ski bum or work an internship on Wall Street. Robinson decided to do a year for the birds. Grubstaked by a grandmother who gave him $2,500, a brownand-white Dodge van, and orders to chase his dream, Robinson retraced much of the old perimeter route—down the East Coast, across the Gulf to Texas and Arizona, then up the Pacific Coast— first promoted by Peterson and Fisher in *Wild America*. By early May, he had posted a startling 600 birds, nearly 150 ahead of Murdoch's record-setting pace, but he had a problem. In the frenzy of spring migration, he had promised to put his Big Year on hold to help a professor with a research project. For two and a half months, he remained stranded with the professor in the decidedly unbirdy

White Mountains of central New Hampshire. When Robinson finally emerged, however, he revolutionized the concept of Big Years with one simple twist: instead of continuing his traditional birding field trips, he started chasing rarities. In the first part of his Big Year, Robinson had met enough birders to be admitted into an informal network of rare-bird alerts, the avian version of a Baptist prayer circle, which spread the news about sightings of unusual species across the continent. Armed with a $500 Eastern Airlines ticket that allowed him to fly unlimited segments almost anywhere in America, Robinson started knocking off toughies one at a time—a loggerhead kingbird in the Florida Keys, a ruff at Big Sur, a Montezuma quail in Arizona. The Big Year record was his.

If a college kid could cook up a plan to knock off a record, what could a real businessman do? James M. Vardaman stewed over that question. A timber consultant in Jackson, Mississippi, Vardaman conceded that he was only a so-so birder. But one thing he did know was business—his middle initial M actually stood for Money (a family name, he said)—and Vardaman's business needed publicity. A Big Year, he concluded, would be the cheapest, easiest, and most fun way to make a national name for James M. Vardaman & Co.

As a business consultant, Vardaman strongly believed in writing a plan and sticking with it. One hitch: he didn't know enough about birding to draft his own Big Year plan. So Vardaman hired a who's who of birding to meet in Mississippi and serve as his Strategy Council. There was Kenn Kaufman, the 1973 Big Year hitchhiker who now lived in Tucson; John Arvin of McAllen, Texas, a virtuoso on the birds of the Rio Grande Valley; Larry Balch of Chicago, a top lister who operated Alaskan bird tours; Will Russell of Seal Harbor, Maine, an owner of the Northeast Birding tour group; Rich

Stallcup of Inverness, California, author of *Pelagic Birds of Monterey Bay, California*; and Paul Sykes, of Delray Beach, Florida, a U.S. Fish and Wildlife Service specialist in endangered species. The idea, Vardaman said, was not only to hire the best experts, but to hire the best experts from different birding regions who were tied into local hot lines whenever rarities showed up.

Still, Vardaman worried that his paid posse might sometimes find itself out of the rarity loop. As a backup, he got the addresses of 850 North American bird clubs, then added 300 top members of the American Birding Association and National Audubon Society. Everyone on this mailing list soon started receiving a regular newsletter, *Vardaman's Gold Sheet*, that told everyone about the progress of his Big Year. Though the sweetener in the newsletter was the description of his latest birding adventure, the business end was a box with this plea: *Call collect 601-354-3123, ask for Birdman.*

Vardaman had created the first North American birding hot line. He picked up an extra twenty species because of it.

Not all went according to plan. While Vardaman, fifty-eight, was gallivanting around the continent on his Big Year, his wife, Virginia, was home alone with the couple's six children, ages six to seventeen, including two sets of twins. At one point, after Vardaman took off on an Arctic swing for gyrfalcons, bluethroats, and crested auklets, Virginia told a *Wall Street Journal* reporter, "I would have sold him for a dime when he went off to Alaska and left me for weeks with the kids." By the middle of the year, when Vardaman phoned home, his children stopped saying, "We miss you," and started saying, "What's your count?"

From the beginning, Vardaman wisely decided to make his Big Year above reproach. Every time he saw a bird, he made sure a witness saw him seeing the bird. Vardaman showed off both his witness list and species list to all comers. Even so, many birders were soured by the spectacle of a rank amateur—whose repeated flights made him an official Flying Colonel of the Delta Air Lines fleet— spending wildly to see birds that he sometimes couldn't identify by himself. When Kenn Kaufman guided Vardaman outside Phoenix to find Le Conte's thrasher, a notoriously elusive soil-digger of the saltbush desert, he excitedly pointed out the bird and started to pull out his scope for a better look. "Oh, no, that's okay," Vardaman told Kaufman. The bird was checked off his list. Time to move on.

Vardaman ended 1979 with several major accomplishments. He shattered the Big Year birding record, with 699 species. He broke the Big Year spending record, with total expenditures of $44,507.38—including guide fees of $10,157.12—and an overall cost of $63.67 per bird. He proved conclusively that there was no connection between birding skill and a big birding list. And perhaps most importantly, James Money Vardaman pissed off the North American birding establishment.

Birders had long wrung their hands debating whether their passion was science or sport. In a single twelve-month swoop, however, Vardaman had reduced it to bingo. Bingo was for little old ladies in tennis shoes. Was birding, too?

No way, the Old Guard decided.

The job of defending the honor of competitive birding fell to a chortling Tennessean named Benton Basham. The original membership chairman of the American Birding Association, Basham was an anesthetist nurse with a Norman Vincent Peale–like zeal for birding who joked, promoted, and sweet-talked his way into the front ranks of the sport. A recruiter with an evangelist's fervor, he had helped persuade Floyd Murdoch in 1973 to do his Big Year.

In 1983, it was Basham's turn.

With Basham in the field, the American Birding Association directors left little to chance. While Vardaman solicited rarity news in 1979 by mailing his *Gold Sheet* to bird clubs and three hundred selected birders across the continent, Basham and his American Birding buddies expanded the information network even further. They mailed individual letters to four thousand members of the association telling them about Basham's attempt to take back the record, and urging them to phone in news as soon as any rarity turned up.

This request wasn't as simple as it seemed. Though many birders knew the species around their hometowns, they had little idea how they fit into the bigger continental picture. A black oyster-catcher, for example, would be an amazing rarity in Massachusetts, but it was common on the Pacific Coast. Basham didn't want middle-of-the-night calls about birds that were common somewhere; he wanted calls about true freaks of nature. So he invented a code system that prioritized all North American birds. Code 1 was for the easiest birds, the starlings and house sparrows; Code 2 birds, such as the peregrine falcon, were seen regularly but not predictably; and Code 3 was for tougher species, such as the violet-crowned hummingbird, that required a special trip to targeted areas during a short observation season. Together these Code 1, 2, and 3 birds represented 675 species, the breeding and migratory base of North America. Basham assumed he'd pick up these species somewhere, sometime during his Big Year. These birds weren't worth urgent phone calls; Basham wanted news about Code 4 and 5 birds, the vagrants, accidentals, and weirdos that somehow got lost on their home turf and blew over from other continents. These species were Basham's top priority, the birds that would break Vardaman's Big Year record.

To make sure that birders would remember Basham's quest,

Birding magazine covered his Big Year with the same kind of hoopla that *Sports Illustrated* reserved for Henry Aaron's assault on the Babe Ruth home run record. "703 in '83" began one pre–Big Year article, describing Basham's hope and plan to take back the record from Vardaman, the moneyed outsider, with 703 species. "Benton Basham continues to roll on toward his goal," reported another *Birding* update, "and it now appears that only a miracle will stop him from soaring well over seven hundred." When Basham did finally win back the record from Vardaman, with 711 birds, *Birding* celebrated with eight pages of coverage—led by a cover photo of Basham in conqueror's pose atop a gate with a no-trespassing sign. It was one of the few times a nonbird ever appeared on the cover of *Birding*.

The birding elite celebrated: Vardaman the vulgar was vanquished. Basham had put true birders back on top. The pecking order was restored.

His feat wasn't cheap. Though Basham steadfastly refused to say exactly how much he spent on his Big Year, he did admit that, for the same amount of money, he could have built a nice home and put a car in the driveway. This was in Tennessee, though.

To hard-core birders, Basham's new record was the feat of the century: though 675 species or so lived in North America, he managed to see 36 more. The rarity-chasing game first started by Scott Robinson on Eastern Airlines had been pushed to the hilt. Others tried, but failed, to beat Basham.

But in February 1985, in the living room of a house in Clint, Texas, Basham sowed the seed of his own doom. Waiting for a staked-out, purplish-backed jay to show up at someone's backyard feeder—it was the first record of this species in North America—Basham was plopped inside the living room on the sofa when a stranger knocked. Like

Basham, this man was bearded, boisterous, and seriously intense about chasing birds. The two talked, and Basham extracted three promises from the newcomer: (1) He would join the American Birding Association. (2) He would spend $5,000 on a new top-of-the-line Questar birding scope. (3) He would set aside at least three weeks of his life to run after Asian rarities on a deserted Aleutian Islands government outpost called Attu.

By the time the purplish-backed jay finally landed at that West Texas feeder, the newcomer, Sandy Komito, was a walking tinderbox of bird lust. Benton Basham had just passed him the lit match.

Two years later, in 1987, Komito was traveling the continent on a practice run for a 1988 Big Year. By August, however, Basham had persuaded Komito to shell out a few thousand dollars for a bush-plane camping trip, north of the arctic circle at the confluence of the Kelly and Noatak Rivers, to hunt down Siberian tits. At the end of that successful trip, Komito had 660 birds for the year—and a hunch that he should turn this Big Year practice run into the real thing. On November 6, he broke Basham's record with a Muscovy duck below Falcon Dam on the Rio Grande and pushed on until a long-eared owl on New Year's Eve took him to 721.

Komito had spent $60,000. He had traveled two hundred twenty days. He had become the new and undisputed Big Year birding champion of North America.

He remained unfulfilled. For starters, he had missed at least thirty birds—including a white-tailed eagle on Attu, an eared trogon in Arizona, a Ross's gull in Oregon, Manitoba, and Alaska—that he could have seen. He had wasted precious days chasing some birds in remote arctic breeding grounds when they could have been picked up much more easily, with a little more organizational effort, on the Great Plains and the

Gulf Coast. And he still wasn't enough of a birding insider to be fully plugged in to the national rare-bird alert networks. (In contrast to the hero's parade of publicity lavished on Basham, Komito's Big Year record didn't even rate a story in *Birding* magazine; Komito eventually self-published a book on his 1987 record, titled *Birding's Indiana Jones*.)

Komito knew he could do better. Even worse, he knew that others could do better, too. He even knew them.

Dr. Bill Rydell was one of Komito's best birding buddies. They had roomed together at Attu, where Rydell had considered Komito an ideal bunkmate because he didn't snore, didn't drink, and didn't lug his muddy boots into the room. While playing bridge and cribbage and hearts by the hearth, Komito had told Rydell more and more about his 1987 Big Year. Rydell had listened—and learned.

By 1992, Rydell was prepared to retire from his general-surgery practice in Las Vegas. But he was too restless for retired life, and his wife, Mary, wasn't ready to have her husband around all the time, especially when she was decorating their new house in Pebble Beach. So Rydell stockpiled $50,000 and ten frequent-flier airline tickets and took off on his Big Year.

At the Kelly and Noatak Rivers in northern Alaska, Rydell flew the same bush plane to see the same tits as Komito. Rydell knocked off two of Komito's nemesis birds, the long-eared owl and Muscovy duck, ten months earlier than his friend had in 1987. The surgeon who had spent four decades in the emergency room was so caught up in the frenzy of seeing a Bahama mockingbird and La Sagra's flycatcher that he somehow locked his keys in his car twice in the same day—in the Florida Keys and Big Sur, California. Racing on his Big Year roll, Rydell then prepared for the all-out trump of his old bridge partner: a weeklong boat trip, on the private yacht of a California millionaire, two hundred miles off the Pacific

Coast. Rydell and the rest of the birding world could hardly contain their excitement. Never before had a boat toured so far, and so long, just for birds. Who knew what rarities lived way out yonder?

As it turned out, not much. While Rydell did pick up one hot species, a red-tailed tropicbird, on the first day out of San Francisco Bay, the remainder of the trip was a bust. Rydell returned from sea with only five new birds, and all but the tropicbird were commoners. A Big Year was always a race against the clock, and Rydell had burned seven full days of precious time. When a prized spotted redshank turned up in New York on December 21, Rydell decided he'd rather spend Christmas at home with family. He finished with 714 birds that year.

Komito's record still was safe; Rydell had ended seven birds short. But watching one of his best friends travel with the same budget to the same haunts for the same birds had re-kindled something inside Komito. He missed competitive birding. Komito knew his record had barely survived. Someday, he figured, someone would break it. If not Rydell, then who? Komito considered the possibilities, but kept returning to the same conclusion.

He wanted to do another Big Year.

But no man in history ever had done it twice. He had the time and money. But the strength? The stamina? The mono-maniacal devotion to a single cause?

It was time for the rematch, Komito concluded, me against the birds.

He never even considered the possibility that it could be man versus man versus man.

FOUR

Strategy

Greg Miller went straight for the bedroom and dug for the Christmas present from his brother. He had stashed away the gift for the same reason a dieter stashes away a box of chocolates—to make it hard to find. But Miller was over the guilt phase now. He wanted that birding book.

After a few minutes of excavation he found it, maroon and gold, with a songbird on the cover. It was *Kingbird Highway*, the story of Kenn Kaufman's 1973 Big Year, and Miller devoured all 318 pages in a marathon reading session, splayed on the frameless futon that was plopped on his bedroom floor. Miller couldn't believe a man could see all those birds and travel all those miles for less than $1,000. Maybe a Big Year wasn't so unattainable after all. Miller started thinking. His Ford Explorer had survived the divorce, so he wouldn't have to repeat Kaufman's feat of thumbing his way across America. Could Miller really afford a Big Year?

He unfolded a blue metal card chair and set it up in front of his wood-laminate computer desk. He navigated his PC straight to the Internet travel site www.travelocity.com and saw, amazingly, the spoils of an airline fare war. He pulled out a Visa card and started clicking.

One hour later, Miller had booked round-trip flights on the

no-frills carrier Southwest Airlines to Arizona, Texas, and Minnesota in February; Oklahoma and California in March; and Texas again in April. His total airfare cost for these six trips was $1,000, or roughly the same as Kaufman's entire Big Year.

Miller wasn't done yet.

For years he had dreamed of a May trip to Attu, the Holy Grail of serious birders. A treeless Alaskan spit seventeen hundred miles from Anchorage but just two hundred miles from Russia—the international date line actually curved around the island to keep North America on the same calendar page—Attu was where Asian rarities landed when storms in the Bering Sea turned brutal. A two-week trip to Attu, plus another week of tours to other forsaken Alaskan isles, cost $5,000, or more than a year's worth of rent in this two-car-garage apartment. Miller knew he couldn't afford Attu. But he couldn't afford to sacrifice his mind to work and despair, either. Attu would be the trip of a lifetime, if he could only live until May. He bought Alaska with a $500 deposit.

Never in his life had he booked so much travel. Never in his life had he felt so exhilarated. His whole body tingled; he nearly expected to look up and see a Bonaparte's gull land on his home computer monitor.

Miller pulled out his favorite reference book, the *National Geographic Field Guide to the Birds of North America*, and tried to steel himself with some cold reality. At work he still had thousands of Y2K bugs to slay, and at home he had little money. If he missed a bird on the coast during spring migration, he would have neither the time nor money to chase it later on the tundra breeding grounds. Wild races for one-of-a-kind rarities were out of the question. He might see six hundred birds.

In the middle of the night, alone on the futon in his garage apartment, Greg Miller still felt lucky.

A Big Year ultimately is a numbers game. There are 675 birds that commonly live in North America, and there are 365 days to see all of them. Find two new birds a day and you're the new champ.

Doing the math is easy. Living it is madness.

For starters, birds don't all live in the same place. Ornithologists say 440 species live on land, 190 stick to shores, and 45 stay far at sea. Many of these species remain extremely picky about where they live. Though a purple sandpiper and rock sandpiper are nearly identical in looks, voice, and flight, the purple chooses to live only in the pounding surf of the North Atlantic. The rock prefers the Pacific. Why does one creature with the freedom of flight require an ocean sunrise, while the other demands a sunset? Nobody knows, but a successful Big Year birder must spot them both.

The problem is, spots move. Migration is one of the planet's most powerful natural forces, and at least three hundred North American species succumb to it each year. The Canada warbler, for example, remains true to its name every May by nesting in the moist North Woods. But by August this yellow-and-gray songbird turns into a fair-weather friend, flying a thousand feet above the treetops until it reaches its wintering grounds four thousand miles away in the eastern Andes Mountains of Peru. That gives Big Year birders a five-month window to see the Canada warbler in North America. Almost everyone does; a Canada warbler is so easy to find while migrating to and from its nesting turf that it's considered a "gimme" bird.

Many others aren't. The northern wheatear looks like a pale, half-sized robin, but with a rugged behavioral quirk: it insists on sex only in the rocky tundra of Alaska and northern

Labrador. Chicks happen. But after a summer of love above the arctic circle, the wheatear replaces its appetite for romance with a new craving for particular kinds of beetles. So the northern wheatear ditches the Western Hemisphere— Alaska birds travel over Siberia, Labrador birds go over Greenland—for the beetle-rich wonderland of Africa. This remote migration route makes the wheatear a tougher species for birders, but one that Big Year contestants still can't miss.

And so it goes. Each species poses a different problem. To succeed, a Big Year birder must research each of the continent's 675 homegrown species and figure out when, where, and how to see it. Does this bird migrate early or late? Over land or water? Which flyway route—Atlantic, Pacific, Mississippi, or Central? Alone or with other species? Does it winter in the American South or flee the continent altogether?

Many species must be seen on a moment's notice.

Strategy is king.

Scheduling is a bitch.

The challenge is setting up a whole year of travel around the sweeping pendulum of the migratory clock. For Big Year contestants, spring migration is the easiest and best way to see dozens of species on a single trip. Most springtime action centers on so-called migrant traps, the crucial oases where exhausted birds rest after surviving a major water crossing. For birders these are magical places—High Island of Texas, Dauphin Island of Alabama, and Point Pelee of Ontario are three of the most famous—that brim with a continent's cornucopia of species, but are also conveniently near major airports. A bird seen in a migrant trap is a bird that doesn't have to be chased again in a more inaccessible breeding ground; Big Year birders turn frantic trying to see everything possible. Only a rookie would arrive at Point Pelee after sunrise in mid-May and expect to find a parking spot.

The second migratory sweep, in fall, is desperation time. The only birds being sought then are the ones missed in the spring migration, missed during nesting season, and missed throughout the summer. Miss a bird in fall migration and kiss it good-bye for the year. Big Year birders don't like to depend on fall migration.

Around the two great migrations, contestants must fit in other stops at birding's stations of the cross: South Florida for tropical species and shorebirds; northern Minnesota for owls and other cravers of cold; West Texas for desert specialties; southeast Arizona for hummingbirds and goatsuckers; the Great Plains for longspurs and inland sparrows; coastal Alaska for Eurasian breeders; Colorado for sage grouse and other wild chickens; and California and North Carolina for seabirds and land leftovers.

A birder who arrives at all these right places at all the right times can expect to see all 675 homegrown North American species. The problem: the Big Year record is 721 species. How can a birder see 721 species in a continent that is home to only 675? Vagrants and accidentals.

During migration, birds get lost. Some are blown off course by hurricanes or typhoons. Others, like a father on a family road trip, refuse to stop for directions. The result, though, is the same: a bird that doesn't belong in North America ends up in North America. These lost species quickly get categorized: a vagrant is a species that has wandered off its typical migration path; an accidental is a species that has been seen only a few times in an area a long, long way from home. Vagrants and accidentals have a nasty habit of turning up on the side of the continent farthest from Big Year birders.

Sandy Komito knew that drill better than anyone. In 1987, he had sensibly tried to save money by booking airline tickets far in advance to traditional birding hot spots. Just as he was about to take off according to plan, he'd get word of a vagrant or accidental spied somewhere else. Should he continue his existing plan to see a dozen native species or ditch the cheap trip for the chance at a once-in-a-decade accidental? The dilemma always gave Komito heartburn—and an adrenaline rush.

This time, in 1998, for his second Big Year, Komito was ready to stop the hand-wringing. Always chase rarities first, he decided, and worry about the checkbook later. Still, Komito was too frugal to burn $100 bills. Besides, few things gave him more pleasure than working out a better deal. Komito started working.

First he walked his wallet over to Continental Airlines, which sold special senior-citizen ticket booklets for $999. Each booklet contained eight tickets; each ticket allowed him to fly a segment anywhere in the continental United States or Canada. Because Komito had traveled 60,000 miles the previous year, mainly chasing birds, he almost always got free upgrades. Combine the senior booklet with all the upgrades and Komito expected to fly first-class to almost any bird on the continent for $125. Komito bought three booklets, or twenty-four flights.

Komito also knew he had to get to Attu. But he had a problem—a lingering dispute with the Attu tour director over a $48.06-a-night hotel room. In 1993, Komito and other birders were ready to fly their tour-chartered plane to Attu when a fall storm slammed Alaska. The group was grounded in Anchorage for four days, so the tour director, Larry Balch, former president of the American Birding Association, booked rooms for all stranded birders at a local hotel. Komito believed that Balch should pay the resulting $192.24 hotel bill because he had selected the hotel and given Komito no choice about where to stay. Balch said the room was Komito's responsibility. For months afterward, the two men exchanged nasty letters—Komito could, after all, type eighty words per minute—until Balch finally shut off argument with one sentence: "As a matter of policy, Attour will not accept reservations from persons with delinquent accounts." Komito seethed. But there was no way for Sandy Komito to get to Attu without Larry Balch, and Balch would not let Komito on Attu until he paid the $192.24. So Komito wrote the check. He also worried about a repeat of the infamous Attu tour of 1995, when bad weather canceled that year's trip altogether. Komito cringed at the prospect of having thousands of his dollars tied up in a birding tour that might be washed out. His solution: pay the deposit to Balch, but withhold the remaining $5,000 until this year's trip was guaranteed to happen. Attu wasn't until May. In the meantime, Komito told himself to focus on birds, not people.

Al Levantin, by contrast, had no people problems. For years, while Komito and the rest of the birding elite had been traipsing around the continent, Levantin was cooped up in his office. Few top birders even knew him. That meant he didn't have anyone who would call him in the middle of the night to tell him about a vagrant or accidental. But he also didn't have anyone trying to settle an old score against him. This was a distinct advantage.

Levantin was determined to go it alone. He'd had enough of assistants setting all his lunch dates, all his meetings, all his plane travel. He was a chemist. He loved solving problems. And a Big Year was a giant logistical problem.

For inspiration, Levantin read Jim Vardaman's book, *Call Collect, Ask for Birdman*. Like Levantin, Vardaman was a businessman with money to spare but no insider status among the top flight of birders. Levantin admired Vardaman's executive approach—when he didn't know something, he hired the best expert to tell him how to do it. True, many birders spat out Vardaman's name the same way a sick man spat phlegm—can you *believe* that guy *bought* himself a Big Year record? He was so *clueless*, he had to *hire* somebody to *show* him all the birds—but Levantin really knew his birds. He wouldn't have to hire anybody. He wanted to prove that an outsider could break the Big Year record without being led around like a cruise ship tourist.

Levantin had read Komito's self-published book, *Birding's Indiana Jones*, so he knew how the 1987 record was set. Ever the scientist, Levantin analyzed Komito's strategies and concluded that one change could score him a lot more birds.

That change was boat trips. Komito had admitted that he missed at least six seabirds during his record-setting run because he hadn't scheduled enough ocean journeys. Levantin would not make the same mistake. He scoured through catalogs, the Internet, and *Birding* magazine and bought tickets for as many offshore tours as he could find. From his home in the Rocky Mountains, he prepared for victory at sea.

All was well—until he actually tried to book a plane seat. This was the last problem he'd ever expected. As he'd climbed in his career from laboratory man to middle manager to vice president to chief executive, he also rose in the pecking order of United Airlines frequent fliers—from Premier (25,000 miles a year) to Premier Executive (50,000 miles) to the most perk-laden of all passenger peaks, Premier Executive 1K, for the 100,000-mile-a-year traveler.

But he still couldn't get a flight out of Aspen. From January through March, Aspen was a capital of North American skiing (or at least après-skiing), and nearly every flight was already booked solid. Levantin called the special line for top United customers and tried every argument possible: He was

Premier Executive 1K, not some first-time tourist. He was flying out of Aspen, not in. He was packing binoculars, not heavy bags of ski gear. After a few minutes of this, Levantin realized he may as well have been trying to cut a better deal with the post office—it just wasn't going to happen. Levantin scooped up the few airline tickets he could and braced himself. As long as the skiing starlets and trustafarians flocked to Aspen, Levantin would have a hard time finding vagrants and accidentals. Who'd have thought that the airport in Aspen— rich, glamorous, fast-paced Aspen—would be such a bottleneck? He shared this complaint with only his wife. Levantin knew he could never win sympathy among birders by lamenting the difficulty of life during an Aspen ski season.

Greg Miller could only dream of such riches. He started the year with $7,000 in his checking account, but nearly all that money was already spoken for to pay for the big Alaska trip. He also had $10,000 of debt spread across three Visa cards, one MasterCard, and one Discover card. Though he hated paying 19 percent interest on some monthly balances, Miller believed he had little choice. Credit cards gave him financial wiggle room. His credit limit still allowed another $6,500 of charges. He wanted to pick up more cards, but didn't hold out much hope. Sometimes in his work binges he had forgotten to pay a few monthly bills. Visa made him feel grateful for the plastic he had.

Miller's Big Year, then, would have to be all hand-to-mouth. He got $45 an hour at the nuclear power plant. He worked as a contractor, so there was no time-and-a-half overtime. But his bosses encouraged him to rack up the hours. A twelve-hour day, after taxes, would pay for a Miami flight, if the airfare wars lasted. A fourteen-hour day could get him to Vancouver. He calculated the office time required for a flight to Point Barrow, Alaska, and he shivered.

If he worked the hours, he could afford the travel. But if he worked the hours, he didn't have time for the travel. Y2K was two years away, and the software was still rife with bugs. Would Miller's boss risk a meltdown for the birds?

No way. Miller would have to work hard and bird hard. If the year went well, he would have nothing left in his desk, his wallet, and his dreams.

Nobody ever had tried to work a full-time job during a Big Year. But Miller was a man of extremes. He knew he could do it.

FIVE

Bodega Bluff

At any given time, there were billions of birds in millions of places watched by thousands of people. So why in the world, Al Levantin wondered, did *that* man have to show up right here, right now?

There was no mistaking it: a half hour before dawn in Bodega Bay, California, Sandy Komito had just walked onto the same birding tour boat. Or, to be completely accurate, it was Komito's voice—that booming, bass voice—that entered the boat far in advance of his feet.

Before that moment, Levantin could think of no improvements to his Big Year. It was only nineteen days into January, but he had already tallied 245 species. That was one new bird every two hours. He felt invigorated. He had traveled to three states and one Canadian province. And that British Columbia bird, a green microburst of energy called a Xantus's hummingbird, was exceedingly rare—so rare, in fact, that it had been reported north of the Mexican border only two other times in history. Rarities build a Big Year record, and Levantin hoped to find even more with the promise of new seabirds on this offshore trip.

Enter Komito, with bluster. Levantin, of course, knew exactly who Sandy Komito was. In two earlier spring migrations, they had spent weeks together, along with the hardest of birding's hard core, in that lonely Aleutian Islands outpost called Attu. After all that time in such close quarters, Levantin concluded that Komito was rich and relentless. He also knew Komito was the undisputed owner of the Big Year record, 721 birds, set in 1987. Levantin knew he was going to beat Komito's old record. He just didn't know if he would tell him.

"Good morning, Master," Levantin told Komito. Levantin had given Komito that nickname on a long-ago birding trip, and Komito had never really disputed it. Levantin was so jovial that it was hard to tell if the nickname was sarcastic. A career in the Fortune 500 had taught him that a smile in business, even unpleasant business, went a long way.

"Hello, Al," Komito replied. "How you doing?"

Decision time. Should he tell Komito that he was out to get him?

Before Levantin could open his mouth, Komito walked away. It was the first big offshore birding trip of the year, and Komito saw fifty other birders on this charter. He was a volcano brimming with a winter's worth of war stories, and he was about to erupt.

For Levantin to run into Komito here felt especially odd. Bodega Bay was the same harbor where Alfred Hitchcock had filmed his 1963 horror classic, *The Birds*, the movie that made the world think twice about backyard feeders. Hitchcock knew the worst shocks came from the mundane, and few creatures were as widespread, and as taken for granted, as birds. So the great director had western gulls dive-bombing children at an outdoor birthday party, raspberry-dipped house finches pouring into a living room through the fireplace, and American crows slashing at Tippi Hedren while she cowered in a bedroom. Suffice to say, *The Birds* was not a popular movie with birders on board this tour boat. After lifetimes of weekends in the field, they knew birds didn't attack humans. The only way Hitchcock had got ravens to chase actors was to sprinkle their hair with seed. Crows lurked on the gutters of the old schoolhouse because he affixed magnets to their feet. Children fleeing swarms of blackbirds in the movie were actually running on a studio treadmill with birds tied to their necks. It all seemed silly to Levantin. The only menacing thing birds ever did to him was poop on his patio.

A single human, however, was about to cause him more trouble. Komito returned from the bow of the boat. Was that a new bounce in his step, or just sea legs? Either way, Komito seemed to be accompanied by that eerie whEE, whEE, whEE of Hitchcock horror music.

Should I tell him? Levantin wondered. Should I tell him?

Komito, as usual, cut to the chase: "You been out lately, Al?"

What Levantin thought was: I have been out lately. A lot. I'm at 245 and I'm gunning for your record.

What Levantin said was: "I just got back from British Columbia. Got the Xantus's hummingbird there. Nice bird."

"Excellent bird," Komito replied. "You know, I was thinking of trying for Xantus's."

That's odd, Levantin thought. Komito had seen the Xantus's years earlier. It was on his life list. Why would Komito spend the time and money traveling to see the same bird again?

If Komito wouldn't tell Levantin what he was up to, then Levantin wouldn't offer anything, either. Information was valuable. One of the main challenges in a Big Year was identifying the competition. Every top chaser had some weakness—a shortage of cash, a surplus of hubris, an aversion to long separations from a spouse at home—but no soft spot could be exploited until a foe was conclusively identified. Levantin didn't want anyone, especially a Big Year champion, to know what he was up to.

Waves lapped. The boat rumbled. Finally Levantin couldn't suppress it. The helpful side of his personality, Mr. Nice Guy Engineer, took over. "Well," Levantin told Komito, "I came straight from Vancouver and I've still got my maps and ferry schedules. You want them?"

Did Komito want them? What kind of question was that? Levantin just offered Komito the birding equivalent of a treasure map. Without Levantin's ferry schedule, Komito could spend good money on a plane flight to Vancouver but then sit around and wait on a dock until who knew when. In a Big Year, there was nothing more precious than time, and Levantin was giving the gift of a 366th day.

The extra day became even more valuable when the boat motored to the mouth of the harbor, near the Bodega bluff where Jessica Tandy's house had withstood the monumental cinematic crow attack. Waves in the ocean beyond were ten feet and blasting. It was unsafe to continue, the captain announced, and he called off the trip. The day was a bust. When the boat turned around to the dock, Levantin had no birds to count, but he did have plenty of time to think. His own Big Year secret was still safe. But what was Komito up to? Why would he want to see a lifer twice? Could Komito be on a Big Year, too? Nah, nobody ever did a Big Year twice. He knew Komito was a birding lunatic. But that kind of lunatic?

Levantin felt tinges of dread and suspense. The Tides restaurant, same as in *The Birds*, loomed above the bay. Western gulls tailed the boat, but the engine groaned too loudly for anyone else to hear a note of that Hitchcock music.

Three days later, at another dock two hundred miles down the California coast but three thousand miles from home, Komito walked onto Levantin's boat again. This was too weird. Komito had time for the Xantus's hummingbird in British Columbia—*and* this boat in Monterey Bay? When Levantin and Komito finally greeted each other, it was hard to tell who eyed the other more suspiciously. There still was no talk of a Big Year, but Komito did confide he hadn't had a chance yet to zip up to Canada for the hummer. Komito seemed strangely preoccupied. He had his own worries.

Eleven years earlier, during his first Big Year, Komito had had a legendary run-in with the operator of this very boat, Debi Shearwater. In the birding world, Shearwater was the High Queen of the High Seas, the Pacific Coast's leading organizer of offshore trips, called pelagics, that gave birders their only chance to see about seventy-five different species that live almost their entire lives far at sea.

There was no disputing that Shearwater loved birds; in fact, she had legally changed her name in 1980 from Debi Millichap to Debi Shearwater in honor of the thirteen species of shearwaters, the tube-nosed seabirds that coursed the deep waters of the Atlantic and the Pacific. (Her favorite bird was a land-based raptor, but Debi Golden Eagle sounded too Indian for a woman with Swedish grandparents.)

For Komito, the problem was that Shearwater loved more than just birds. She also had the hots for whales and dolphins and often called time-outs in the middle of birding trips just to watch sea mammals. Birders put up with this partly because her trips produced fabulous birds, but also because Shearwater was intimidating. In a pastime filled with the shy, bookish, and polite, Shearwater had the temper and physical presence of a linebacker. She yelled.

Not everyone cowered. In 1987, when Shearwater once again stopped her charter far offshore to watch some cavorting gray whales, Komito finally had enough.

"Hey, we paid to see birds, not whales!" he called to her.

Shearwater ignored him. The whales *were* beautiful.

With no birds in sight, Shearwater kept the engines cut next to the spouting cetaceans. Komito couldn't take it. He went customer to customer on the charter and asked a single blunt question: Do you want to watch birds, or whales? With a crush of these customers waiting outside the captain's cabin, Komito confronted Shearwater with the results.

Forty-seven of fifty customers on your boat want to see birds, not whales, Komito told Shearwater. Let's stop this whale nonsense right now and get on with the reason we're here—pelagic birds.

Shearwater was not happy. A mutiny at sea over birds? The gall!

Miles from shore, Komito had found the one person, a woman, who could match his stubborn streak. Shearwater refused to move the boat. So Komito relayed the voting results to the actual skipper, who, like most captains on Shearwater boat trips, was used to running lunch-bucket fishermen, not persnickety birders, out to sea.

The skipper looked at the New Jersey industrial contractor, then looked at the woman who had changed her name to a bird. "I do what she tells me," the captain told Komito. Shearwater told him to stay put.

So they did.

Shearwater and Komito refused to speak long afterward. She bet that Komito needed her more than she needed Komito. She turned out to be right. Here it was, eleven years later, and Komito was back for another Shearwater trip. He knew, and she knew, that he had no other choice: if you wanted to see Pacific pelagic birds, you had to start at Shearwater's dock.

The two bumped into each other as the seventy-five-foot boat throttled up its engine. How would she treat Komito? What if a good bird was holding on the other side of the boat? Would she move the boat for him?

Komito had been on so many pelagics—he'd stopped counting at two hundred—that he had already memorized the usual onboard safety lecture. But Levantin, who had been at sea only twice before for birds, paid closer attention.

Shearwater barked: No smoking, life jackets are over there, make sure you take a pill for seasickness. Drink a lot of water and go easy on the coffee. If you have to throw up, don't go in the bathroom, because that'll just make a mess. And don't go off the front or sides because it'll just blow back. Go off the back, okay? Any questions?

There was good reason why Shearwater ran trips from Monterey Bay: it was a biological wonder. Monterey is one of the few places on earth with just the right convergence of parallel-to-the-coast winds, an unusually deep canyon, and rich undersea life. The result is a natural phenomenon called an upwelling.

To most humans this upwelling is barely discernible—a slightly off-color rip with cooler water temperatures. But to marine life, it's an open pipe from a food factory. The upwelling traps microscopic life, phytoplankton, from the depths of the Pacific and blasts it on a nonstop elevator ride to the top. Phytoplankton attracts baitfish, which attract tuna and dolphin and whales, which attract birds.

When Shearwater began hiring fishing captains for birding trips in the 1970s, she found that they saw the same natural phenomenon, but from a different angle. A lifetime of searching for fish at sea had taught skippers to look for "tuna birds," the agile white dive-bombers that trailed schools of albacore and feasted on the predator's leftover anchovies. But on her first trip with fishing skippers to the albacore grounds, Shearwater discovered that "tuna birds" were arctic terns—a species prized among birders and the greatest migrant of the animal world, a four-ounce creature that flies ten thousand miles every year from the endless summer sun of the North Pole to the endless sun of the South, and then back again.

If Shearwater could teach skippers the real names of pelagic birds, she could also show them how to pilot a boat for birders. Some species, such as northern fulmars, were so common that skippers could blast right by them. But others, like the streaked shearwater, had to be chased. How could manly fishing captains learn to identify dainty birds on the wing? Shearwater had to speak their native language: a rhinoceros auklet flew like a football, she told them, and a Cassin's auklet flew like a golf ball. The tutoring process looked a lot like the maritime version of *My Fair Lady*, but with the young woman instructing the old salts. Slowly, but inevitably, fishermen became birdmen.

By 1998 Shearwater was running seventy birding charters a year, and the drill was well established. The boat first cruised the rocks to find harlequin ducks, gaudy inshore birds with a seeming suicide wish: every time surf crashed against the jetty, the ducks dived for crabs and mollusks. Somehow the harlequin returned to the surface with head intact.

Just beyond the white water worked the pigeon guillemot. Black with a white wing patch, it seemed smarter than the duck, avoiding the pounding waves and diving down a hundred feet for deep crabs and mollusks.

As sunrise crept over the coast, sea lions and harbor seals basked on the jetty. Komito and Levantin checked out birds, not each other. Life was good.

The boat barreled out to deeper water. The great thing about Monterey was that the upwelling was less than five miles off-shore. Some East Coast trips, dependent on the Gulf Stream, had to motor fifty miles before seeing their first pelagic species. But here were northern fulmars and pink-footed shearwaters and pomarine jaegers, all within sight of land.

Someone called, "There she blows!" Just off the starboard side spouted a pod of gray whales.

Komito braced himself. The Big Year clock was running. He needed every minute for birds. Would Shearwater paralyze him with the torpor of whale watching?

Amazingly, the boat continued on. It was fifty degrees with ten-knot winds, but Komito felt an undeniable warmth. Maybe, just maybe, an old hatchet was buried. (The truth was that Shearwater had lost some of her fascination with gray whales. When she'd first started running trips in the 1970s and 1980s, the giant mammals truly were unusual sights. But decades of conservation policies had finally let the populations bound back, and gray whales weren't unusual enough today to cause her to throttle down the engines.)

Off the stern, birders started a chum line, tossing out popcorn and anchovies and attracting a wave of gulls, including black-legged kittiwakes. Komito hated fouling his hands with anchovy slime, which he believed could take a week to properly scrub off. Levantin and some others did work the chum. Levantin couldn't help wondering again: Why was Komito here? Waves rolled. The boat was out of the harbor.

Attracted to the diving and splashing and fighting throng of gulls, a black-footed albatross glided by. On board, near bedlam broke out. An albatross was always a star attraction: eight feet of effortless wingspan that rarely came within eye-shot of land, the albatross was payoff for all the hassles and expense of a trip to sea.

A guide unpacked the secret weapon of every pelagic trip—a big bucket of cod-liver oil—and poured it off the stern.

The birds went wild.

Cod-liver oil—whew!—Levantin hadn't smelled that in years. It really stank.

More waves rolled.

Diesel fumes wafted from the engine.

Waves. Cod-liver oil. Diesel. Waves.

Why did Komito want the ferry schedule?

Feeling tension in his toes.

Komito seeing a life bird again?

Cod-liver oil.

Levantin upchucked over the rail.

He felt embarrassed, very embarrassed. But his embarrassment was part of the chum line now. He staggered into the cabin, closed his eyes, and tried to recover. Why did he get sick? Was it waves or nerves?

While Levantin ruminated, Komito remained out on the rail, where he spotted Cassin's auklets and short-tailed shearwaters. By the time Levantin could stand again, those birds were gone. Komito was two species ahead of Levantin, with directions in pocket for that rare hummer. Levantin knew he had to hustle, if only he could keep his face from turning green.

SIX

Whirlwind

Sandy Komito was worried. He thought he had a competitor, and not just any competitor. Al Levantin possessed a dangerous mix of time, money, and birding smarts. Komito had seen Levantin in action at Attu. He knew Levantin was tireless and at ease with people, a personality advantage that could translate into a few goodwill birds. Plus, Levantin was from the Bronx. Komito had learned long ago that there was a word for people who ignored driven men from the Bronx. That word was *loser*.

If Al Levantin wanted a contest, then Sandy Komito would give him one. In the month after the two met on a boat ride on Monterey Bay, Komito tore off on a travel schedule that was ridiculous and exhausting, but designed to deliver one defiant warning:

Don't mess with Sandy Komito.

January 20. Gibsons, British Columbia. 1,100 miles. $366 Second Street, Second Street. Where the hell was Second Street?

Sandy Komito knew men weren't supposed to ask for directions, but this was different. He was in a strange city in a foreign country and it was raining. Somewhere out there was a rare bird, the Xantus's hummingbird that Levantin had told him about, in Canada for the first time in recorded history. Levantin had told Komito the bird was diving to a house feeder on Second Street. Komito needed that house. He needed that bird. He needed help.

In a town that seemed to ban older people, Komito finally spotted a fiftyish woman on the sidewalk walking through the drizzle. A mature woman, he figured, might understand his plight. "Excuse me," Komito called, rolling down his car window and pulling his rented Taurus alongside. "Can you tell me where Second Street is?"

The woman stopped.

"Oh, you're looking for that bird!" she said.

Komito burst out laughing. In his mind, most people couldn't tell a hummer from a Humvee. But he had somehow picked the one person on the streets of Gibsons, British Columbia, who knew the exact home address of the Xantus's hummingbird.

Just up the hill, on a panhandle lot jutting into Georgia Strait, stood 221 Second Street. At the moment, it was the center of the Canadian birding universe.

When Gerrie and Lloyd Patterson had first reported that something weird and green was poking its bill into their fuchsia flowers, few birders twittered. After all, the Pattersons were nice people with a few feeders, but they were hardly chasers. Besides, the bird they described wasn't in any field guide common to the Pacific Northwest—or North America, for that matter. Even the local experts were puzzled, so they called in Mike Toochin, globe-trotting birder extraordinaire, from Vancouver, who confirmed it: the rufous tail and buffy underparts made it a Xantus's.

How it got here, nobody knew. The Xantus's was a sun-lover that was supposed to winter twenty-two hundred miles south of B.C., along the tropic of Cancer in the lower tip of the Baja. In fact, this bird had been found north of the Mexican border only twice before, and both those spottings had come in Southern California more than a decade earlier. Some ornithologists thought this bird had been blown north during a freak West Coast hurricane in October; others thought it must be an escapee from a local zoo, even though no one had reported a missing Xantus's.

How could a tropical pip-squeak live through the dankest depths of a Pacific Northwest winter? Luckily, hummingbirds were one of the few animals that could, at will, survive a cold night by dropping into semihibernation; in this temporary state, a hummingbird cut its body temperature in half, to fifty-five degrees, and braked its heart rate from twelve hundred beats per minute while flying to just fifty or so pumps in torpor.

Once word of this biological miracle spread on the Internet, the house on the island at the top of the hundred-foot drive-way became an international tourist sensation. By the time Komito arrived, more than fourteen hundred people from twenty-eight states, eight provinces, and five countries had signed the visitors' log at 221 Second Street. Most came on the morning ferry from Vancouver, which offered a bustling coffee concession. By the time these latte-loaded birders reached the Patterson driveway, they were performing a wiggly gotta-pee jig. The Pattersons giggled—until the jigglers started ringing the doorbell and begging to use the bathroom. The Pattersons took up a collection and rented a Porta Potti.

Knowing that coffee could not be bought, only rented, Komito had taken care of his morning beverage lease before arriving at the Pattersons' door. He signed the visitors' log, but a raindrop turned his hometown into a blob.

Six days earlier, Al Levantin had signed the same book.

Komito tried making small talk with Lloyd Patterson, who

was polite but not foolish enough to walk out from under his porch overhang in a fifty-degree drizzle to greet his latest visitor. In the rain, behind a chest-high cedar fence, twenty feet from a red, plastic feeder filled with sugar water, Komito waited. The Xantus's hummingbird stayed long enough for Komito to snap a few pictures.

Take that, Al Levantin.

January 21. Vancouver. 200 miles. $120
Over a lifetime of birding, Komito most fondly recalled his times in wild places—the swifts darting behind waterfalls, the grouse exploding through the North Woods, the albatrosses gliding through the sunrise.

This was not one of those times.

He parked at the Wild Coyote Bar and Grill and walked south toward the roar of jets just across the water at Vancouver International Airport. At the Arthur Laing Highway Bridge, rush-hour traffic streamed up and over the causeway.

Komito ducked beneath the bridge. He was in the last lair of the crested myna.

One hundred and one years earlier, legend had it, a careless sailor or customs official had opened the cage of some captive crested mynas from South China and set them free on a dock in Vancouver. The birds went forth and multiplied. And multiplied.

By the 1930s, the streets of Vancouver were rife with tens of thousands of crested mynas, a dark, chunky, robin-sized bird with white wing patches and a scruffy forehead. Homesick Chinese laborers kept crested mynas as pets. But Canadian wildlife biologists, who valued tried-and-true native species over spicy exotics, regarded the myna as winged vermin. They feared that the bird would keep moving and breeding until it had plagued all of North America. There was, after all, a horrible precedent for this: 120 European starlings, released in New York City at about the same time the myna was set free in Vancouver, had already multiplied a millionfold and conquered the continent.

Then Mother Nature, in her unsentimental way, hosted a strange encounter on the streets of Vancouver. Asian invader met European invader. It turned out that the myna and starling enjoyed having sex (though not with each other) in the same urban environments—in the crevices of old buildings, amid the grime of noisy underpasses, around the trash of unkempt alleys. The difference was that starlings made better mothers. Whenever a myna grew bored of incubating eggs and decided to take a quick flight around the neighborhood, the starling moved right in, taking over the same habitat, and, sometimes, the very same nest.

The starling—pushy, pesty, and promiscuous—now ruled the streets. By the time Komito got here, fewer than fifty breeding pairs of crested mynas survived in North America. Vancouver was its Alamo. Though there were steady reports of crested mynas going Dumpster-diving for french fries at local McDonald's, the Arthur Laing Highway Bridge was supposed to be the myna's last, best remaining roost.

If only Komito could stand the racket. Overhead, cars and trucks and buses rattled the girders so loudly that he could hardly hear himself think; no chance of hearing any bird's call here. His eyes watered from the stench of exhaust. How could any animal that managed to live here still teeter on the brink of North American extinction?

He checked the girders, the posts, the sign brackets, but the myna was missing. Maybe the Golden Arches were a better bet, after all. He did not relish the thought of chumming for any bird with a Happy Meal.

So he walked the underpinnings of the bridge, northbound to southbound, merge lane to exit ramp. He looked up so much that his neck hurt. A headache started to take root, and the diesel fumes didn't help. Finally, from a pipe supporting a highway sign, out popped one myna. Then another.

Komito got the hell out of there.

January 22. Seattle. 2,500 miles. $300

There was a report of a rare Siberian bird in Alaska. On a layover in the Seattle airport, Komito called all four people he knew in Anchorage. Nobody was home. Should he grab the 9 P.M. flight anyway and hope the bird was there when he arrived? Decisions, decisions, then he remembered: since New Year's Day, he had been home in New Jersey a total of ten hours.

He flew to Newark.

January 23. Fair Lawn, New Jersey

At home, he paid bills, saw a red-breasted nuthatch at his backyard feeder, called Alaska, ate dinner at a restaurant with his wife, and announced he would be leaving tomorrow by dawn. He fell asleep by 9 P.M.

January 24. Superior, Arizona. 2,400 miles. $266

As a teenager in the rough-and-tumble copper town of Butte, Montana, William Boyce Thompson played high-stakes poker in bars. His parents, aghast, shipped him off to prep school at the elite Phillips Exeter Academy in New Hampshire. He failed to graduate. He was admitted anyway to Columbia University, where he tried studying mining. He quit after his freshman year. He mined back home in Montana, but failed there, too. So Thompson moved back to New York City.

In the canyons of Wall Street, where they moved paper instead of earth, William Boyce Thompson got rich—tens of millions of dollars rich. His stock plays financed some of the vast Western mining pits that today are some of America's nastiest toxic waste dumps. But his booty also built a spectacular desert arboretum fifty-five miles east of Phoenix. Naturalists, aghast at the mining scars, loved the arboretum. So did the rufous-backed robin, a secretive Mexican that occasionally enjoyed wintering up north in Arizona.

At the Boyce Thompson Arboretum, near a tree labeled "Netleaf Hackberry," Komito bagged a rufous-backed robin. The soul of William Boyce Thompson moved one step closer to being freed from environmental purgatory.

January 25. Portland, Oregon. 1,400 miles. $189
Komito leaned into a pay phone and slowly repeated three words: "Long. Eared. Owl." He felt like an undercover agent. Would the password work?

Success! He had been admitted to the select society of the North American Rare Bird Alert, or NARBA. His $25-a-year membership gave him instantaneous access, no matter the time or place, to a Houston phone hot line that told where the latest rarities roosted. For $15 a bird more, he would be guaranteed a drop-everything phone call anytime a particular hottie was sighted.

Sure, this service did little more than duplicate what the local rare-bird alerts across the continent were already doing. But NARBA put all this information in a single place, one-stop shopping for the seldom-seen. It was a critical time-saver, and if there was one thing Komito needed during his Big Year, it was time saved.

His password, *long-eared owl*, was a reminder of his nemesis bird from his 1987 Big Year. Though that bird usually was a gimme in the West End parking field at Jones Beach, New York, Komito repeatedly missed it there—and in Toronto; San Diego; Casper, Wyoming; St. Louis; New Haven, Connecticut; and the New York Botanical Garden. He finally got it one hundred miles from home on December 31, 1987, the last day of that Big Year. Komito picked that long-eared-owl password to keep himself from feeling too cocky during his 1998 Big Year. So far it was working.

> *January 26. Lower Klamath National Wildlife Refuge,*
> *California. 600 miles. $79*

Komito had driven eleven hours from Portland to northern California and back to Portland again, and he was spent. He wanted to sleep. But before his head would touch a pillow, he had to repeat his nightly on-the-road ritual. He had to shake down a motel clerk.

To Komito, there was little difference between a desk manager at the Hilton and a trinket peddler at a flea market. Both advertised prices that were negotiable. Komito had stayed thousands of nights in hundreds of motels. He didn't sleep well unless he knocked off at least 10 percent from the desk manager's first rate.

He had this down to a system. He walked into the lobby of the Fairway Inn and tried to look as untired as possible. He didn't ask if the motel had any available rooms; only hopeless tourists did that. Instead, he said, "What's your best available rate for a room tonight?"

When the clerk told him, he didn't take it. He asked to see the room. He took the keycard and noted in his walk across the parking lot that few cars were there. An empty motel offered more chances to negotiate.

Inside a room, he always found something wrong—a faucet that dripped, a touchy thermostat, a curtain that reached the windowsill instead of the floor. He returned to the clerk loaded for bear.

There's a problem with the room, he told the clerk, sliding the keycard across the counter as if he were about to walk away. He rattled off the woes, but the clerk refused to budge. He mentioned the half-empty parking lot, then pulled out his travel agent card—he was his only customer—and asked for a travel agent discount.

He got the room for $31.80, with tax.

January 27. Seattle, Washington. 180 miles. $343
Komito needed to get to Alaska—now. But there was no easy way to Alaska from Portland. So he negotiated a no-drop-fee arrangement with the rental car company, drove to the Seattle airport, and called Alaska again. The man in Anchorage said: You need to get here now.

January 28. Anchorage, Alaska. 1,500 miles. $176
Why was a bug-eater visiting Alaska in January? Komito had to admit that it was a strange question. But it was no stranger than another question: Why would any sane creature visit Alaska in January?—which he didn't want to contemplate, much less answer.

Komito couldn't ignore reports that a Siberian accentor, an Asiatic connoisseur of mosquitoes and other flying nasties, had decided to winter somewhere in an old neighborhood of central Anchorage. The accentor was a good bird, a really good bird, a once-a-decade visitor to North America that looked like a mere chickadee but made a chaser's heart race faster than a hyper hummer's.

Lucky for Komito, the accentor had virtually been adopted by an old Attu roommate, Dave DeLap. A retired junior high school biology teacher, DeLap had made the first ID on the bird when it had showed up on a tree behind the home of former teaching colleagues Phil and Carolyn Kline. When the Klines had fled Anchorage over Christmas break for a two-week vacation in Florida, they'd given DeLap their house keys. No point in having birders wait outside for the accentor when there was a warm and empty house with a big living-room window. By the time Komito called, the homeowners were tanned and back to teaching seventh-graders. But DeLap still had their keys.

For Komito, this was another birding miracle. Though he prided himself on his relentless powers of persuasion, he had never before finagled the house keys of complete strangers in the darkest hours of an Alaskan winter. But here he was, cozy in a comfy chair with a straight-on view of Mr. Accentor's expected perch.

Komito liked to talk. DeLap liked to listen. They could have sat together in the Klines' house for hours and hours. So they did.

The wait actually wasn't their choice. Komito wanted a quick in-and-out. The bird, however, was nowhere in sight. DeLap had already shown the Siberian accentor to more than a hundred birders, and no one had come farther to see it than Komito. DeLap felt terrible.

As the winter sun set at 4:50 p.m. over Anchorage, the two men called off the day's hunt. Komito walked out of the Klines' house without leaving a thank-you note. When the Klines returned home that day, they never knew a stranger had spent the day in their living room.

January 29. Anchorage, Alaska. 50 miles. $96
Time for Plan B. There were rumors that the accentor some-times favored a backyard cottonwood just up the block from the Kline house. DeLap moved the accentor hunt two houses west.

The owners there welcomed Komito and DeLap inside their yard, but not their house. So Komito and DeLap bundled up at dawn and waited below the home's second-story deck. Though it was a natural hiding spot, the yard beneath the deck was frozen for a reason: it rarely saw sunlight. Komito zipped his parka to his chin. He wanted to shuffle his feet to generate body heat, but concluded that any movement might scare the bird. He stayed still and hoped for something to happen soon.

When he pressed his binoculars to his face, they fogged over with body heat. Ah, winter in Alaska. No question it was far too frigid for insects. Was it too cold for a bug-eating accentor?

At first light, Komito checked the cottonwood.

"Dave, I've got bird!" Komito whispered hoarsely.

"Sure you do," DeLap replied sarcastically. Did Komito ever stop telling tall tales?

"No—really!" Komito replied. "Eye level. On that horizontal branch."

Sure enough, there it was—five and a half inches of buffy brown with an orange eyeline. They watched it flit until Komito couldn't stand the cold any longer. He had his bird. Even better, Levantin didn't.

Walking back to their cars, DeLap spied something that stopped him in his tracks. The mystery of the insect-eating Siberian accentor was finally solved.

Above the home's deck was a bug-zapper. On the deck and beneath it was a wide splattering of electrocuted bugs.

He connected the biological dots: the accentor had foregone its migration to warmer Asian climes to subsist on freeze-dried food in Anchorage.

That night, Komito himself opted for steak, medium well, and reserved a plane seat for south Texas.

January 30. Bentsen State Park, Texas. 4,000 miles. $369
The first time Komito birded Bentsen State Park, he hated it.
Most of it was at least a mile from the Rio Grande, scraggly
with mesquite and crawling with people. At Bentsen, you
didn't go birding on trails. You birded on a long, paved trailer
loop filled with senior citizens from Minnesota, the Dakotas,
Kansas, Ohio, Idaho, and other cold points north. These
"campers," if you could call them that, watched television in
their Winnebagos and Airstreams and fifth wheels. Some even
had air conditioners and, worst of all, electric bug-zappers.
How were you supposed to spy a great crested flycatcher when
mosquitoes made the sparks fly?

Over the years, though, Bentsen had grown on Komito.
These trailer people weren't birders, but they had learned to
help. Now most had nailed up a half-orange (to attract
orioles) or tossed out seed (to attract everything else). He had
to admit: the campers were friendly. And they generally didn't
make fun of pale strangers pointing $800 binoculars and
$1,000 spotting scopes into the bushes around their campsites.
Today most of North America's best birders passed through
regularly, turning Bentsen State Park into a station of the
cross—and social circuit—for serious chasers. Komito himself
had been here at least two hundred times. He knew all
seventy-eight spaces of the trailer loop as well as his backyard.

NARBA reported that a clay-colored robin was feeding
reliably on a marshmallow at Trailer Space No. 19.

By the time Komito got there, the marshmallows were out.
The clay-colored robin wasn't. He left after a few hours. Had
the bird grown tired of marshmallows and moved on to new
dietary horizons—Twinkies, perhaps, or maybe even night
crawlers? This question kept Komito up all that night.

> *January 31. Santa Ana National Wildlife Refuge,*
> *Texas. 50 miles. $229*

Fifteen miles east, on the banks of the Rio Grande, the Santa Ana National Wildlife Refuge also reported a clay-colored robin. Komito ate breakfast at Denny's—the usual ham, eggs, hash browns no oil, and dry toast—and walked the refuge's B trail. No alarm clock needed here; few places in North American birding were as loud as Santa Ana at dawn. Grackles crackled and catbirds meowed, but loudest of all were the chachalacas, the Mexican thicket-dweller that sounded as if Ethel Merman had swallowed a rusty trombone. No way any living creature, especially a clay-colored robin, could sleep through all that. Two miles of trail-trudging, however, produced nothing.

Luckily, Komito did spot another birder, Marcel Holyoak of Davis, California, who claimed to have just observed the winged suspect. Holyoak started relaying detailed directions—at the second bridge, look under the lone palmetto—when he stopped and thought the better of it and decided to make the whole hunt easier by simply taking Komito there.

Holyoak, it turned out, was doing a Lower 48 Big Year—a nonstop year of birding strictly in the continental United States. Because his lunacy had limits, he was no threat to Komito. He also was offering to help. Komito's conclusion: good man.

Five hundred yards up the trail, at the second bridge and under the lone palmetto, was a dull olive-brown bird that looked like a typical backyard robin, but with the color bleached out. It was the clay-colored robin, and it had apparently not moved for the past half hour.

Quarry conquered, Komito walked easier. For the first time in weeks, he actually had time to bird at leisure. Days of target birding—ignoring everything but the species he really needed—was efficient, but joyless. His mood lightened.

At the visitor's center, he joined a stranger, Sharon Smith, as she pushed her husband, Ron, in his wheelchair. Limited by infirmity, Ron marveled in the freedom of birds. It was a sweet moment, but Komito made sure it was just a moment.

As the three birders scanned the brush, hoping for a Cassin's vireo, Sharon told how she and Ron once were trailed by a hawk.

"Maybe," Komito interrupted, "you looked delicious to the hawk."

She shot right back, "I'm not buying any of your New Jersey blarney."

"You know," Komito said, "birds are creatures of instinct and are motivated by just two things—to eat and to mate. I'll let you decide what it may have had in mind."

For some reason, the Smiths continued birding without Komito.

February 1. Allendale, New Jersey. 2,000 miles
When a man loves a woman and has seen her for a total of one day in the first month of a new year, he wants to see her. But what does he do with her?

After a morning at home, Komito got fidgety. And more fidgety. He finally couldn't ignore nature's call. He took his wife birding at the Celery Farm, a nature preserve near their house, and for the first time during this Big Year he spotted everyday Eastern birds such as blue jays and tree sparrows. He and Bobbye enjoyed their time outdoors together. But the day trip also boosted Komito's Big Year total to 342 birds, nearly sixty birds ahead of his record-breaking 1987 pace. He wouldn't stay fidgety at home for long.

February 4. Jericho, Vermont. 310 miles. $69
Komito left his house well before dawn to drive seven hours through an ice storm to a country house in Vermont with a big lump in a backyard tree, but nobody was answering the doorbell. The northern hawk owl was supposed to be somewhere in Jericho. What if the lump was the owl?

He knocked again. Still no answer.

He had already checked all the NARBA-recommended perches—the hardwoods behind the hardware store, the roosts around the restaurant, the timber by the U-Store-It warehouses. No owl. If he had to drive the streets of Jericho one more time, these small-town cops were going to get suspicious.

He really wanted this bird. Northern hawk owls rarely ventured south of the Canadian border, and even then, they preferred the rugged and remote over a quaint town with fresh decaf in the café. Hawk owls looked like a mix of their two namesakes: they were long-tailed day-hunters that could hover like a kite and snatch sparrows in midair. Komito didn't want to miss a prized bird like that.

Well, if nobody was home, no one would ever know that he trespassed, right? Deep in the throes of hot-bird fever, Komito could convince himself of almost anything. He hoped the no-answer house didn't have a no-bark rottweiler. Komito traipsed around the side, then the back, hustled through the clearing, and pointed his glass up that massive, leafless tree.

Did that lump just move?

It was the northern hawk owl! He ran off two pictures for proof.

Nobody home, nobody harmed. He glided back to Jersey.

February 5. Washington, D.C. 250 miles. $80
Rain fell in sheets, then blankets, and flood warnings were everywhere. Komito was headed to Virginia Beach, Virginia,

for another offshore birding trip, but the weather didn't bother him. He was safe with his SKUA.

The vanity license plate on his Lincoln Town Car, SKUA, was Komito's kind of joke. Any mild-mannered bird lover could go for GULL or WREN or EAGLE, but it took a hard-core chaser (or crossword puzzle nut) to get the humor behind SKUA.

The skua was the bully pirate of the open seas, a barrel-chested brawler that combined intelligence and intimidation to survive comfortably in some of the earth's most in-hospitable places. When south polar skuas nested in the Antarctic, they lived off the eggs of penguins. When they worked the coasts of North America, they traveled patiently with gulls and shearwaters until it came time to spirit away their food. Unless the pickings were unusually abundant, skuas stayed solitary. They were experts at letting others do the hardest work.

While one skua rode the trade winds of the mid-Atlantic, another drove I-95 down the coast.

February 6. Virginia Beach, Virginia. 210 miles. $96 Komito's two-day drive ended with bad news: the offshore trip was canceled because of foul weather. The good news, though, was that someone else had found a real rarity, a white-throated robin, back at Bentsen State Park in Texas. The skua in Komito booked the first flight in the morning.

February 7. Bentsen State Park, Texas. 1,800 miles. $268 From his Virginia Beach motel room he drove to the Norfolk airport, where he hustled onto the first flight to Houston, where he caught the first connection to McAllen, where he drove the first available rental car to Bentsen State Park. So rushed that he didn't bother trying to score a free admission, he cleared the park gate by 11 A.M.

Komito wasn't alone. Word of the white-throated robin had spread rapidly, and two dozen chasers from Arkansas, Florida, and Washington, D.C., among other places, had already joined the hunt.

The main binocular focus was on Trailer Space No. 73, an unoccupied campsite fifty-four spots past the former haunt of the marshmallow-baited clay-colored robin.

NARBA reported that the white-throated robin was visiting a "water drip," an idyllic way of saying the bird was hanging by a rusty campsite spigot left running by some trailer person. From sixty feet away, the crowd trained its glass on the galvanized faucet.

Drip. Drip. Drip.

Scrub shook. Binoculars rose.

Orange-crowned warbler. Ho-hum.

Drip. Drip. Drip.

For ninety minutes this continued. The only change: there now were three seconds between drips.

Komito realized he had no clue what this bird looked like; it wasn't even pictured in his trusty *National Geographic*. Luckily, someone had carted along a Mexican field guide—this bird was supposed to live in tropical Mexican mountains—so Komito studied it. Frankly, the white-throated robin looked so much like a clay-colored robin that some wondered if the bird had actually been here for weeks, but misidentified. The key field mark was a narrow white collar band. Forget about its rare status; this bird was a dullard. Show it to a nonchaser and the reaction would be, So what?

Drip. Drip. Drip.

"I've got the robin!"

A few hundred feet south on the trailer loop bend, someone

called. A wise man does not stand between Komito and a lifer. He ran—fast.

At Trailer Spot No. 61, an arsenal of optics trained on a bush. Komito's heart pounded so rapidly that it was hard to focus. But there, thirty yards away, something darted forward to snare a berry.

It was the white-throated robin. Eighteen hundred miles with a prayer for this wing and it worked. He wanted to dance a jig, but first whipped out his Nikon and peeled off five shots. The bird vanished back into the underbrush.

Komito backed out and found the nearest pay phone.

"Long. Eared. Owl."

About an hour north of Bentsen, on U.S. Route 77, NARBA reported a ferruginous pygmy-owl, a spunky predator that weighed less than a pack of cigarettes but still struck fear in the hearts of smaller songbirds. It made Komito's heart warble, too.

He met an owner of the El Canelo Ranch, Monica Burdett, just outside her house. A few months earlier, this ranch was swarming with $750-a-day hunters and lots of nervous quail and deer. Right now, though, Komito only needed $25 to see a pygmy-owl. He paid without negotiating.

He needed only one lap around the lawn to find the famed yardbird of the El Canelo Ranch. It was so easy that the Texas rancher offered him something more for his money. She pointed him to a stepladder next to a palm tree. Atop the palm was wired a portable dog kennel.

A few weeks ago, three baby barn owls had fallen from a nest in this tree. The ranchers had rescued them, but then worried about the owls falling again. They stuck the birds in the dog kennel, hoisted it eight feet up the palm, and covered the whole shebang with fronds. Mama owl kept feeding her babies as if nothing had changed.

Komito climbed the ladder and poked his camera into the kennel. There they were, three downy owlets. One hissed at Komito, making it wild enough to count. Bird No. 360—in a doghouse.

On the walk back to the rental car, the rancher passed along another great tip. In a pond behind a Wal-Mart in the town of Raymondville was a Central American rarity. Komito raced the sunset to the loading dock and landed a ruddy bird with blue bill and black face. Watch out for falling waterfowl: it was a masked duck.

From Virginia to Texas for a one-day sweep of a white-throated robin at a leaky trailer spigot, a ferruginous pygmy-owl in a rancher's front yard, three barn owls in a dog kennel, and a masked duck behind a Wal-Mart—Komito wasn't exactly seeing Wild America. But he was here, and Levantin wasn't. (Levantin would come a week later.) To Komito, the only scenery that mattered was the kind that served up birds.

February 8. McAllen, Texas. $242
This trip was a grudge match. During his 1987 Big Year, Komito had looked for longspurs on their great migration through the eastern plains of Colorado. It didn't take much to find McCown's and chestnut-collareds and Laplands. But he never spotted the cagiest longspur of all, the Smith's, a thin-billed bird with pale eye ring, two white outer tail feathers, and an infuriating knack for taking wing just beyond the 10× range of a birder's binoculars.

By the end of that spring migration, he finally admitted that he had missed the bird. He was left with only one choice—find them where they breed. That meant Alaska. So he spent a small fortune on a special trip to Denali National Park in June for a bird he should have seen near a major airport on the Great Plains in February.

On his Alaska trip, he endured rain, sleet, and ice-water swamps, but he did not quite endure the mosquitoes. No mortal could. Early summer in the marshes of Denali: eleven years later, the mere thought still made Komito break out in shivers and scratches. He had to find those bastard Smith's in the Lower 48 before they up and left for their bug-infested sex hovels to the north.

Komito was desperate and determined, but mostly desperate. He called a politician and pleaded for help.

Meet me tomorrow in Oklahoma City, the politician told Komito, and we'll see what we can do.

February 9. Oklahoma City, Oklahoma. 1,500 miles. $70 Bob Funston knew how to make promises. A man can't work all those years as an Oklahoma state senator, a state Democratic Party chairman, and even a Democratic candidate for governor without knowing something about how to appeal to hopes and dreams. But were these promises that Komito could trust?

Komito and Funston sat across the table at a local Denny's— the restaurant was Komito's idea—and spread out their paperwork. Funston pointed Komito to Aristida grass. The Smith's really liked the Aristida grass.

It was a Monday morning, and Funston wore a coat and tie. On anyone else, the work clothes might lend an air of credibility. On a politician, though, those same clothes made Komito wonder.

Whenever Komito met a nonbirder, the question was always the same: How do you know that somebody actually sees a bird? Why do you believe them? Can you really just take it all on *faith*? Invariably, Komito would answer the question the same way: the only way to get a reputation in birding is to earn it. In a way, birders were like golfers: everyone in country

club locker rooms always knew whose golf handicaps were real
and whose weren't. After decades of experience in both sports,
Komito had learned to trust more birders than golfers.

Still, a trustworthy politician?

Komito had known Funston from only a few chance
encounters in the field. But now he was entrusting the
politician with a full day of his time, precious Big Year time,
to find a Smith's longspur. Funston was matter-of-fact about it
all. Komito had to find open fields that weren't fenced in,
Funston told him. The birds would be moving in flocks. If he
moved deliberately through the short, tan grass, he should find
them.

The politician poked at his refolded map: There, southeast
of Norman, the fields and the fences should be just right. It's
about an hour away. Go try there.

Shortly after slamming the door on his rental car, Komito
heard trilling overhead. Five birds dropped from the sky into
the short grass at his feet. Smith's longspurs—every single one.
Damned if the politician wasn't right.

Somewhere in Denali, mosquitoes wept.

Komito, however, had no time to celebrate. He hustled
back into his car and beelined one hundred miles for the
Wichita Mountains National Wildlife Refuge, which had
bison, elk, and prairie dogs. Four-legged creatures were fine,
but he struck out on the real stars of that plains state—the
greater prairie chickens.

He could stay there and feel sorry for himself, or he could
keep driving. If he couldn't find greater prairie chickens in
southwest Oklahoma, then maybe he could find lesser prairie
chickens, a smaller but distinct breed, in northwest
Oklahoma.

Eight hours and three hundred miles later, Komito finally
slowed down. There were fields with no cattle, towns with no

stoplights, streets with no people. The sun had set hours ago. He was hungry, but couldn't find a restaurant. He was tired, but couldn't find a motel. His chin bobbed to his chest. Whoa! He really was tired. It was 10 p.m. He pulled to the side of the road and parked.

February 10. Somewhere, Oklahoma. 320 miles. $276
He shuddered awake at 5 a.m. His car was still running.

What had happened? Where was he?

Oh, yeah, right—driving last night and got tired. Fell asleep in the front seat. Good thing he left the heater on—cold outside. Oh, his back hurt. The SKUA had room for resting, but not a rental Taurus. The sun rose behind him. That meant go forward—the lesser prairie chickens were west of here, wherever here was.

Road sign . . . Road sign . . . Finally! Highway 95. Elkhart, Kansas, was north. Lessers were north.

At Pawnee National Grassland, Komito tried to remember: Where were the lessers' leks? Funny thing about the lessers was that they always met at the same place every spring for mates. A lek is where the boys strutted and the girls cooed and somehow all these chickens got together and did it, though not often enough ever to become a common bird. If Komito could only find the lek, he was sure to list the lesser. He had been here years ago with Larry Smith, but Larry was dead now and Komito hoped he could still remember the directions.

Wrong turn. Back up. Wrong turn again. Where was he?

Just in front of his car hood something moved.

Three lessers flushed.

Was this the lek? Were the lessers mating?

Komito had no clue. He was relieved to finally get an easy bird. He drove back to Oklahoma City to catch a flight East.

February 11. Norfolk, Virginia. 1,900 miles. $30
At the Norfolk airport he picked up the SKUA and drove north until he stopped for lunch in Delaware, where he was served by a toothless waitress with an open lip sore. Komito considered ordering something in a can, but then thought better of it. She did have a nice smile.

February 12. Fair Lawn, New Jersey
Home. Paid bills. Checked rare-bird alerts. Got ready for the road.

February 13. Hammonasset Beach State Park,
Connecticut. 325 miles. $27
It was cloudy and thirty-seven degrees and the National Weather Service reported wind gusts of thirty-five miles per hour, so Komito decided to go to the beach, where there was a report, appropriately enough, of an Iceland gull.

One thing about Hammonasset Beach in winter: birders were never alone there. When Komito drove up in his Town Car, he saw a man pointing a massive 800mm telephoto lens up a pine tree. Experience taught Komito that the easiest way to spot a good bird was to spot the birders first. He walked up and asked what was happening.

Look there, Komito was told.

Up the pines was a tight flock of red crossbills, wandering Canadians with freakish crisscrossed beaks that gave them leverage to snap down and pop open pinecones, their favorite food. Crossbills were tough to find in the Lower 48. The drive here had been worth it.

The photographer worked closer and closer to the trees. Komito cringed. This guy may have had a big lens, he thought, but he is still making a very amateur mistake.

A few years back, Komito had edged underneath a similar

tree that was quaking with four hundred starlings. If there were four hundred birds in a tree, he figured, they couldn't all be commoners. So he had moved even closer for a better look.

Just then a powerful predator, the peregrine falcon, had shot by. Four hundred scared starlings took flight—and simultaneously crapped on Komito. His coat coated with gooey, globby, and greenish bird poop, Komito made one unbreakable vow that day: never, ever stand beneath flocks in trees.

February 14, Brigantine National Wildlife Refuge,
New Jersey. 140 miles. $125

Komito birded en route to Cape May, where a pelagic trip was scheduled for the next day. He didn't get much besides an early bed.

February 15. Cape May, New Jersey. 225 miles. $27

He rose at 3:30 A.M. and was so excited at the prospect of Eastern seabirds that he arrived at the dock at 4:30 A.M. He was first in line. A half hour later came the announcement: no pelagic trip today. The boat had mechanical trouble and couldn't go out.

Komito was crestfallen. This was his third canceled offshore trip this year. From Cape May, the drive home on the Garden State Parkway was seldom enjoyable, but it was even worse when the SKUA had missed its prey.

February 16. Plum Island National Wildlife Refuge,
Massachusetts. 650 miles. $41

Thick-billed murres were supposed to be here. Was that them?

Komito jogged fifty yards up the shore. The birds took off across the water. They looked like they had fat bills. Maybe they were the thick-billed murre. Problem was, maybe they weren't.

He hustled up another fifty yards. The birds went two hundred. He jogged. The birds paddled and were gone again. This was getting tiring.

Still, he knew it could be worse. The murre was called the "penguin of the North" for a reason. It wore the same tuxedo and its plumage was waterproof, but it also swam underwater faster than a man could walk on shore. With flipperlike wings for propulsion, murres could dive three hundred feet for baitfish. One plunge like that and Komito would be hopelessly out of range.

He needed this bird. There just weren't many chances to catch it. The thick-billed murre spent almost all its life far offshore in the High Arctic. But in spring, it always returned to rocky cliffs and islands to breed. (It required the least privacy of any breeding bird, with as many as forty murres nesting on every square meter of flat sea rocks.) These breeding grounds, alas, were distant and inaccessible.

If Komito could ID a thick-billed murre today, he'd save himself an offshore boat trip later. So the I-Go-You-Go game continued up the seashore.

Finally, after a mile, Komito drew close enough to positively note the shorter bill, dark cheeks, and dark nape. Komito's heart pounded, but he had to admit, it was the chase, not the bird, that made his chest throb.

February 17. Fair Lawn, New Jersey
Home with Bobbye. He set up another trip to Texas.

February 18. Austin, Texas. 1,800 miles. $412
A double rainbow split the sky. Somewhere out there was the bird Komito wanted. Did the double rainbow signal good luck? He would find out tomorrow morning.

February 19. Amistad Reservoir, Texas. 300 miles. $88
Miles from the nearest road, stranded after dark on a boat with
a crippled engine, Komito was trying to shut up. His friends in
the bow were banging around in the night. His first instinct,
as usual, was to give some direction or make some wisecrack,
but he knew that would only make this mess worse. So he
summoned all his willpower and zipped his lips.

Oh, it wasn't easy.

He had come here with dreams of another big score. His
quarry was the rufous-capped warbler, a Costa Rican native
that, according to the Internet rare-bird alerts, had wandered
to this vast reservoir just below the Big Bend of the Rio
Grande. The south shoreline of the border lake belonged to
Mexico; the north was in Texas. Luckily—or so Komito
thought at the time—the bird had decided to spend the
winter on the Big Year side of the line, up a dry wash called
Pink Cave Canyon.

The only way to get to Pink Cave Canyon was by boat. The
only way for Komito to get a boat was to call for help.

His first call went to his longtime Texas birding friends
Barbara and John Ribble of Austin, who in turn called two of
their friends, Sue and Egon Wiedenfeld of Comfort. The
Wiedenfelds had a boat. When they'd motored out from Del
Rio that morning, the boat had seemed just large enough for
four Texans, Komito, and some of his stories.

Just offshore, however, gales blew. When whitecaps lashed the
bow, Barbara and Sue joined the skipper, Egon, in the cockpit,
safe from the spray. Komito was stuck in the unprotected stern.

When the first wave crashed over him, he yelped. The
second soaked him. The next sent him scrambling for a
flotation seat cover, which he held up as a water shield. It was
no use. The 35 mph winds kept slamming in water, and
Komito kept getting drenched.

"I expect the black swifts to start nesting on us!" Komito shouted, referring to the peculiar species that lays eggs behind waterfalls. His fellow birders got the joke, but didn't laugh too hard.

The mood turned more tense fifteen miles into the trip, when the boat motor conked out. Running at one-third throttle, the boat crawled. What was supposed to be a half-day jaunt had turned into a marathon. This did offer one advantage, though. Against the slow pace of a sputtering boat, the two-foot waves of Amistad Reservoir finally stayed below the gunwales.

More than three hours after leaving the dock, the water-borne birders finally spotted Pink Cave Canyon. The boat turned for a shore landing. The engine sputtered again. This time, it was out of gas.

There was a spare tank, but Komito and the others were too antsy to fiddle with the connections. They paddled ashore.

Pink Cave Canyon was 100 feet high and 180 feet deep. The walls were limestone and steep, and the canyon floor was thick with mesquite. If there truly was a pink canyon here, Komito couldn't see it. There was, however, a refrigerator stuck in the muck near the mouth of the canyon. Thirty-five miles into the backcountry on a boat and somebody had dumped a large kitchen appliance. What a place.

Onshore, Komito worried about his legs, which still wobbled. It was the first time he had gotten sea legs from a reservoir ride.

The five birders quickly organized a bushwhacking party, each person standing twenty feet apart and striding carefully, purposefully, into the canyon.

"I've got the bird!" Barbara soon called, and indeed she did. Long-tailed, with a yellow breast, rusty hat, and white eyebrow, the rufous-capped warbler carried more color than most rarities. But it was hard to ignore that Komito had traveled 1,800 miles by jet, 240 miles by car, and 30 miles by boat for a bird that would fit inside that refrigerator's butter tray.

It was 4:30 P.M. The winter sun was sinking fast. They were thirty miles from the dock with a misfiring boat that would go no faster than 7 mph. Could they get back before dark? Komito started to say something, then looked at his companions' faces. For once, he stayed silent. He didn't want to be left behind.

Back on the reservoir, the sun moved faster than the boat. Komito repeated to himself: Don't say anything. Don't say anything. Don't say anything.

He almost did once, but looked up and thought he saw a red-billed pigeon. Though the bird wasn't there, Komito got an idea: every time he thought about cracking some comment—about the impending sunset or the pokey boat or the fact that no one had eaten for hours—he simply raised his binoculars and searched for red-billed pigeons.

If something moved in that sky, his 7×42s were all over it.

At 6:30 P.M., the sun set. At 7:15 P.M., twilight was gone. At 7:45 P.M., everyone realized there was no moon. At 8:15 P.M., the last flashlight exhausted its batteries.

Thwomp!

The boat hit a submerged tree. Komito tasted panic. The front of the boat now had three navigators. More submerged trees. Where was the dock?

Sue Wiedenfeld plunged through the darkness onto shore. No one on board said a word. She returned a few minutes later with some disconcerting news: they appeared to be stuck on an island. Maybe they should motor farther through the dark to find the mainland.

Others debated. Komito thought: Don't say anything. Don't say anything.

At 9 P.M., they spotted the lights of the deserted dock. They were too tired to trailer the boat, so they tied up, loaded the gas can into their van, and drove fifteen miles to the nearest motel.

Komito was raw and grimy and too exhausted even to try eating. But as he fell asleep alone in his motel room, he wondered:

Could anyone else on a Big Year do all that for one bird? Would they?

SEVEN

El Niño

GREG MILLER

It was a windup alarm clock, black with gold trim, and it had hands that glowed a sickly green in the dark. It cost $4.95. After comparing it to a dozen competitors on the shelves at Wal-Mart, Greg Miller picked it for one simple reason: it clanged like a fire bell. Miller needed a loud alarm clock. At night, he didn't sleep. He hibernated.

After another fifty-four-hour week at the nuclear power plant, Miller collapsed into bed on Friday night and set his trusty alarm for 3 A.M. He dreamed of birds. In the morning he was leaving on a flight for Arizona. Six weeks into 1998, his Big Year would finally begin in earnest.

He woke up in a pitch-black apartment, but something wasn't right. His alarm clock was silent, but its spring was sprung. He rolled over and double-checked the time on his digital watch. It was 4:30 A.M. Somehow he had slept through the entire two minutes of his clanging wake-up bell. Miller was in trouble. He lived eighty miles from the airport, and his flight left in two hours. He was so panicked that he skipped breakfast. He raced 80 mph on 55 mph roads to Baltimore-Washington International Airport, where there was no time for $5-a-day economy parking. He nabbed a $12 space and bolted for the terminal.

In the years before he got away with murder, O. J. Simpson was the universal image of a scrambling traveler in Hertz commercials that showed him leaping like a gazelle over suitcases and seats until he finally made his gate. Even the little old ladies yelled, "Go, O.J., go!" But in this airport, nobody cheered Greg Miller's mad dash. He had six minutes. He ran with all the grace of a tank—and this tank was in serious danger of overheating. He plowed past the ticket counter, through the security station, down the concourse. Two minutes. His wheelie bag wobbled. His attaché slammed his thighs. He made the gate just as they announced final boarding. Then he remembered: he was flying Southwest Airlines, the no-frills carrier with no assigned seats.

The gate attendant shut the skyway door. He was the last one on this flight. He was breathing so hard, and perspiring so profusely, that he stripped off his windbreaker. He walked onto the plane and dozens of faces creased with horror. Only middle seats remained on this flight, and nobody wanted to sit next to the guy with half-moons under the armpits and a smear the size of Jupiter on the chest. Luckily, in the back, way in the back, Miller found an empty aisle seat. It was in the last row of the plane, so the seat didn't recline. At least there was one empty chair between him and the traveler by the window. Miller looked over at him. The man refused to acknowledge him. Miller considered saying something, apologizing for his smell and the streams of sweat gushing from the band of his Cleveland Indians hat, but decided that he couldn't say anything that would help. He cranked open the overhead air vent—when he reached up, he saw the half-moons in his armpits had gone full—and hoped the jet would soon move. His stomach grumbled. No breakfast. Southwest served only snacks— peanuts over America, Miller called it. He pulled off his cap to mop up more sweat. The window guy shot him a disgusted sideways glance. Miller feigned sleep.

He woke when they landed, rested but embarrassed. He was physically incapable of sleeping without snoring. His snores were so bad, in fact, that his wife often made him sleep on the couch even when they weren't fighting. Miller shuddered to think what noises had erupted from his hibernation during this flight. The window guy was too nice to say anything—or too scared.

After a cold, wet winter at home by the Chesapeake in southern Maryland, Miller longed to feel his face blasted with Arizona desert air. He didn't get it. Rain pelted Tucson. By the time he had driven to Sonoita, seventy miles later, rain had turned to sleet. Another half hour up the road, in Sierra Vista, the sleet became snow, and the Huachuca Mountains above were blanketed white.

Miller blasted the defroster on his rental car and shivered. His suitcase was packed with clothes for chasing roadrunners and cactus wrens—not the abominable snowman. Twenty miles from the Mexican border, he still hadn't seen his first desert bird, and he was wishing that his Arizona rental came with snow tires.

This wasn't right. This wasn't normal. This wasn't how he hoped to start his Big Year. What was happening here?

In the tropical Pacific, a few hundred miles off the coast of New Guinea, an ocean buoy bobbed five inches lower than usual. A government satellite detected the shift and beamed the new measurement to a data collection station in Wallops Island, Virginia, which forwarded the news to computer banks in Largo, Maryland, and Seattle, Washington.

Those five inches launched an international scientific sensation: El Niño, the bad boy of global weather, was back.

In the equatorial Pacific, westward trade winds are so strong, and so consistent, that the sun-warmed seas at Indonesia are seventeen inches higher than at Ecuador. At least once every seven years, though, the trade winds mysteriously ebb. Without gusts to hold it back, water from the tropical Pacific sloshes back, warming South American coasts that are supposed to be cold. Peruvian fishermen called the phenomenon El Niño, after the baby boy Jesus, because it tended to show up around Christmas.

No matter the time, the result is the same—weather havoc, all over the planet. Storms that usually pelt the western Pacific instead hammer the Americas. Indonesian rain forests wither. African deserts flood.

In 1982, scientists were caught so flat-footed by the onset of a strong El Niño that they deployed seventy buoys, sixteen feet high and tethered to the ocean floor, across the Pacific. Each buoy measured surface winds, water temperature, and subtle changes in the depth of the ocean. All information was transmitted to passing satellites; the hope was to predict El Niño–related weather far enough in advance to warn people of the dangers.

By the fall of 1997, the buoys from New Guinea to the Galápagos were detecting a new El Niño, and scientists sounded the alarm loud and often. That was a good thing. By early 1998, when snow pounded Greg Miller in southern Arizona, the new El Niño was easily the most intense in recorded history—packing more energy than a million Hiroshima atomic bombs.

The freakishly warm waters spawned a slew of wild weather—236 mph winds on Guam; the earliest onset of monsoons in a century in India; rainfall forty inches above normal in Kenya; and drought so terrible that wildfires in Indonesia spewed more carbon dioxide in four months than all of industrialized Europe pumped in an entire year. Record high temperatures were recorded in Washington, Mongolia, and Ho Chi Minh City. Record floods devastated Poland and the Czech Republic. So much rain pooled up in South America that Peru suffered its worst outbreak of malaria in decades.

All told, the El Niño of 1997 killed at least two thousand people and caused at least $36 billion of economic damage.

It did, however, make for excellent birding. The Xantus's hummingbird in Vancouver, the Siberian accentor in Anchorage, the white-throated robin in Texas—these birds all were a long, long way from home. The same El Niño winds that caused so much grief for so many people were depositing an unprecedented cornucopia of lost birds on the shores of North America.

In 1998, El Niño was responsible for dozens of new weather records. It just might make a birding record, too—if a birder could grit through a snowstorm in southern Arizona.

If this were a vacation, or even an ordinary birding trip, Miller might have slept in. He had checked 250,000 lines of software code. He had traveled twenty-five hundred miles. He was exhausted. And after last night's storm, the Arizona roads were slippery and the backcountry was a frozen mess. But he had to meet a special person.

In Miller's mind, Stuart Healy was living the dream. For fifteen years, the diminutive British expat had toiled, like Miller, as a round-the-clock software jock. But after braving the brutal work schedule first in Silicon Valley, and then in Microsoft's shadow north of Seattle, Healy had decided to chuck it all and move to Sierra Vista, Arizona, where he had established himself as one of the state's premier birding guides.

It all made Miller jealous. In the depths of those window-less, fourteen-hour days at the nuclear power plant, he thought about Stuart Healy and his life as a professional birder. Healy seemed to know everything about the birds of southeastern Arizona—where they lived, when they migrated, how they sang—and Miller couldn't imagine anything better than being paid to do exactly what he loved. Then Miller learned that Healy was paid only $10 an hour. Maybe that dream wasn't so idyllic after all.

Miller never liked to put a price on birding, but he had to admit, $10 an hour was a terrific deal. Other Big Year contestants might be too cheap, or too proud, to hire a guide. Miller didn't think twice. He was six weeks late in starting his Big Year and was playing catch-up. All he had so far were birds commonly seen around his Maryland nuclear power plant. If an out-of-state guide had to lead him by the nose to get tough birds, he wouldn't feel embarrassed. A mountain-climbing guide had short-roped a customer up Mount Everest, but she still was a conqueror, wasn't she?

Nobody ever achieved greatness by whining, so Miller buttoned his lips when Healy led him from his warm car into the aftermath of an Arizona ice storm. The sun was barely up. Steam rolled from Miller's nose. And the ground, frosted stiff, crunched with every step deeper into the bush.

Healy hiked like a man on a mission. Miller labored to keep up. They trained their binoculars in the shadows and searched.

When the sun crept high enough to illuminate the mesquite, Miller rejoiced. Finally, some warmth. Soon, though, he recoiled. The sunrise thawed the mesquite, and ice water was drip, drip, dripping from the branches onto his

Cleveland Indians hat. No Jolt needed this morning; Miller snapped awake.

From somewhere inside the thicket, Healy called. Miller ran, even faster than in the airport. Mesquite slashed his thighs, his ribs, his face. He was a 215-pound rocket. He stopped at a thirty-foot tangle and pointed his glass exactly where Healy directed.

The bird called, "Wheek."

There, in the thicket of Patagonia Lake State Park, was the Nutting's flycatcher.

It was the same bird Sandy Komito had seen on January 1.

It was the same bird Al Levantin would see six days later.

It was No. 160 on Greg Miller's Big Year list.

At night in his motel room, Miller should have been happy. In five days in Arizona, he had hustled 125 new birds onto his year list. He had reveled in twelve hundred miles of spectacular scenery. He had wrung every dollar of Arizona birding knowledge out of Stuart Healy.

Still, he moped. What was the point of a great time if you couldn't share it with someone? Though he loved finding out-of-the-way places during the day, he longed for friends by dinnertime. It was just Miller and the motel and the Weather Channel, night after night after night. He was starting to feel like New Year's Eve all over again.

He clicked off the television and picked up the phone.

His father answered.

Dad, Miller said, I'm in Arizona and you won't believe the birds.

Really?

Really.

Even though his father had an impressive life list of more than five hundred species, he had never even heard of a Nutting's flycatcher. He was enthralled. He wanted to know what it looked like, where it lived, how his son had found it. He got his son to imitate the flycatcher's call—Wheek!—over the phone.

Miller didn't need more prodding. His mouth was off to the races. He told his father of the ruddy ground-dove in a pecan grove outside an airpark with dogfighting biwings, the Le Conte's thrasher in the desolation fifty miles west of Phoenix, the failed search for a spotted owl in the foot-deep snow of the Huachuca Mountains, the successful score of the rufous-backed robin at the Boyce Thompson Arboretum. (*Dad, in Arizona they call it a botanical garden, but back home in Holmes County they would say it needed a lot of water.*)

His mother popped on the line and asked about his health. Miller said he was fine. The mother had her doubts—she knew that her son, when excited, could push himself beyond exhaustion—but whatever she said as a caution was just a blur to Miller. He kept thinking about his father.

There was no hint of disappointment in his father's voice. The whole issue of the failed marriage hadn't come up. If anything, his father sounded thrilled. Miller realized that his Big Year could be more than just about birds. It was a way for him to connect again with his father. Miller could heal a relationship that he feared was hurt by divorce. With a mentally retarded son and only a modest government paycheck to support him, the father had neither the time nor the money for a Big Year. But he could understand one. He could appreciate one. Miller wished his father could help him on one.

Even in the strange world of a Big Year, this was a strange problem. Miller still had eight more hours in Arizona, but he had already spotted nearly all the winter birds of the desert Southwest. He couldn't grab an earlier flight; Southwest Airlines would make him pay too much to change reservations. He couldn't try again for the spotted owl; the Huachuca Mountains were a slushy and muddy mess. And he wasn't about to go off and blindly beat the brush for some undiscovered species; after five days of predawn wake-up calls, he hardly had the energy to roll out of bed. What to do?

Miller drove north from Nogales on Interstate 19, the only freeway in America with distances marked solely in kilometers, and blew past the sprawl of Tucson and the brown cloud of Phoenix. He drove west until all human habitation stopped, then drove ten miles more. He parked. This was the desert that was never on postcards. Flat, brown, and barely vegetated, the moonscape stretched as far as he could see. There were no other cars. He was alone.

In the distance, he heard something. He pointed his binoculars and saw movement. He walked in that direction. Whatever it was—it looked brown, with a long tail, probably some kind of thrasher—it moved again. He followed. Soon he couldn't see his car anymore. He could hear the bird, though, farther away. He trailed it.

In typical Miller preparation, he had brought no water bottle. At least the desert wasn't hot today. Miller had been so intent on chasing the bird that he hadn't seen the sky clouding over. When El Niño began leaking on him, he was at least a half mile from the road.

He ignored the rain. He had three more hours in Arizona and had no interest spending them on some vinyl chair at Sky Harbor International Airport. He followed the birdsong. He got wetter.

After concluding he could sneak no closer than one hundred yards to the still-unidentified thrasher, he turned back. He squished when he walked.

In the car he was so hot and wet that he fogged all the windows. He flipped on his tape recorder and fast-forwarded straight to the thrasher section to match the call of the bird that had just turned him into a sopping mess.

Someone knocked on his window. He jumped. He wiped away the fog and saw a Border Patrol officer peering in.

"What are you doing?" he asked.

"Birdwatching."

"Birdwatching? What are you watching for?"

"Sage thrasher, curve-billed thrasher, Crissal thrasher, Bendire's thrasher."

"Well, I've never seen anybody out here before. It's a rainy day today."

Miller didn't know what he was supposed to say to that.

"What have you got in your hands?"

"Tape recorder."

"Play it."

"Huh?"

"I want to hear the tape recorder. Play the tape recorder. Turn it on."

Miller turned it on and felt relieved. The tape was proof: that bird *was* a sage thrasher.

The Border Patrol agent still looked perturbed. Nobody came out here to look at birds, he said. What they looked for was airdropped drugs.

Miller showed the agent his binoculars and field guide. The agent turned and left.

"Birdwatcher. Huh."

Miller drove an hour to the airport and passed airport security with a wet T-shirt. When he boarded the plane, his sneakers still squished. Luckily, the flight was so empty that he had a whole row to himself. He snored an opera.

AL LEVANTIN

Some birders called it the Tamaulipas Crow Wildlife Sanctuary. Others preferred the Brownsville Nature Preserve. Those with a Latin flair opted for Corvid National Park.

Al Levantin, who was never one for pretense, simply called it the dump.

For the past thirty years, the Brownsville, Texas, Municipal Landfill had been the only reliable place in the United States to see a Tamaulipas crow. Nobody besides the crow liked going there. To say it stunk did injustice to the word *stunk*. It reeked. It rotted. It marinated decades of throwaway table scraps in the fecund humidity of the Rio Grande Valley and then roasted it under the south Texas sun. It smelled so bad it made grown men cry.

Not Al Levantin, though.

Whenever Levantin went to the dump—and he had been there before, always to search for the Tamaulipas crow—he carried a secret weapon. Levantin had no sense of smell. All those years in the Rohm and Haas chemical lab had done a number on his nose. When his wife had picked him up from work, she had to drive all the way home with the car windows rolled down—the solvent stench was that bad. Levantin, however, remained oblivious. When he walked in the door at home after a day in the lab, he stripped over the washing machine and dropped his clothes straight in. French food never tasted quite the same anymore, but all those years in the corporate suites had taught him the importance of turning a liability into an asset.

Let the others swoon from the stench at the Brownsville Municipal Landfill. Levantin was ready to strut.

He idled in line behind a parade of garbage trucks—even they drove with their windows up—until he finally reached the gate. Levantin veered away from the truck scale and waved his binoculars at the guard, who waved him in. The road was rail-straight with a partition that, in more northern climes, would be called a snow fence. Here it captured blowing trash. Spackled with snags of newspaper, grocery bags, and twelve-pack boxes, the fence was a spiderweb of man-made detritus. Levantin drove on.

Brownsville was one of the few major landfills anywhere that still admitted birders; most insurers and city attorneys refused to let passenger cars share a dump road with trash haulers en route to their honey hole. But Brownsville was a border town anxious to promote nonborder businesses. If bird-watchers wanted to spend their tourism dollars pointing $1,000 binoculars at heaping mounds of trash, the city elders here weren't about to block their view.

Levantin finally arrived at the key road fork with two signs. The orange-and-black one on the straight fork warned: *No Bird Watchers Beyond This Point*. The black-and-white one, with a silhouette of a soaring crow, had an arrow pointing right: *Landfill Birdwatch*. These signs, Levantin surmised, were not mass-produced.

He parked his rental and ambled toward the viewing area. Other birders had already formed a neat line of scopes and tripods. Everyone seemed to be breathing through the mouth. Levantin inhaled through his nose. He had to admit, even a man with a hapless honker could tell this place was skanky.

Levantin snapped open his tripod and zoomed in on Mount Trashmore. He felt lucky. New garbage was still being dumped in this part of the landfill. A connoisseur of refuse, the

Tamaulipas crow liked fresh best. If anyone needed proof, he just had to check with Manuel Vela, the landfill scalemaster, who had spent two years teaching a crow, whom he had named Jack, to snag and eat bread crusts tossed in midair.

The Tamaulipas crow was a species common in its home turf, but rare in the United States. Tens of thousands of them lived south of the border in Mexico, but a hardy few—three dozen in good years—spent the winter feasting on Brownsville trash. The challenge was identifying them. The Tamaulipas crow looked a lot like other all-black birds. At fifteen inches, it was slightly larger than a common grackle, slightly shorter than a Chihuahuan raven, and roughly the same length as a great-tailed grackle. If the crow, grackles, and raven were side by side in the sun, the ID would be easy. But at the Brownsville dump, the crow rarely flew within a quarter mile of birders. It wasn't easy to estimate size, distorted by heat waves, through the lens of a sixty-power telescope.

Fortunately, Levantin had played this game before. When he spied a black bird on a faraway fence post, he suspected he had his crow. To make sure, he scanned the disgusting countryside for a similar, but much closer, fence post. Now he had his size comparisons.

With heat waves shimmering in the midday sun, Levantin ticked the Tamaulipas crow off his list. At the dump, he knew his nose gave him an advantage over most birders. He could not honestly say, though, that he enjoyed it.

Cocooning himself in the cool refuge of his car, Levantin heard something. He had been so focused on the Tamaulipas crow that, until this point, he had ignored all other sounds. The sky above him was filled with dozens of laughing gulls. They were cackling.

"Well, Ethel," Al Levantin said over the phone that night to his wife, "today I was in Brownsville, Texas, and I saw the Tamaulipas crow."

"A Tamawla what?"

Ethel Levantin was not a birder. Years ago, she had tried. She had joined her husband on birding trips to the sea and the desert, the mountains and the valleys, but she never quite got it. Her husband could stand for hours in the sticks and marvel at the beauty of a single bird. Ethel got bored. At first she felt bad about it. She wanted to be excited about the same thing that excited her husband. She was a marriage counselor. She knew the importance of common interests. When Al asked Ethel about doing a Big Year, Ethel was determined to do something to share the experience. Maybe she could write it up for a family keepsake. Her husband's thing about birding, she never understood. But traveling the continent on a moment's notice, going to exotic places where few people had trekked before, that would make a fun travelogue. Al just had to supply the material.

"A Tamaulipas crow. A Mexican crow. I saw it today."

"How nice. What does it look like? Is it a good-looking bird?"

"It's a crow. It's black."

"Where did you see it?"

"At the dump, Ethel. The Brownsville dump."

The dump. He had paid hundreds of dollars to fly fourteen hundred miles from Aspen at the height of ski season to look for a crow at a dump. The news would make some wives scream. Not Ethel, though. This was travelogue material. She did her best reporter's imitation.

"Was it a nice day?"

"I got the bird."

After thirty-seven years of marriage, she realized her

husband wasn't being short. He was just so focused on his singular goal, finding birds, that he blocked out, or never took in, anything else around him. He would have his fun. She would put away her pen and paper.

From the dump in Texas to the dead of winter in Duluth—Al's travels were becoming harder and harder for Ethel to understand. Al was insistent. He kept telling Ethel, there are a few birds that usually live high in the Arctic, but drop down into northern Minnesota in January. Duluth for these birds was like a Caribbean cruise for people—a midwinter change of scenery with decidedly warmer weather. Big Year birders who didn't score these species in Minnesota would have to bushwhack for them in northern Canada sometime in summer. Chasing them now meant you didn't have to battle the mosquitoes.

He flew to Minneapolis—finally, a birding hot spot with a direct flight from Aspen—and drove north. He hardly had the heart to tell his wife that he wasn't really aiming for Duluth. That was just a city most people had heard of. His true destination was another forty-five miles northwest of Duluth. Officially, this place had no name; even the roads had only numbers. But by driving Highway 53 to County Road 232 and then looping up 7, 28, 788, and 213, Levantin would be on cherished ground—the place birders called Sax-Zim Bog.

The North Woods of North America have spruce bogs that are bigger, wetter, and birdier, but Sax-Zim is famed among birders for another reason: it's easier. Sax-Zim is the only big bog within a half day's drive of a major airport. And it's crisscrossed with country roads that make two hundred square miles of foreboding spruce, tamarack, and white-cedar swamp open to anyone with binoculars.

On the road to Sax-Zim, Levantin started learning how much of Big Year birding wasn't even birding; it was traveling to birding. If Sax-Zim was so convenient, how come he couldn't find a radio station with classical music? At least there wasn't much traffic.

That was fortunate. About a half hour beyond Duluth, where the spruce really started towering, Levantin spotted a clump on the flat road, one of those dirty ice clods that builds up and falls off the rear tire wells of country cars. The closer he got, though, the less the clump looked like a clod. Clods should be on the side of the road; this was on the yellow line.

At 60 mph, he saw that the clod had a head.

Levantin slammed his brakes and raised his binocs. Ten powers of magnification showed that the clod was actually a wild chicken of the north, a ruffed grouse, with crested head, black-banded tail, and absolutely no fear of a fast-approaching Hertz rental sedan. Levantin drove within forty feet of the bird and grabbed his camera. Before focusing, however, he checked his rearview mirror for a speeding logging truck. (In these parts, "speeding logging truck" was redundant; there was no other kind.)

With reassured rear, he resumed focus through the windshield.

The bird was gone.

He slammed his hand on the steering wheel. Though a ruffed grouse was a good bird, a tough bird, it still wasn't an extremely rare bird, and there would be no reason for anyone to doubt his sighting. He really wanted the photo, though, to prove the location. Birders were accustomed to whacking brambles to find good birds, but Levantin had found this specimen, a game bird that had just survived a Minnesota hunting season, in the middle of a highway. Somebody once told him that grouse groused on winter highways because they ate ice-melting road salt. He also wondered if the bird was attracted to black pavement because it held the sun's warmth longer than the eighteen-degree air temperatures around it. These were only conjectures. Without a photo, they all sounded like more birder bar stories.

By the end of his time in Sax-Zim, he had accumulated whole shot glasses full of stories. He lucked into the Arctic's two toughest dainty birds, the sparrowlike common and hoary redpolls, gorging themselves at feeders in someone's backyard by a frozen lake. He found a snowy owl camouflaged on the jammed ice and drifted snow of Duluth harbor. Most unlikely of all, though, was the way he scored his great gray owl. The elusive flat-faced nemesis of so many accomplished birders, the great gray owl stared at Levantin with brilliant yellow eyes atop an electrical pole in the frozen bog flanking the road from Sax (a wide spot in the road discovered by Rand McNally's mapmakers) to Zim (no McNally).

When he phoned home to Ethel, he sounded like a Boy Scout. The birds were great, he told her, and then he passed along the hows and wheres of each discovered species. Everything else, she had to ask about. Yes, he was outdoors three days and the thermometer had never climbed above twenty-five degrees. No, he never saw the sun. Yes, he always had the whole bog to himself. It was all birds, birds, birds, no distractions, and all the time.

Ethel admired his passion. She questioned his sanity.

I worry about you, she told Al. I wish you'd go to some of these places with someone. What if your rental car broke down? What if you got hurt?

Whatever you do, she told him, make sure you're safe.

The mountain lion was so close that Levantin could count its whiskers. They were twitching. Levantin would scream if he could force air into his throat.

He was two miles into a hike a hundred miles from nowhere, and he was alone, helplessly alone. At first he had thought that rustle in the bush behind him was a bird. But when he'd wheeled around, he'd seen the cat, big and bulky, ready to pounce on his neck. The lion stared. Levantin stared back. It was gray eyes versus blue eyes, a glaredown at twenty feet.

Slowly, steadily, he raised both hands above his head. If another hiker chanced upon this confrontation, here in the high desert of West Texas's Big Bend National Park, he would think that the man with binoculars was surrendering. Levantin hoped the lion thought otherwise. With hands up, Levantin was trying to make himself appear larger, a stunt he had read about in the predawn gloom on a trailhead sign.

The lion didn't flinch.

Finally wind filled Levantin's throat.

"Get out of here! Lion! Get out of here! Go away! Get out of here!"

Five seconds passed. Then fifteen. The lion wasn't budging.

"Get out of here! Get out of here!"

The four-foot lion sprang up and away and hightailed it back down the trail. Levantin hurled fist-size rocks at the lion's fanny. He hit nothing, but threw more. He wanted the lion to think it was being chased.

Levantin stopped and listened. Nothing. He kept staring ahead while stooping down for more rocks. Still nothing.

His instincts told him to run to the safety of his car. But the lion had run that way, too. So with rocks in hand, he turned uphill and quickly, cautiously, continued along the Boot Canyon trail. He had another four miles to go. He hoped the lion wasn't also prowling that way.

The whole reason he had come here was to see a Colima warbler, a singing bugeater of southwest Mexico that fancied trysts north of the border. Turn-ons: out-of-the-way oaks and maples in the Chisos Mountains above 5,900 feet. Turn-offs: dry weather. Thanks to El Niño's showers, Levantin figured that Boot Canyon would be crawling with Colimas by now. He hadn't counted on carnivorous cats.

Every rock and tree suddenly looked suspicious. Though he had heard other birders groan about the long, steep hike into the lair of the Colima warbler, Levantin shrugged it off. He was in excellent shape. Back home, he pedaled his bike over mountains for sport. After weeks of wintertime birding out the window of his car, he was looking forward to a pore-opening hike under the high border sun. Now he worried that his perspiration smelled like cat food. His neck grew sore from all those looks over his shoulder. It would have been the fastest four-mile hike of his life if he hadn't spent so much of his time hiking backward.

Luckily, just shy of his destination, Levantin met up with two other birders who had spent the night camping in the canyon. He told them about his lion encounter. The birders banded closer together.

Finding the warblers themselves was anticlimatic. There were dozens of them flitting around the brush, yellow-rumped with flanks washed in brown. It was another bird that was rare in the United States, but not the world. He was glad to get it out of the way.

He hustled six miles back to the trailhead and confronted a National Park Service ranger with his news: There's a mountain lion out there that stared me down from twenty feet! He thought the ranger would hike the trail to caution others or at least post a warning sign.

Instead, the ranger smiled. "Are you lucky!" he told

Levantin. "I've worked here eight years and I haven't seen a mountain lion!"

Levantin, sore neck and all, could have popped the guy.

That night, after a hot shower in the comfort of his motel room, Levantin felt better. The Colima warbler was the 435th bird of his Big Year. He was twenty ahead of Sandy Komito's record-breaking 1987 pace. But he still had a serious problem: What would he tell his wife?

Ethel, who knew her husband had scheduled a backcountry trek, cut to the chase:

"Did you see the bird?"

"I saw the bird," Al replied.

"Did you go with somebody?"

"You know how you don't like it when I go birding alone? Well, today I went out with a gorgeous blonde. Slinky. Athletic. Hotblooded. Biggest eyes you've ever seen."

By the time he uttered the words *mountain lion*, Levantin feared his phone connection had gone dead. It hadn't. When Ethel finally responded, she sure didn't sound a thousand miles away.

SANDY KOMITO

April Fools' Day started early for Sandy Komito. The motel alarm clock beeped at 3:30 A.M., and he was out of his room a half hour later. The temperature outside was fifteen degrees, but Komito was flush with excitement. Today he would spy wild chickens having sex in the cheatgrass of Colorado's high desert.

He could imagine no better stunt for April 1. Let the

amateurs make do with mere whoopee cushions. Komito needed something more. Among birders, he was the Sultan of Slapstick, the Guru of Guffaws, the Bigshot of the Biological Borscht Belt, and he had a reputation to uphold. So he rose before dawn with a plan to spy on sharp-tailed grouse in the throes of copulation.

Komito felt so good about this adventure that he shelled out the extra money at the rental car counter for a Lincoln Town Car. As he nosed the land barge onto Highway 40, he saw through his high beams that every driveway in Hayden, Colorado, was filled with a pickup truck, many with gun racks. This was cowboy country. A guy from New Jersey was as common as a vegetarian at a rodeo. But a New Jersey guy in a Town Car—that was the punch line to a local joke, not something that ever showed up here in real life. Luckily, at this early hour, the cowboys and sheepmen were quiet.

South of town, past the towering smokestack of a coal-fired power plant, Komito turned onto a dirt road. About five miles beyond, the directions said, lay the lek of the sharp-tailed grouse.

A kind of singles bar of the grouse world, a lek is a grassy knoll where hot-to-trot birds meet year after year to search for mates. Leks are all about dancing. Males stomp their feet, shake their tail feathers, spin in circles, and fend off rivals; females swoon over the best strutters. The whole peculiar mating dance repeats every dawn for about a month, after which the females start nesting, the males drop from exhaustion, and the Peeping Tom birders take long, celebratory drags from cigarettes.

The Hayden lek was infamous as one of the horniest places in the world of grouse. Problem was, Komito's Town Car was spinning its wheels a long way from the action.

Three miles up the dirt road, just after the *No County*

Maintenance Beyond This Sign warning, Komito was high-centered in ruts ten inches deep. He rocked the car forward, then backward, and then forward again, but all he heard was the dismal whine of rubber digging deeper into mud. Komito popped out and discovered that he had stopped just shy of a seven-foot snowdrift. (Thank you, El Niño!) When the weather was warmer, that melting snow turned this road into quivering mass of slop. But now that the thermometer inside the Town Car read sixteen degrees, that slop was black ice. Komito was stuck.

Dawn was an hour away. He saw no sign of lights, or help, anywhere. He had no food or water. He wore only two light sweaters and one windbreaker jacket. For the first time in his Big Year, Komito was scared. He shivered.

He could wait in the warmth of his car, but for how long? With a seven-foot drift looming over his windshield, he could tell no one was coming down this road anytime soon. Komito started walking back in the direction of his tire tracks.

Fifteen minutes of trudging and he still found nothing. No danger of human overpopulation here: it was darkness and sagebrush and barbed wire for as far as he could see. A cold wind blew. His face hurt. He wished he had warm gloves. He wished he had long underwear. He wished he knew where the hell he was.

Finally, a cow brayed. He trudged another mile and saw a porch light on his left. Civilization! Two dogs tore down the driveway. Komito ignored them. Dogs didn't frighten him as much as a wasted dawn in a Big Year. The mutts barked to high heaven, but never bothered nipping at Komito's heels. Rescue was within reach.

Then his day took a truly weird turn. From the dark a Vietnamese potbellied pig suddenly confronted Komito. The man of a million words was dumbfounded. Did these things bite? He didn't intend to find out. When the potbellied pig grunted at Komito, Komito grunted back. The pig eyed him suspiciously. Komito grunted again. His Vietnamese finally worked—the pig retreated. At 5:30 A.M., with pig at his side, Komito walked onto the lit house porch and rapped on the ranch house door.

Nobody answered. Komito peeked inside. A man ducked in the kitchen. Couldn't he hear the knocks? Komito rapped again. Still no answer. That pig was sniffing Komito's calf. Three more hard knocks. The guy finally opened his door.

Komito explained his problem, but the pig-propagating cowboy said he was too busy to help. He gave Komito a cup of coffee and the phone numbers of two local towing services. Komito, oblivious to the fact that most of the world was still in bed at 5:45 a.m., called both. Neither answered. Now he was really stuck.

Maybe the cowboy sensed Komito's desperation. Maybe the cowboy sensed a new punch line to a local bar joke.

"Get in the truck," he told Komito, and up the road they went, cowboy in hat behind the wheel, birdman with hope in the passenger seat.

When they found the Town Car, even Komito had to admit that it looked pathetic. The sun was up, and it illuminated acre after acre of wide-open ranchlands. Komito had managed to get stuck in the only rut for miles around. At least the cowboy could see that Komito wasn't exaggerating his mess. Of course, Komito had no idea how to fix it.

The cowboy parked well short of the mud bog and extricated from the back of the truck a long length of chain, the heavy, rusty stuff that looked and clanged as if it had just come off the anchor of an old warship. This shouldn't take long, the cowboy said.

It did. For people who lived in sage country, every vehicle

was equipped with an undercarriage hook to rectify situations like this. But a Lincoln Town Car, to the surprise of Komito and the disgust of the cowboy, had no easy place to affix a tow chain. A Town Car was not made for tugging.

After the cowboy lay on his back in the snow—Komito stood safely aside; he wasn't about to roll in the cold—he finally found some metal strong enough to support a grappling hook. One jerk from the truck and the Town Car was liberated at last.

Komito was so grateful that he pulled out his wallet to reward the cowboy with $50. Alas, Komito carried nothing smaller than a Ben Franklin. He gave the cowboy the hundred—oh, the horror of overpayment!—and plopped down exhausted in his car.

What were you doing out here, anyway? the cowboy asked.

Looking for a bird—the sharp-tailed grouse, Komito replied.

The cowboy shook his head. What lived on the range was for eating, not looking.

Komito goosed his Town Car heater and sped away.

Somewhere deep in the brush, a sharp-tailed grouse cried "April fool!"

Komito rested at home, but he needed a good bird. He thought about Newfoundland, where a redwing from Iceland had somehow survived an Atlantic crossing, but Newfoundland was a grueling trip. He was tired. He reconsidered his need. No, he didn't need a good bird. He needed a good, easy bird. But nothing new was being reported in Florida. Minnesota was quiet. Arizona was dead. Texas—toast.

He picked up his phone and repeated his code words: Long.

Eared. Owl. The North American Rare Bird Alert responded
with big news: a pink-footed goose was paddling just 130 miles
away in Pennsylvania.

A native of Europe, the pink-footed goose was so common
on its home turf that it was a bigger hit with hunters than
birders. On this side of the ocean, however, the goose was a
bona fide Code 5 bird—one of the 155 rarest species in North
America. Komito backed his Town Car out of his garage by
dawn. SKUA was on the prowl again.

He made a beeline for Lake Ontelaunee, near Reading, and
ran out of his car. In the reservoir was a white mass of five
thousand snow geese. On the shore before them was a
battalion of binoculared birders. Komito, breathless, recognized one, Paul Guris, a veteran of many pelagic trips.

"Is the goose still around?" Komito asked.

The other birder checked the focus inside his scope. "Take
a look," he told Komito.

The eyepiece filled with the unmistakable image of the
pinkfooted goose.

Komito was stupefied. After all his wild-goose chases—the
days in the sleet in Alaska, the hours in the summer stench of
the Salton Sea, the nights among the border swimmers on the
Rio Grande—his hunt for the pink-footed goose was over in
thirty seconds. The only way he could describe his feelings
was to use a word that, until this point, had been alien to his
vocabulary.

He felt guilty.

EIGHT

The Wise Owl

The question was simple: Where is the best place to see a long-eared owl?—but the answer to Greg Miller was fraught with complications. This bird was fickle. One day it would gather in groups of thirty along oaks in a parking lot; the next day all would be gone. Though long-eareds did tend to show up most often in New England and the Rocky Mountain West, Miller had his own little stash. The tricky part: those long-eared owls were back home in Ohio.

Since his first trip to Arizona, Miller had started calling his father nearly every night, sometimes to compare birding notes, other times just to break the loneliness. The divorce never came up, and Miller was grateful. His father was sick with congestive heart failure. His heart worked at only 15 percent efficiency. After he had open-heart surgery, doctors gave him only six months to live. That was two years ago, in 1996. Now his father was savoring every extra day of life, and Miller didn't want to do anything to make him worse. He debated the issue again and again in his mind: Would a birding trip with a divorced son help or hurt his father's fragile heart?

When Miller finally broached the subject, his father quickly cut him off. Of course he wanted to go birding with his son. He was sixty-eight years old. He already knew what he would die of. This trip would give him something more to live for.

His father was weak. Miller could see it in his face and hear it in his voice. Every step was an effort, but his father kept taking them, one after another through the snow and wind of Killdeer Plains. For the past hour they had searched every tree for any sign of a long-eared owl, but all they had found was a single pile of scat beneath a maple. Daylight was vanishing as quickly as his father's energy. Maybe this wasn't such a treasure trove after all.

From the next grove emerged another birder, a teenage girl with the strength to ignore the sideways snow. Miller's father knew the search could be helped by an extra set of eyes.

You two go ahead, he told Miller, and I'll see what I can find back here.

Miller tried to protest, but his father would hear none of it. Miller and the girl pressed on together to a distant woods.

The girl had a sharp eye, a keen ear, and identification skills good enough to name their first dozen birds in Killdeer Plains without a field guide. She was gung ho enough to believe that the owl was always just in the next tree, but careful enough to keep herself from moving too quickly and flushing the bird. She reminded Miller of himself, twenty-five years earlier.

But teenage optimism wasn't enough to produce a long-eared owl. After a half hour, Miller worried about his father. The snow blew sideways again. Miller and the girl redoubled their steps back to the original forest.

Miller's stomach pitted. Why had he left his father behind? What if something had happened to him? Even in the cold, Miller broke out in sweat. He quickened his pace.

Beyond the next field, luckily, thankfully, he spotted his

father standing beneath a tree. He looked okay, but he wasn't moving. He was looking up.

Miller raised his binoculars.

In the maple above Miller's father was a long-eared owl, perched and wheeling its head from father to son, father to son, father to son.

The eyesight of a long-eared owl is extraordinary, but this particular bird could not tell which two-legged creature beneath it wore the broader smile.

NINE

Yucatán Express

On a sultry April night deep in the Yucatán jungle, a ruby-throated hummingbird stirred. She was hungry, but that was nothing new. For the past two weeks she had done little more than eat. She had downed so many aphids and spiders and bees and nectar—especially nectar—that she had nearly doubled her body weight. Now she weighed as much as two pennies. Her breast bulged with yellow globs of fat. She needed those globs. Her life depended on them.

At her tail a steady breeze blew. It had been 106 degrees during the day, and the heat stifled everything in the jungle, even the keel-billed toucan, that screeching, big-honkered bird made famous by Froot Loops. But the sun had dropped below the beach a half hour ago. Trees were coming alive, not with calls of local birds, but with the trills of travelers like her. Everything felt right.

She lifted off her perch and so did waves of others. There were tanagers as red as fireplugs and buntings as painted as Vegas showgirls and warblers—warblers!—with orange faces and blue backs and yellow bellies and sides with zebra stripes. Beside that thousand-winged art show, the female ruby-throated hummingbird was a mere plain Jane, a pinkie-size creature with green back, dull belly, and brown flanks.

Her goal, however, was astounding

Tonight she would try to fly five hundred miles over the Gulf of Mexico. If she stopped just once to rest, she would die. If she made it, she would earn the chance for two or three seconds of copulation on the ground with a promiscuous male with a brilliant red throat.

To navigate her nonstop, nighttime ocean crossing, the ruby-throated hummingbird would rely on a brain smaller than a pea. Humans, with noggins ten thousand times larger, were still trying to comprehend this incredible journey—the marvel of migration.

Bird migration has dumbfounded humans ever since they started scanning the heavens.

In the Bible, when a miserable Job had to be reminded of the Almighty's might, the Lord asked him, "Doth the hawk fly by thy wisdom and stretch her wings toward the south?" In Jeremiah 8:7, migration was cited as proof that birds could be smarter than man: "Yea, the stork in the heaven knoweth her appointed times; and the turtledove and the crane and the swallow observe the time of their coming. But my people know not the judgment of the Lord." The quail that fell from the sky to feed Moses and his wandering band in the desert was, scientists now say, part of the biannual migration between nesting areas in Eurasia and African wintering grounds.

Even the pagans knew something was up. Homer began the third chapter of the *Iliad* by likening the battle cries of the Trojans to "a flight of wildfowl or cranes that scream overhead when rain and winter drive them over the flowing waters of Oceanus."

But recognizing bird migration was a lot different from

understanding it. Aristotle, the renowned expert of logic and metaphysics, was stumped by swallows. He believed the speedy bug eaters vanished from the autumn skies of ancient Greece because they hibernated in tree holes. When black-faced Eurasian redstarts skipped town for warmer climes and were replaced by orange-faced Eurasian robins, Aristotle came up with a novel explanation—the redstart and robin were part of a glorious transmutation, the seasonal change of one animal into another. (At least he kept his feathers together; Romans thought swallows turned into frogs.)

In 1703, an Englishman who identified himself only as a "Person of Learning and Piety" published the "Probable Solution of This Question: Whence come the Stork and the Turtledove, the Crane, and the Swallow, when they Know and Observe the Appointed Time of their Coming?" His answer: birds wintered on the moon.

By the late 1800s, after Linnaeus had classified the birds and Darwin had figured out how they evolved—his famed thirteen finches of the Galápagos helped inspire the *Origin of Species*—migration became less of a mystery. For the first time, ships and railroads made it possible for man to match the travels of featherweight creatures. When biologists crossed the globe from north to south, they found many of the same birds from home. Bird migration became the new conventional wisdom.

The hows and whys of migration remained elusive. Clearly, one of the world's great flyways linked South America with North, but the exact route was unknown. Noting that land birds such as warblers sometimes landed on tankers and shrimpers in the middle of the Gulf of Mexico, most scientists concluded that migrants simply flew over water. In 1945, though, Texas professor George Williams rocked the ornithological boat with a simple question: Why would tiny songbirds risk their lives in a five-hundred-mile ocean crossing when they could fly around it? To make sure no one ignored his point, Williams even revived a twisted form of the old Person of Learning and Piety moon-jab. The belief in trans-Gulf migration, he wrote, was like the belief that "the interior of the moon is made of green cheese"—there was little scientific proof of either. Even though Williams knew that many species tended to appear magically on the same spring days on the Gulf Coast of the United States, he concluded that these were land-bound migrants, blown out to sea by storms and trying desperately to return.

Williams's green-cheese raspberry was so troubling to ornithologists that they soon began staying up nights to disprove it. The most successful was a Louisiana State University researcher, George Lowery, who spent the spring of 1948 peering at the moon through a 20x telescope from the southern coast of the Gulf, in Progreso, Mexico. What Lowery saw in the dark was vindication. Songbirds were taking off within an hour of sunset and flying high in the night past the glow of the moon. Each one was headed due north.

In all his nights on the shores of the Yucatán, Mr. Moonwatcher rarely saw more than a meager thirty birds per hour—a telescope, after all, takes in only a minute percentage of the sky—but it was still enough to spoil Williams's cheese. A Gulf flyway clearly was open. But no one knew how many travelers used it.

The big breakthrough came from an ornithologist who, strangely enough, made his most important discovery indoors. In the mid-1960s, Sid Gauthreaux learned about a new battery of government radars rimming the Gulf from Brownsville, Texas, to Key West, Florida. Though the equipment was built to forecast the weather, Gauthreaux figured out that the sensitive radars also picked up something else moving in the sky—evidence of migrating birds. One small blob on a radar screen represented a small flock of birds; a bigger blob was hundreds of birds. When Gauthreaux started looking through old weather records, he found blob after blob after blob. Fortunately, the government, being the government, had archived nearly every weather radar image since the network had been built in 1957. Gauthreaux hunkered down and reviewed thousands of radar pages. It was mind-numbing work, but the weather records proved that the Gulf of Mexico was one of the planet's most important avian flyways. It came to be known as the Yucatán Express.

At peak migration, Gauthreaux estimated, as many as 45 million songbirds arrived in a single night along three hundred miles of the Gulf Coast, from Corpus Christi, Texas, to Lake Charles, Louisiana. That's 150,000 birds per mile, or 15,000 per city block.

The overall numbers were amazing, and they contained incredible individual feats. Curious about the endurance of songbirds, a University of Illinois researcher named Richard Graber captured a gray-cheeked thrush—a smaller, plainer relative of the American robin—and attached a tiny transmitter to it. With Graber in hot pursuit in a small aircraft, the thrush took off in central Illinois and flew straight north at an average speed of 50 mph. (The bird was boosted by a 27 mph tailwind.) At Lake Michigan, the airplane played it safe by hugging the shoreline, but the one-ounce bird flew smack-dab up the middle of the vast lake. The eight-hour four-hundred-mile chase finally ended at the northernmost point of Lake Michigan when the pilot was forced to land to refuel. The bird continued north without stopping.

Birds indisputably had the ability to complete staggering flights. Humans just had to believe them.

Migration was lonely work. While other species banded together in aerodynamic flocks or majestic Vs, the ruby-throated hummingbird always flew apart. She neither gave nor received chirps of encouragement or hints on direction. She was, by nature, a solitary cuss. Hers was the only bird family that could hover, fly backward, or even upside down, but tonight she was interested in going only one direction—north.

Beneath her the land gave way to water, and the great blackness of the Gulf stretched before her. She climbed until she found her tailwind, which tonight was a steady 14 mph. Different species favor winds at different elevations. On the long flight north, sandpipers and red-necked phalaropes often fly so low that they could be seen only after cresting a wave. Above them are hummingbirds and songbirds, which typically stay five hundred to two thousand feet over the Gulf. (Most songbirds are too small to be seen without binoculars above one thousand feet.) At the top of the sky are the strongest flyers, mostly shorebirds, which often exceed three miles above sea level. Of course, nature never fails to make exceptions—or to astonish. Twenty-one thousand feet above the Nevada desert, a commercial jet once whacked a migrating mallard. Climbers gasping for breath on oxygen bottles atop Mount Everest, elevation 29,028, have been shocked to see geese flying overhead.

Five hours into her Gulf flight, the hummer was averaging 30 mph and still pointing toward America. Why don't birds get lost at night? Some university studies have concluded that birds may follow the stars—Polaris, the North Star, is the one light in the sky that never moves—but other researchers have found stronger links to polarized light that wafts from the sun in the evening sky. Neither theory explains how birds successfully navigate hundreds of miles in the dark through clouds and fog. The truth is, the best scientific minds in the world still don't know how bird brains find their way.

By the time the sun rose, the little ruby in the sky was becoming a mere shadow of herself. She had covered three hundred miles and was burning fat fast. A hummer's metabolism is so high that, on a typical land-bound day, she must feed every twenty minutes or so just to stay healthy. That means she eats half her weight in food and drinks eight times her weight in water—every day. For the past ten hours on migration, however, she could consume nothing. Her wings flapped fifty times a second. Her heart beat a thousand times a minute. Her weight was down about 25 percent.

On the horizon, trouble loomed.

From two hundred miles away, Greg Miller could see it: billowing black storm clouds, closing on the Texas coast. Miller knew exactly what to do. He raced to the heart of the storm.

Al Levantin was already there. Sandy Komito was getting soaked by it.

In the thick of spring migration, competitive birders dreamed of foul weather. Actually, they lusted for it, the nastier the better, a gale-force thunderstorm or a cold front that took two sweaters.

The reason: fallout.

Fallout is a fabled natural phenomenon where migrating birds, confronted by a sudden head wind or downpour, literally drop from the sky to seek safe refuge. In many years fallout simply doesn't happen; steady tailwinds and calm skies conspire to let birds cruise easily to their northern nesting locations. But when fallout does occur, it is the stuff of legends. Fallout looks as if a *Star Trek* transporter is beaming creatures from outer space and down onto the coast—birds, thousands of birds, come from nowhere. Tree limbs bend with scarlet tanagers. Lawns are carpeted with warblers. Yard bushes with bare spring buds are transformed into Christmas trees laden with brilliant winged ornaments.

For most birders, a fallout is an amazing spectacle. But for Big Year birders, a fallout is a shortcut, a time-saver, a Cliff's Notes that gives the answers to most of that semester's final exams. Every bird seen exhausted on the ground during a fallout is a bird that doesn't have to be chased later on its breeding grounds. No competitive birder can afford to miss a fallout.

Greg Miller pushed his rental car to 80 mph and then floored it.

The hummer was fading fast. When the storm first hit, sweeping from land to coast, her fat globs were already thin. Now they were gone. All she had for energy stores was muscle. Each wingbeat ate more away. She was cannibalizing herself.

Sixteen hours of southerlies had brought her within twenty miles of land. But the tailwind that had carried her so far so fast had been spun around by the storm. The wind now blasted her face. She needed twice the work to go half the distance. All around her the storm had knocked down birds from their migrating altitudes and left them struggling just above the water. She was almost on the waves, too. The Gulf was really rolling. She couldn't float or swim. One dip and she was history.

Humans have long understood the dangers of Gulf crossings. At the turn of the twentieth century, seamen on a ship thirty miles off the Mississippi River delta watched in amazement when hundreds of migrating warblers, confronted by a cold snap, braced against a head wind, struggled, and drowned. After another spring storm in April 1995, David and Melissa Wiedenfeld of Louisiana State University walked the beaches near Grand Isle, Louisiana, and found seven thousand dead birds per mile. That single storm, they concluded, killed at least forty thousand songbirds of forty-five species.

Gulf catastrophes were common enough that Mother Nature, through evolution, had hedged her bets. To prevent the destruction of an entire species by one horrible storm, many species, including the ruby-throated hummingbird, had two kinds of birds—those that migrated over land, and those that migrated over water. Land migrants knew about raptors. Water migrants knew about willpower.

The hummer was finally within striking distance of the coast. Rain fell in sheets. She had the biggest heart, proportionately, of any warm-blooded animal, and she was pushing it to the hilt. Her lungs, like those of all birds, remained fully inflated, but hers were turbocharged by nine special air sacs that pumped like bellows and kept the oxygen coming. She was turning weaker faster.

Then, over the waves, she saw it: land!

Not just the usual swampy coastal plain, but trees, big honking trees, stretching just beyond the ocean froth. She was almost there. She might be saved. Her wings were being battered by rain and wind. She fought hard. The closer she came, the better she saw—hackberries and honey locusts and water oaks fifty feet high, yaupon and privet bushes in the thicket below, and Indian paintbrushes and grass in the fields around.

She dropped on a hackberry like a hailstone from the sky.

She was weak. She had lost so much fat and muscle on her eighteen-hour journey north that she now weighed one-tenth of an ounce. She and nine friends could be mailed together for the price of a single postage stamp. But she had done it. She had conquered the Gulf. She was alive.

A two-legged creature approached. It made a loud, deep sound.

"Ruby-throated," announced Sandy Komito, dripping wet in the rain.

For the past ten days, Komito had been hanging out at the famed fallout hot spot of High Island, Texas, and he was going stir-crazy because of it. There just wasn't much to see; on a bluebird day, High Island didn't even have bluebirds. Komito was so bored that he took to scolding children in Boy Scout Woods—"Screaming and loud noises bring mosquitoes!" he lectured a preschooler—and teasing foreigners. ("God bless the Brits!" he proclaimed to a tour group of twenty. "If it wasn't for them acting as decoys for us, we'd all be eaten alive by these mosquitoes.")

Now the waiting game was over. The fallout hummer on the twig before him was so spent, so oblivious to his presence, that Komito didn't even need binoculars to identify her. Besides, her species was so common around summertime flowers and gardens along the East Coast that he expected to see hundreds during his Big Year.

She was no big deal.

He moved on. The sky was raining birds onto High Island, and Komito had more to find than ruby-throated hummingbirds.

Like some of the people it attracts, High Island is a little unusual. For starters, it isn't an island. It's a small town seventy miles east of Houston and twenty miles south of the interstate, a full mile from the roily Gulf, and surrounded by rice fields, oil rigs, and humidity.

High Island also isn't very high. In fact, it rises only thirty-two feet above sea level, the crest of the bubble of a subterranean salt dome. But its fertile soils support a canopy of fifty-foot trees, a green oasis that can be seen for miles offshore, the most prominent point on hundreds of miles of Gulf coast from the Yucatán to Mobile, Alabama.

The island's reputation exceeds its size. Though it regularly draws birders from Los Angeles to Long Island to London, the prime fallout area covers only fifteen acres. Every year, more than six thousand people converge upon this tiny preserve with high hopes for a spring fallout.

High Island is not the most popular place on the continent for birding—Santa Ana National Wildlife Refuge in south Texas and Cape May in New Jersey each attract about one hundred thousand visitors a year. And it isn't the richest—High Island birders pump $2.5 million into the local economy, a fraction of the $15 million spent to view the sandhill and whooping crane migration at Grand Island, Nebraska. But for three weeks in April, High Island is the undisputed center of the serious birding universe.

It even has grandstands. Determined to make birding a spectator sport, Houston Audubon built bleachers beneath the hackberries to hold as many as forty people—fifty if the birds were really good—with views of a puddle birdbath that was fed by regular drips from aquarium tubing. A sign on the grandstands warned *Beware of Berry Bottom*, but many intemperate birders still walked around all day with silly purple stains splotched across their seats. The most-trafficked walking paths were boardwalked, with benches at strategic locations. All other paths were hard-packed from the repeated laps of so many birders.

Though everyone came here for the birds, some of the most interesting spectacles are put on by bipeds.

There are vanloads of touring Brits, earnest but business-faced, always lugging their tripods and telescopes for the closest possible looks even though the fallout birds are so weary they can nearly be touched. For Englishmen—and they are, overwhelmingly, men— obsessed with ticking off as many New World species as possible, High Island is the trip of a life-time. Their months of preparation mean they often know more about North American birds than most North American birders.

Close behind are the roving bands of middle-aged women, two or three abreast, wearing sensible shoes, uncolored hair, and plain pants. They care not one whit what any man thinks, unless he can help solve an especially difficult bird identification. When the women coo over the discovery of a rose-breasted grosbeak, crowds gather. Otherwise the women keep mainly to themselves and grin and chortle and have as much fun with each other as with any winged creature.

The noisiest bipeds in the woods are the married types. A typically disastrous trip to High Island occurs when one spouse, an inexperienced birder, insists on tagging along with the other to see exactly what this birdwatching thing is all about. Usually it takes four mosquito welts or one downpour for the inexperienced spouse to demand how the hell this fits into any normal person's idea of a vacation. Inevitably the day ends with one angry spouse in the car, another angry spouse in the field, and both insisting over dinner that night that the other remain ensconced on his or her side of the motel bed.

Prowling, prowling, and never resting are the Young Turks, most easily distinguished by their absolute refusal to wear a foppish hat. The headstrong ones stare intensely, quote their *Geographics*, and generally talk as if they know it all, which they seemingly do until a tough call on a plain female warbler makes them into monkeys. The smart Young Turks ask for help from Brits and middle-aged women and say a lot of "Yes, ma'am," "No, sir," "Thank you."

Then there are the standoffish types, almost all men, who lurk around as lone eagles until someone else calls out a particularly rare bird. Then they pounce. These guys are either seriously competitive or highly susceptible to competition fever. They talk about life lists.

All these people walk around and round the four-block circles, craning their necks to the heavens and speaking in the hushed tones usually reserved for Sunday morning in the pew. It is all so neat and proper and civilized.

It made Sandy Komito crazy.

He tried to keep quiet, oh, he really did. But with as many as five hundred birders a day walking the High Island boardwalks, he couldn't resist some showmanship.

At one point, two tour groups clustered around a low oak branch adorned with an apparent chuck-will's-widow, a robin-size bug-eater that hunts at night, sleeps during the day, and wears such perfect dead-leaf camouflage that it is usually overlooked as just another lump on a log. Komito was happy to join the crowd. A chuck-will's-widow was rarely seen during the day; people usually drove the back roads at dusk with hopes of headlighting the glowing eyes of this bird.

Yes, the defending Big Year champ confirmed, it's an excellent bird.

Just as Komito started puffing with the discovery of another toughie, Jon Dunn, the chief birdman for the *National Geographic Field Guide to the Birds of North America*, ambled by. Dunn parted the tour groups like Moses at the Red Sea.

Dunn studied the bird and issued a new proclamation: "That's no chuck-will's-widow. That's a whip-poor-will."

Though the two species were similar, the whip-poor-will was about 25 percent smaller, with more white in the tail.

Komito glassed the bird more closely and saw that Dunn was right. Komito felt the humiliating splat of egg on his face. Mistakes were always part of the game in birding, but Komito didn't like to commit his in front of the game's master, with two tour groups so up close and personal with his misfortune.

High Island was a small place, and Komito was a proud man. He really wanted something better out of High Island. He had spun his wheels the past ten days waiting for a storm to bring him fallout. All that was falling out now, though, were the usual suspects—ruby-throated hummingbirds, golden-winged warblers, summer tanagers. Nice birds all, but nothing that was going to break any Big Year records.

Perhaps sensing the hurt, Dunn gave Komito a heads-up on a hunt for another tough bird, the elusive yellow rail, only a short drive away. Komito decided to chase it.

On his way out, as he shuffled on the boardwalk past the women and the warblers and the Brits and the buntings, Komito bumped into something that was totally unexpected: Al Levantin.

"Hello, Master," Levantin said, his customary greeting to Komito when encountering him in an uncustomary place. It was the third time they had met in the first four months of the year. The hellos were about the extent of their conversation. Levantin could make small talk for hours, but was Mr. Secret Agent Man when it came to personal details.

So the two Big Year competitors passed on the boardwalk as quickly as they came. Komito went to dog the Dunn bird. Levantin stayed to score thirty-two songbirds.

Once safely out of each other's sight, however, both men pondered the same question: What was *he* doing here?

The yellow rail was the Greta Garbo of the bird world: it wanted to be left alone. Few birds were camouflaged so perfectly; few animals were so obsessed with remaining unseen. It wintered only in coastal swamps with spartina grass so dense that it rarely saw its own shadow. It never walked in the open. If chased, it ran. It hated flying so much that scientists once suspected that it migrated alone at night—on foot.

For competitive birders, this all meant the yellow rail would never win any Miss Congeniality contests. It used to be an easier target, thanks to the federal government. For years, the U.S. Fish and Wildlife Service had driven something called a rail buggy—a monster Rolligon truck with wheels three feet high and four feet wide—through the skankiest depths of the thirty-four-thousand-acre Anahuac National Wildlife Refuge. Birders rode on top. Rails ran for their lives.

But federal biologists grew concerned about the smushing damage inflicted by five-hundred-pound tires on five-day-a-week rumbles through a supposed nature preserve. In 1988, the buggy was officially derailed.

For the next decade, many birders simply wrote off the bird. Without the buggy to flush it, the yellow rail was just too difficult to see.

So when Jon Dunn mentioned a plot to spot yellow rails at Anahuac, Sandy Komito jumped. Though birders no longer could ride for rails, they could certainly scurry for them. Vanloads of birding tour groups, plus Komito, converged at Anahuac headquarters and organized a rail walk. The Fish and Wildlife Service even endorsed the whole scheme by opening up a part of the swamp that had long been off-limits to human visitation.

There was, of course, a catch. All this was to happen in a place called Gator Marsh.

Anahuac was home to alligators. Big ones. Hundreds of them. Usually they stayed under the boardwalks and off the gravel roads, but they were most definitely there. They used to be one of the main attractions on the old rail buggies. They were fun to watch from the top of a truck with four-foot-wide wheels. But alligators at ankle level were an entirely different proposition. Some birders decided to play it safe by standing atop the levee well above Gator Marsh.

The rest got their marching orders. The only way to see yellow rails was to force them to take wing. This was no easy task. Even with a line of birders this long—there were sixty people—a rail could still move fast enough on the ground to escape detection.

So the birders decided to use a secret weapon: terror.

On long ropes they tied dozens of plastic milk cartons and poured gravel into each. The result was a noisemaking dragline. If the birders tugged this contraption quickly through the swamp, they might just frighten a yellow rail into the air—if a gator didn't do something about the racket first.

For a good bird, Komito would risk danger. But to many other birders, Komito seemed to avoid extra work.

While fifty-nine other people trudged into the thigh-deep swamp grass with the dragline, Komito flanked to the left, hoping to be in a position to photograph anything that might pop up. Though the people in the middle of the dragline were the main brush-beaters, Komito knew they were less likely to reap any payoff. If a yellow rail couldn't outrun a dragline, it often tried to sidestep the threat. That meant the prime viewing location was on the ends, or the wingtips, of the dragline.

Komito positioned himself in the perfect spotting position and waited for the others to scare the birds to him.

After a few hundred yards of lugging rock-filled milk jugs through ankle-deep water and thigh-deep grass, some in the dragline started muttering about the Bataan Death March. But even a short rest would give a chance for a desperate rail to outrun its pursuers. They trudged on.

Finally a bird flushed out. It looked like a rail, but flew low enough to prevent a positive identification. Half the dragline hightailed it to the general area of landing.

A circle quickly formed and closed tighter. And neater. And tighter.

By the time three dozen birders were actually moving in a circle in the swamp—Komito hadn't tried anything like this since falling victim to the hokeypokey at a wedding reception—the rail was finally spotted. It was black, brown, yellow, and mottled, and it looked as if it had been squished between bricks. Narrow flanks allowed it to squeeze through such dense cover. These flanks were the reason people talked about being as thin as a rail.

To justify his decision to stay outside the dragline, Komito joined the circle around the bird and put his camera in. He took his camera out. He put his camera in and clicked it all about. He got his yellow rail and he turned himself around.

That, he thought, is what it's all about.

The yellow rail fled.

Greg Miller made it to High Island without a speeding ticket. That was saying something. More than two hundred miles in less than three hours through a nasty storm—there was nothing like the chance of a High Island fallout to focus his attention. The hardest part came after he finally reached the boardwalk. His adrenaline kept getting in the way of his birds.

He was able to calm himself enough to spot something chesthigh up a hackberry. It was a female ruby-throated hummingbird, perching long enough to digest her latest load of bugs and nectar.

For Miller, it was the first ruby-throated hummingbird of the year.

For her, it was a brief rest. Five hundred miles after crossing the Gulf, she would stuff herself with more food and, once again, migrate on. She might fly as far north as Canada. She had to find a man.

TEN

The Big Yak

Five miles at sea, on a course for the Dry Tortugas of Florida, Al Levantin was riding the wake of history. All the great birders had traveled this way. In 1832, John James Audubon had sailed the seventy miles from Key West to the Tortugas and found five new species for his landmark *Birds of America*. On their buddy trip 121 years later, Roger Tory Peterson and James Fisher had boated the old Audubon route and discovered rare boobies. This was where, in the heat of their Big Year competition, Floyd Murdoch had contemplated pushing Kenn Kaufman overboard, and Benton Basham had scored his first neotropical rarity. Though Jim Vardaman took a plane to the Dry Tortugas instead of a boat in his big-money Big Year, he was so pleased with the birds of the coral atolls that he served himself a triumphant dinner of one can of Vienna sausages, one box of crackers—and a double bourbon.

Levantin, alas, was in no mood to celebrate. Doubled over the stern rail of the *Yankee Freedom*, he was vomiting his guts out. Seasickness again. Oh, the pain, the misery, the embarrassment. How could this be happening?

The first time he had grown green at sea, on that January pelagic in Monterey with Sandy Komito, Levantin had chalked it up to the jitters. After he had recovered, he did his research and loaded up on all the mal de mer remedies—pills of Dramamine and Bonine for the stomach, Scopolamine patches for the ear, and acupuncture bands for the wrist. He tried big breakfasts and no breakfasts. He ate only pasta for dinner until somebody advised him to switch to all-protein steaks. Others urged ginger, honey, or three tablespoons of bitters. He nibbled pretzels and stoned-wheat thins and drank plenty of water and got lots of sleep.

Everybody had a seasickness cure. Nobody's worked.

He couldn't set foot on a boat this year without losing his lunch, and breakfast and dinner, too. The California ferry to Santa Cruz Island, the Cape Hatteras trip to the Gulf Stream, Monterey the second time, and Monterey the third—his stomach never had a chance. All the seasickness literature warned against two things: never look through binoculars and never look at a book. But no mortal could get seabirds without magnification or field guides. Levantin needed pelagic birds. He wished the consequences were cheaper.

Now Levantin was dry-heaving his way to the Dry Tortugas. Seasickness was the great equalizer. Sure, he might be a business chief executive with a mansion near Aspen, but on the hundredfoot *Yankee Freedom* he was just another chum-maker. It was impossible to put on airs in this position. Would any of his employees spot him?

At this point, Levantin could not have cared. It's not easy being green. He felt like dying. His only solace in the back of the boat—as soon as he felt queasy, he moved quickly away from the in-your-face head winds at the bow—was that he wasn't alone. The stern of every pelagic trip had a Technicolor choir. They were kindred spirits, these Dukes of Hurl, and they had heard all the cracks about bad sailors. Napoleon conquered Europe but never his ferocious seasickness. Harry Truman was a landlubber, too. Even Admiral Lord Nelson, the greatest naval commander in British history, the hero who vanquished both the French and Spanish fleets in a singular war at Trafalgar, suffered from seasickness so bad, and so consistent, that he rarely planned battles until he had spent at least three days at sea.

"Want a surefire cure for seasickness?" asked one stern sufferer to another. "Go stand under a tree."

At least Levantin tended to recover quickly. After contributing to the sea, he would drink a little water, rest a little while, and within a half hour or so, be ready for a little birding. On a pelagic trip, getting sick was something many people did at some point. But missing a bird because of it was unforgivable.

So he suffered, lay down, and then tried, ever so feebly, to raise his Leica glass again. With a black-and-white seabird far out above the rolling waves, he played peekaboo—binoculars up until his stomach soured, binoculars down until it calmed—long enough to see that the bird was massive, fork-tailed, and soaring almost effortlessly. Fortunately, he didn't have to use the binoculars again; there just weren't any other fork-tailed seabirds with eight-foot wingspans.

The magnificent frigate bird was Levantin's 500th species of the year. It was April 23, and he was eighteen birds ahead of Sandy Komito's record-breaking 1987 pace.

To celebrate, Al Levantin pampered himself.

He sat down.

On his sixteenth-century search for the fountain of youth, Juan Ponce de León discovered seven small islands in the tropical seas north of Cuba. Though the coral isles were rich in sea turtles (the Spaniard collected a hundred for dinner; hence the name Tortugas), Ponce de León found no magical fountain there (he died a few years later) or even freshwater (hence the name Dry Tortugas).

The Tortugas have offered up a mix of natural riches and man-made trouble ever since.

Sailors had good reason to fear the islands. Pirates such as Jean Lafitte gathered on Garden Key to plot attacks on passing merchant ships. Seamen who outran the pirates still had to contend with treacherous currents; the Tortugas' shifting web of shoals and reefs are today littered with hundreds of shipwrecks.

By the mid-1840s, the U.S. Army grew interested in the strategic advantages of the Dry Tortugas and imported slaves to build a fort. First slaves and later enlisted men struggled for fifteen years to build an outpost impervious to military attack. The walls of Fort Jefferson were ten feet thick, forty-five feet high, and millions of dollars overbudget. By the time the top layer of stone was finally laid in 1862, other engineers had invented a powerful new weapon, the rifled cannon, that could demolish fort walls in a single eighthour assault. Fort Jefferson, the Gibraltar of the Gulf, was a bust.

Determined to make something out of its wasted investment—some estimated that the fort had cost $1 a stone—the government turned the whole complex into a prison and first filled it with hundreds of Civil War deserters. Soon, though, it also incarcerated some even more notorious, including Dr. Samuel Mudd, who had set the broken leg of John Wilkes Booth after the assassination of President Lincoln.

As a prison, the Dry Tortugas failed terribly. The sewage system was designed to empty into a self-cleaning moat, but ocean tides were rarely strong enough to flush out the waste. The result was an island prison ringed with a doughnut of turds that bobbed and stewed in the tropical August sun. In 1867, yellow fever struck more than half the four hundred prisoners, and the prison doctor died. One survivor worked mightily to fight the epidemic. His name was still Mudd, but he won a pardon from President Andrew Johnson for saving the lives of dozens of inmates. There was no saving Fort Jefferson. Fed up with the disease, hurricanes, and general hardship of a place seventy miles from civilization, the army abandoned it in 1874. The navy revived it a few years after as a coaling station for ships on patrol, but technology soon rendered that use obsolete, too.

The Dry Tortugas did excel at one thing: producing birds.

When Audubon first arrived at the Tortugas on a government ship, the captain warned the birdman with this bit of hyperbole: "Before we cast anchor you will see them rise in swarms like those of bees disturbed in their hive, and the cries will deafen you." Sure enough, when the revenue cutter cast anchor, Audubon reported seeing a "cloudlike mass arise over Bird Key . . . On landing I felt as if the birds would raise me from the ground, so thick were they all round, and so quick the motion of their wings."

The sailors had been here before. They carried sticks and, like explorers slashing through the jungle with machetes, cleared themselves an eye-level path. In less than half an hour, the men had knocked down more than a hundred terns and filled baskets with their eggs. "I considered them delicious, in whatever way cooked," Audubon wrote, "and during our stay at the Tortugas we never passed a day without procuring ourselves a quantity of them."

Others had the same idea. During Audubon's visit, a crew of Spanish eggers arrived from Havana and collected eight tons—tons!—of tern and noddy eggs. Unless Audubon himself had lapsed into hyperbole, that was nearly a quarter million eggs. Sailors said they would sell their load in Cuba for the princely sum of $200.

Needless to say, when Al Levantin landed at the Dry Tortugas 166 years later, the tern and noddy populations had been severely dented. Instead of millions of birds, a mere hundred thousand or so nested. They remained a stupefying sight with a prodigious sound. Still, Levantin could only wonder what used to be. Bird Key was no more; the catastrophic Florida hurricane of 1938 had submerged it and two other islands. Yet Fort Jefferson stayed hulking over the turqoise seas, its moats clear of waste but its masonry crumbling from decades of salt and abuse.

Levantin couldn't do a Big Year without the Tortugas because of their geographical quirk: though the species here were common for the planet, they were rare on this continent. For example, the sooty tern, dark-plumaged fighter pilot of the warm seas, bred by the millions throughout the tropics, but it was hardly ever found in the colder climes of North America—except on the Tortugas's Bush Key. Other birds, such as the masked booby, were difficult to find because they usually stayed so far offshore until it came time to return to their Tortugas nesting colony. (Though old salts named the birds boobies because they seemed stupidly tame, Audubon noted how quickly they wised up. The Bird Key boobies, victims of repeated raids by egg-hunters, became so wary of man that the sharpest shooters on Audubon's boat struggled to sneak close enough to blast one for dinner.)

Besides all the tropical seabirds, the Tortugas offered one other sideshow—migrating land birds. At times the walls of Fort Jefferson looked like a man-made High Island; the masonry literally crawled with fallout warblers and swallows. Levantin picked up many of these birds—a bank swallow, a bobolink, a veery—but it was with a heavy heart. The song-birds on the Dry Tortugas were hurting. They landed only out of desperation and scrounged madly for insects that weren't there. How would they ever grow strong enough to complete the seventy-mile, nonstop flight to Key West? Levantin knew most wouldn't. So did a hungry peregrine falcon that waited, patiently, atop the fort walls. Even though many songbirds here were so spent that Levantin could flick them with his finger, he gave them a wide berth.

If anyone ever felt sympathy for a creature about to struggle with an ocean crossing, it was Al Levantin.

When the gangplank was finally lowered onto the dock at Key West, Levantin felt like kissing the ground. He was a survivor.

For Sandy Komito, however, the misery had just begun. Komito would soon walk onto the same boat for the same trip to the same place. A veteran of dozens of pelagic expeditions, Komito would not get seasick. But he faced his own special hell: triple bunks, deep in the cabin of the *Yankee Freedom*, stacked so close together that a man couldn't even sit up in his own bed. The frames were cold metal. Beds sagged so much that the middle bowed six inches deeper than the sides. There wasn't even room in Komito's berth for a toilet kit; he had to cram the kit in his duffel with everyone else's in the cabin walkway.

Levantin had lived quite well with this arrangement; at night he was so grateful not to be seasick that he rested like a rock on his mushy berth. But Levantin's relief was a Komito nightmare. So fussy about his sleep that he traveled with his own pillow and night blinders, Komito was now shoehorned into a boat cabin with three dozen strangers who snored and wheezed and did God knew what else in a place with absolutely no privacy. Even worse, Komito was assigned to the bottom bunk. Whenever the guy above him rose in the middle of the night to go to the bathroom, he stepped on Komito's bed. A stranger's feet—disgusting.

The first night Komito couldn't sleep.

The second night he got two hours.

The third night he couldn't sleep again.

When the boat finally returned to Key West, Komito was in no mood to be messed with. He had gotten the same seabirds as Levantin, just a few days later. He couldn't wait to get out of there.

Greg Miller longed for the luxury of a cramped berth. Three months of Big Year travel had turned his wallet into a hurting unit. His savings were nearly shot, and he needed a few thousand dollars for next month's trip of a lifetime to Attu and Alaska. He still was putting in the time at work—forty hours last week, forty-one the week before—but that was for rent and the monthly minimums on his five credit cards. He wished he could do the Dry Tortugas with a *Yankee Freedom*–style charter trip that came with guides and cooked meals. His checking account said no. These birds would have to come with no frills.

He wrote code for six and a half hours in his cubicle at the nuclear power plant and caught the red-eye to Fort Lauderdale. He drove until exhaustion. In Homestead, the last town before the Florida Keys, he checked himself into a roadside motel room that had trash in the wastebasket, an unflushed toilet, and a shower with someone else's loofah. He turned on the air conditioner and dirt blew out. It was 1 A.M. He was too tired to care. Besides, it was cheap.

His accommodations on the Dry Tortugas were even more Spartan. His room for the night was a $3 campsite. All the birds during the day had been terrific—he got the requisite terns, boobies, and noddies—but the end-of-the-day blues were sinking in again. There were no phones, so he couldn't call his father. He was just a man with his pup tent and the stars. Miller hadn't thought this camping thing through very well. All he had packed for dinner was a tin of SPAM.

The campers around him had spent the day sunning and snorkeling and were now determined to spend the night drinking. Nesting colonies of sooty terns and brown noddies made a racket to remember, but they had nothing on a campground loaded with navy boys and Bud Light.

As he peeled back the lid on his SPAM can, Miller must have looked lonely or pathetic or both, because suddenly, out of the blue, two women in swimsuits called to him. Miller pinched himself. Maybe this really was a Bud Light commercial.

The babes, it seemed, had been snorkeling the reefs earlier that day when they'd attracted the attention of a passing boat of men. (Go figure.) The men had caught loads of shrimp. Each party had specific biological needs, and an arrangement was struck: the men's shrimp for the women's liquor. The result was two women in the campsite next to Miller with an unexpected bounty of shrimp, plus a backup supply of wine.

As Miller barbecued the sea's riches—that SPAM was history—he tried to explain birding and Big Years to the women. They just didn't get it. In fact, by the end of the barbecue, they were so wasted they couldn't even stand up. Miller didn't care. He was the only birder on the island. He was probably the only sober person, too.

He fell asleep that night alone in his pup tent with no sleeping bag and a pillow made of a shirt rolled around shoes. His belly was full. His mind was calm. He had birds to see in the morning.

Sometimes, he thought, it pays to bird on the cheap.

ELEVEN

The Cradle of Storms

Three miles over Alaska, Sandy Komito was flying with his head in the clouds. All the breaks were coming his way. He had scored his favorite seat on the aisle of this chartered plane while the others rushed for the windows. He had picked up a new species, a boreal owl, the previous day by hooking up with a birding tour group whose members each paid a ninety-five-dollar fee. He even got himself a spot on this trip without paying the bulk of his bill until the last minute.

He was headed to Attu.

This trip, Komito knew, would make or break his Big Year. No place in North America produced more rarities more often than Attu. It was out there—way out there. Farther west than Fiji, closer to Asia than mainland America, Attu was the last island on a volcanic chain that split the North Pacific from the Bering Sea. This flight from Anchorage to Attu would cover the same mileage as a flight from New York to Chicago and back again.

Even before he showed up at the gate, Komito recognized half the people on this tour. Since 1985, he had been to Attu twelve times. Others had been even more. In a sport of obsessives, Attu was the most potent addiction, and not just because of the birds. It was the people. Cardiologists and boiler mechanics, pilots and postal workers, seniors in college and on social security, the men and women traveling to Attu were united by little else but their singular obsession. For at least two weeks in May, on an island two time zones from anywhere, they never heard anyone accuse them of being peculiar. They ate together, bunked together, and did their one special thing together again and again and again in undisturbed bliss. At Attu, though, the joy always came with snow, sleet, and gale-force winds.

Just because so many people knew each other didn't mean they all trusted each other. There were secrets on Attu. Komito, in fact, was being a little cagey himself. He wasn't making any public proclamations about his Big Year, though many people had figured it out. Some competitors could be flying on this very plane.

From another part of the cabin—by the wing, realm of the newbie—a big, bearded, bubbly man came and squatted in the aisle and asked Komito about his record 1987 Big Year.

Komito had seen this guy before. Just yesterday, on the group's pre-Attu birding tour of Anchorage, this same man had tumbled like a bad cartoon down a sixty-foot snowbank just to see a ho-hum Alaskan willow ptarmigan. Now he was asking about Big Years. Komito's danger alarm was clanging.

A Big Year, Komito told the stranger, was quite an undertaking.

The other birder agreed. He had been working full-time at a nuclear power plant and cramming his birding in on long weekends and breaks between contracts. He was trying a Big Year.

Komito cut to the quick: So how many birds have you seen?

Five hundred and eight.

Komito snapped upright in his seat. Five hundred and eight? That was ahead of the pace from his record Big Year.

What kind of maniac could be beating his record while still holding down a full-time job? Komito had never met someone more driven than he.

This was surprising. This was strange. This was downright scary.

The other birder's name was Greg Miller. That was a name Komito would remember.

Komito had more to worry about than just another competitor. He was still in trouble with Lawrence of Attu.

Larry Balch had been the dictator, usually benevolent, of the island since 1980. He chartered all the flights. (There was no commercial service to Attu.) He sold all the tickets and paid all the bills. He did all the hiring. He assigned rooms, roommates, menus, and even the regular chores required of all Attuvians. He held the only federal permit to operate tours on the island; when the government threatened to pull the permit, Balch used his contacts with Texas senator Phil Gramm to keep the annual tours coming.

On Attu, Balch was The Man. Komito had a thing about The Man. It wasn't personal. It was his nature. He just had to stick it to the system. He lived to prick the balloon of anyone with an inflated opinion of himself.

The first time Komito had tangled with Lawrence of Attu, Balch had assembled all the birding troops and announced he was changing the island's time zone to maximize sunlight in the field. Under Balch Standard Time, the sun would henceforth rise at 6 A.M. and set at 10 P.M. Komito shot up in protest. He worried about jet lag. He demanded a vote of all birders, but Balch made him sit down and be quiet. A rivalry was born.

They jousted over chores. Balch decreed that all visitors to Attu must do one, a requirement that caused surgeons to scrub outhouses and business CEOs to mop mudroom floors. Komito hated chores. He thought it was outrageous to spend $5,000 for an alleged vacation and still be forced to cut salad for dinner. He started calculating how much money Balch was making off these Attu tours, but Balch, a college calculus professor from suburban Chicago, told Komito his math was all wrong. Lawrence of Attu would not negotiate on chores, so Komito resorted to an old Jersey trick: he bought off his problem. When Komito quietly offered a few hundred dollars to anyone willing to do his chores for him, he found several takers.

Balch never got angered by any of this. He truly liked Komito, who was one of the island's best dinnertime storytellers—and one of Balch's best repeat customers. For Balch, Komito was the class clown in an especially challenging daycare center. The running battle of Balch versus Komito had become as much a part of the lore of Attu as the ever-present runny nose.

But it all threatened to become unhinged over Komito's refusal to pay the $5,000 balance for this year's Attu trip. Ever since losing the 1993 fight over that $48.06-a-night hotel room, Komito seemed determined to make Balch work for every dime of his money. And Komito didn't want to pay for the trip until he was certain it would, in fact, proceed. So when Balch had sent out a bill for this year's trip, Komito ignored it. Balch followed up with a phone message and another bill. Still no word from Komito.

Balch couldn't understand it. Earlier in the year he had begun hearing reports that Komito was chasing birds all over, all the time, with a zeal that surpassed even his usual type-A drive. The rumor mill held that Komito was attempting another Big Year. Balch knew no one could do a Big Year without Attu. He phoned Komito's wife and sent one bill by fax, another by Federal Express. Komito didn't respond. In the weeks before the trip, some Attu staffers lobbied Balch for a simple solution—ban Komito. Nobody else was allowed to get away with nonpayment. Why make exceptions for him?

As a former American Birding Association president, Balch was awed by Komito's sheer audacity. Nobody did a Big Year twice. He didn't want to be the man who killed a Big Year. Five days before the plane was to leave for Attu, Balch was driving a supply van on International Airport Road in Anchorage when his cellular phone rang. It was Komito, who wanted last-minute assurance from Balch that the Attu trip was a go. Balch said yes. Over a van load of whispers from Attu staffers—"Don't let him come! Don't let him come!"— Balch heard Komito promise to finally write the check.

Balch got his $5,000. In return, though, Komito got more than an Attu ticket. He also got the satisfaction of having paid for the trip on his own terms.

A Big Year wasn't just about seeing birds. It was about seeing birds and sticking it to The Man.

The first thing everyone saw on Attu was the snow. In early May, the 2,800-foot peaks were always frosted, but never like this. The island's runway was flanked with two-foot snow walls; the plane landing felt like an emergency brake on a luge run. El Niño had found Attu.

While tour staffers unloaded baggage from the plane, birders fretted about the weather. Komito, however, focused on something else.

He was looking for a killer.

Every year for the past decade or so, museums and federal agencies had quietly sent gunmen to Attu to shoot rare birds for their collections. Nobody announced the names of these collectors. Indeed, many birders, especially the first-time visitors, didn't even know they were here. But some found out the hard way.

In 1986 one particularly obsessed birder became so enthralled with the rarities of Attu that he arranged to camp and live on the island by himself. The University of Alaska museum was so anxious for information on the birds of Attu that it granted the birder a special collector's permit—a license to kill, but in the name of science. The arrangement attracted little attention until just three weeks before the scheduled spring Attu tour, when the birder found a great spotted woodpecker—one of the first records ever for North America, rarer still for the fact that it was discovered on an island with no trees—and summarily blasted it with his shotgun.

As organizer of the Attu tour, Larry Balch was livid. A great spotted woodpecker would have been the bird of the decade for dozens of his paying guests, but now it could only be seen in a government freezer. It was outrageous that someone had added the great spotted woodpecker to his life list, but then killed it before anyone else could see it and list it, too.

The collector became the social leper of Attu, and the solitary life seemed to take its toll. A host of birders claimed the collector began eyeing, then trailing, a young woman during her day trips through the tundra. As she boarded her airplane home, the man supposedly darted out with scissors and collected something else—a lock of the woman's hair. The collector himself denied that any of this ever happened. No matter the truth, the story circulated for years and mainly served to reinforce the notion that bird collectors were creepy and to be avoided.

Still, collecting continued. A few years later, a nature photographer was focusing on a Pechora pipit when another government collector entered the picture with a double-barrel shotgun. In the westernmost point of the American West, one of the civilized world's most precise pieces of photographic equipment was outdueled by a single round of buckshot.

Ever since then, Komito had known he had to do more than beat all the other birders at Attu. He had to quick-draw the collectors, too. If someone on the flight was a killer, Komito was determined to outrun him.

Miller knew little about collecting on Attu, but was too blissful to care. The birds were incredible. On the one-and-a-half mile trek from the runway to sleeping quarters, he saw three lifers—two smews, four common pochards, and a wood sandpiper—that all were supposed to be on the opposite side of the Pacific. As he started to unpack, someone outside cried, "Whooper swan"—the Attu equivalent of "Fire!" in a crowded theater. Miller and dozens of others blasted through the door (no one had seen the Who concert in Cincinnati) and basked in a magnificent flyby of a five-foot creature as white as the mountains behind it. Even commoners on Attu were worth a second look. The same drab brown birds that barely rated a wintertime yawn in Ohio were transformed into brilliant spring eye-catchers in Attu. Lapland longspurs stuck out with a gaudy yellow bill, black mask, and rufous cape; snow buntings were a dramatic white-and-black. Alaska was the Honeymoon Hotel for birds, and everyone wore the finest breeding plumage.

Miller had never seen any place like Attu. Alternately buffeted by the warm Kuroshio Current from Japan and the cold Alaska Current from the Bering Sea, Attu suffers from some of the world's worst weather. Native Aleuts called it the Cradle of Storms, Birthplace of Winds. It rains or snows 250 days a year. Dry days are usually dominated by fog. Home of the fifty-foot wave, the hundred-knot gale, and some of the planet's shortest-lived wind socks, the island is seventeen miles long and forty-two miles wide, but spackled with mountains that make it difficult to travel anywhere but along the coast. There are no hotels, phones, or restaurants. Nobody lives there permanently anymore; the only residents were twenty Coast Guard on one-year rotations to run the region's loran navigation system. Because the seafaring world was converting to satellite-based GPS navigation, the Attu Guard station—and thus the runway relied upon by birders—was threatened with permanent shutdown. After an Attu winter, few Coast Guard enlistees mourned the prospect of base closure. They had a hard time believing anyone would spend money to vacation there.

Even the names on the island reflect horrible hardship. Murder Point, Terrible Mountain—these were products of the 1740s takeover of Attu by Russian fur trappers, who slaughtered the native Aleut men, raped the women, and turned loose the island's first land mammal, the Norwegian rat. Modern visitors never quite knew how to celebrate the discovery of a life bird at a place called Massacre Bay.

Sight-seeing was strange, too. Miller scrambled for snapshots of the mountains and frothy bays on the plane ride in, but Attu was more complicated closer up. Junk was everywhere. Rusty oil tanks on a shortgrass beach, an abandoned bulldozer in a tidal pond, and a P-38 fighter plane rotting on a hillside over a bay were leftovers of one of the most awful battles of World War II. Seven months after their sneak attack on Pearl Harbor, Japanese forces conquered Attu, marking the first time since the War of 1812 that an enemy had captured American soil. At the time only forty-two natives and a schoolteacher couple lived on the island, but the Japanese wanted to gain a psychological foothold on U.S. soil and divert American military attention from the central Pacific. Neither goal proved successful. Because of wartime clampdowns on the press, few Americans ever learned of the Japanese war victory. And U.S. generals were so underwhelmed by the loss of Attu that they let the Japanese keep it for the rest of the year. Instead of battling the U.S. marines, the Japanese were instead confronted with a more relentless foe—an Attu winter. Dozens were stricken with frostbite and respiratory sicknesses. When 12,500 U.S. soldiers finally landed on Attu in May 1943, they found 2,500 Japanese holed up in the fog of the mountains. After eighteen days of U.S. air and ground bombardments, the Japanese were abandoned by their air force, desperately short on ammunition, and living on a ration of just one popcorn-size rice ball a day. On the night of May 29, they decided to end it all. Armed only with knives and bayonets, the surviving Japanese hurtled down the mountains and screamed, "Banzai!" They slashed wounded Americans in their medical tents and bludgeoned the healthy in face-to-face combat. But the attack did not go far without bullets. When capture was imminent, they pressed hand grenades to their chests—and blew up themselves. Of the one thousand Japanese soldiers who mounted the banzai attack, only twenty-eight were captured alive. Five hundred forty-nine Americans were killed, eleven hundred were wounded, and twelve hundred suffered exposure injuries; many required the amputation of their frostbitten feet. It was the first U.S. experience with Japanese suicide attacks, and the only ground battle of World War II fought on U.S. soil. The War in the Pacific was changed forever.

Birders borrowed some elements of military precision on Attu. Every half hour each group reported all field sightings by CB radio. "Brambling at Navy Town," went the call, and

Miller scrambled two miles to reach the rotting Quonset huts at the base of Artillery Hill. By the time he arrived, the birds were gone. He returned to base and the call was repeated. Miller raced back to Navy Town. Finally he saw the bramblings—black-and-orange finches ducking the wind in the lee of a fifty-five-gallon drum.

Ah, the wind. No matter where Miller went on Attu, the wind always seemed to be in his face. This was a serious problem. The only transportation on Attu was by mountain bike, and he was woefully unprepared. Warned that the trip would be physically demanding, Miller had bought a Wal-Mart bike back home and vowed to train on it. Of course, he didn't. After two days of pedaling through puddles, volcanic muck, and 20 mph head winds on Attu, Miller was one hurting unit. His body was not made to perch on a bicycle seat. His butt hurt so much that he tried riding by standing on the pedals. He quickly faced a choice: inflamed butt or instant heart attack. His rear end would not forgive him.

Luckily, other birders did. Miller was always the last one to arrive at a staked-out bird, but the rule of Attu held that no one advanced on a rarity until everyone was ready. When a rustic bunting was radioed in a mile and a half away at Kingfisher Creek, Miller feared his thighs, bottom, and aorta would simultaneously explode. But he pedaled up to find a waiting scope line—two dozen birders, queued up behind a long lens on a tripod pointed at a bush. With Miller's arrival, the scope line began its backcountry ballet. The person in front stooped over the lens and peered at the bird for no more than two seconds, then hastily retreated to the end of the line. The next birder took an identically quick look, and so on, and so on. When everyone in line could say they had had the bird—it was a lifer for most—the whole process repeated, but this time birders were allowed longer looks to study the creature. This time they got lucky. The bunting stuck around. Many times, however, the rarity didn't. No place could be more excruciating, Miller decided, than the end of a scope line on Attu.

On the fourth day on Attu, the storm hit. By 6 A.M. the base was socked in with three inches of snow. By 7 A.M., the snow had turned into driving rain. Miller tried to pass the time at base by taking a shower—a Dolly Varden trout had clogged the water intake valves the morning before—but the pipes were frozen. Indoors at Attu, strange things happened.

For example, women. Or, more specifically, a woman. She was in her late thirties with dark hair, clear blue eyes, and a laugh that carried across the room. She was fun. She had presence. And, most important, she had a life list of 626 birds. You just don't meet a single woman like that every day. Miller was smitten with Carol Ralph, and she seemed to enjoy being around him, too. They spent the storm day cooped up at base swapping bird stories and moaning about bicycling in the birthplace of winds. Miller made a point of sitting by her at dinner. He might be freshly divorced, but he still had feelings. That surprised him. He liked her. Suddenly there was something else to chase at Attu besides rare birds.

While the rain blew sideways outside, Komito lay flat on his back. He was miserable. Sometime between his chases for a brambling and a pigeon guillemot, Komito's back had begun convulsing with spasms. He made it back to the base, somehow, without passing out, but felt as if someone had taken a hatchet from the oven and buried it in the small of his back. If he could have made it to the Coast Guard station, he might have called an air ambulance. Komito throbbed with pain.

For Larry Balch, the only thing touchier than a healthy

Komito was a suffering Komito. From his magic bag of tricks Lawrence of Attu produced a bottle of muscle-relaxant pills, which seemed to reduce the size of the ax in Komito's back. If only Balch's bag had pills that eased other nagging pains.

Komito didn't like the community sandwich bread, which he felt was often stale because people left the bag open. So he brought his own personal stash, four loaves of Wonder bread, and sealed them with duct tape in a corrugated box that carried one word: KOMITO. He hated any kind of spice in his dinner, so shrimp creole and cayenne seafood pasta were out. The dining room was too cold. His door banged. His room was too noisy.

When Komito arrived on the island, he found that his saddle baskets, which he had last used two years ago, were stripped from his favorite bicycle. Komito asked the mechanic, Mad Dog Swertinski, to retrieve the baskets from someone else's bike and return them. Mad Dog—a Harley-riding male nurse whose nickname came from an emergency-room argument that ended with a doctor being deposited outside the emergency room—told Komito to go jump. Komito stripped off the baskets himself.

Then there were the clothes. Komito had been stockpiling clothes, boxes of clothes, at Attu for years. These weren't your typical birding duds. The clothes Komito wore on one of the wildest places on earth were rejects from his New Jersey country club—golf clothes, pure polyester, a ticking time bomb of fashion from the 1970s. The more outrageous he looked, the better. He matched burnt-orange trousers with lime green shirts, blue-and-green madras with red-and-black buffalo plaid. His bell-bottoms could swallow a fire hydrant; his collars were as wide as the wings on a 747. His favorite of all, though, was a patterned plum polyester known as Mr. Pants. If Mr. Pants could talk, he would never shut up. A thirteen-year resident of Attu, Mr. Pants had accompanied Komito on some of the greatest bird chases of North American history—the Narcissus flycatcher on the bush, the white-tailed eagle atop the nest, the Oriental turtle-dove on the gravel. Komito was not a drinking man, but that did not stop him from waxing long and misty-eyed about the incredible adventures of Mr. Pants.

These were the stories that brought birders to Komito. On a foul-weather day at Attu, when seventy-five of the continent's most serious birders were stuck together in a leaky, rat-infested, former Coast Guard building, an industrial contractor from New Jersey was laid out in full polyester with a spasming back—and trying to speak Japanese on the base's two-way radio with offshore fishermen. It was the borscht belt on the Bering Sea. Even in the lousiest circumstances, Komito usually could find some way to make people laugh.

Somebody stuck his head out the door for a new weather report. Rain still pelted the island, but the direction had shifted. Now the wind blasted from the west—straight from Asia.

That made the birders laugh a little harder.

The next ten days were the greatest run of rare birds in recorded North American history. A giant vacuum cleaner of a storm had sucked up whole flocks of Siberian species and dumped them all across Attu. In one amazing day, Miller saw fourteen birds that were too rare even to be mentioned in Roger Tory Peterson's first field guide. Birders accustomed to flying across the continent to see a single accidental were now awash in dozens of them. The wood sandpiper, a Eurasian fan of freshwater marshes, was typically seen in North America perhaps once every two or three years. Miller saw 212 in one day. The sky rained rarities.

These birds, however, came at a high price—sixteen miles of biking and ten miles of hiking through snow, sleet, mud, and forty-knot winds. Miller's rear end no longer was sore. It was raw. A bad intestinal bug was being passed around, too, and Miller was scared to death of No. 2 in the tundra—especially when Carol was around. He ate Imodium like Halloween candy and hoped against hope that there would be no line at the outhouse at the end of the day. He had made the mistake of buying a raincoat that was size medium; he couldn't even fit an arm inside. First he got soaked. Then he got sick. At night Miller had already been assigned to sleep in the loudest room at the base, which everyone called the snore-a-torium. (His remarkable volume and cadence earned him the nickname Chainsaw.) But now a respiratory bug was spreading, and snores in the sleeping quarters were being replaced by oyster-hacking coughs. Miller still refused to give up. His sole concession to sickness was that he sometimes woke up at 7:30 A.M. instead of his usual 6 A.M. This was a once-in-a-lifetime trip and he was going to wring every possible minute from it.

Komito was so paranoid of germs that he washed his hands every time he touched a doorknob. Some evenings this meant eight trips to the sink, but he wasn't arguing with the results. In a building that was becoming a giant petri dish, Komito remained as immune to sickness as the Rock of Gibraltar. Even his back stopped hurting.

After a certain point, when he saw Miller and others running themselves to exhaustion, Komito adopted a different birding tactic. He would venture far afield only for new rarities. This meant positioning himself at some central location, such as Smew Pond, or, when his back was nagging him, by the warm stove indoors, listening to those regular half-hour radio reports. If a good bird was found somewhere—

say, an eye-browed thrush at Murder Point—Komito would chase it. That was grueling work. Otherwise he conserved his energy while everybody else flogged the soggy tundra for new finds.

To Komito, this was called strategy. Others, however, disparaged it as radio-birding. They resented it. They felt like beaters on an English pheasant hunt. They found the birds—Komito got the glory. Though his Town Car was safely garaged back home in New Jersey, the skua was alive and well and scoring prizes on Attu.

While nursing his delicate back in the warm base, Komito ran into other birders. One was Macklin Smith, a poet and professor of medieval English at the University of Michigan who could read and write the language of Beowulf and Chaucer. Smith was the only person who reported a bigger North American life list than Komito. Komito, however, believed that the professor's list was rife with poetic license. Smith had a knack for discovering rarities that were seen by him and only him. There was an Asiatic common crane in Nebraska, a broadbilled sandpiper on Attu, and on and on—more than a dozen birds, all told, that Komito believed Smith had simply made up. For his part, Smith thought Komito should stuff a sock in it and vouched long and often for every bird on his list. He rattled his saber at Komito's own claim several years ago of an Eskimo curlew in Texas. Komito, Smith said, was simply jealous, a claim that Komito has vehemently denied. As the tour group's breakfast cook, Smith had birded on Attu six more years than Komito. (Smith missed 1987 only because of his wedding that year.) Smith was a high-minded professor; Komito was a streetwise night-school dropout who had scrapped his way from poverty to riches in one of the most macho businesses of the industrial Northeast. Smart people didn't stand between them.

This year, the lung virus had hit Smith particularly hard, which meant he was spending a lot of time bedridden in the base. Smith bunked next to Komito's room. His cough was horrible, so loud and so wet that Komito couldn't squelch it with his earplugs.

When the radio call went out for a great knot at Alexai Point, Komito knew that Smith, no matter how sick, would not be able to resist. This brawny Asiatic sandpiper was as rare as a Nutting's flycatcher, a bird seen only once in a generation. If Smith was going to claim it, Komito was going to be there, too.

For twelve miles they biked and hiked through creeks, around waterfalls, and over tundra that squished like a sponge when a boot stepped on it. Sleet sloshed. Smith lost all color in his face. But every time Komito forged ahead, thinking Smith had finally quit, he would hear that disgusting cough again. It was the slowest-motion chase since Captain Hook and the crocodile that swallowed a clock.

Two and a half hours of agony later, Komito finally arrived at Alexai Point. Smith had disappeared, but the great knot was staked out on a distant beach. A scope line of three dozen birders waited to see it. Komito was waiting his turn in the scope line when he heard it—the cough. Smith had pulled up two hundred feet short. He didn't have the strength for the great knot.

Komito got his look at the bird—Miller was in line in front of him—and then walked back to Smith. It's a great rarity, Macklin, Komito told him, and you really should see the bird. Smith was tired. Komito wanted Smith's eye on that scope. It wasn't good enough to be in the neighborhood of a rare bird; if Smith was going to list the rarity, he actually had to see the rarity.

Finally Smith mustered the strength to conquer the extra

two hundred feet to the scope. Komito saw his nemesis see the bird. Now, he was satisfied. How Smith got himself back to the base— that was his business.

Now there were other birds to chase. Komito was especially interested in a report of a pin-tailed snipe at Pratincole Beach. The snipe was a notoriously difficult bird to identify, but the call had been made by James Huntington, an Iowa postman who was unique among top listers for three reasons: he was soft-spoken, humble, and painfully careful with his field calls. He spent so much time staring at tricky birds that his name had become part of the birding vocabulary. A Huntington look was when somebody stared at a bird long after others left. It also was what some people were accused of taking when they lingered at the head of an antsy scope line.

Because Huntington was one of the few birders with a life list that rivaled his own, Komito hadn't been able to resist taking a few jabs over the years. On one of his first trips to Attu, Huntington had raced too close to a rarity and scared it off. Komito had memorialized the mistake by calling him Flush Gordon. On another year in Attu, the weather was oddly pleasant, and Huntington was sunburned so badly that he smeared white zinc-oxide cream all over his face for protection. For that one, Komito called him Casper, after the cartoon ghost.

Komito took his Huntington look through Huntington's scope and proclaimed himself unsure of the snipe identification. A fine line separated a pin-tailed snipe from its Asiatic cousin, the Swinhoe's snipe, and none of the differences appeared clear to Komito. He thought the folded wings of a pin-tailed should extend beyond the tail; Huntington focused more on the central crown stripe. This was birding at its highest level, the ornithological equivalent of doing a Sunday *New York Times* acrostic in one sitting in pen. No one had ever seen both species of snipe in North America. Even on their home continent, where the two snipes were far more common, birders struggled to tell them apart. Most of the world would look in the scope and see nothing more than a brown bird with a long beak in a swamp.

Huntington remained convinced the snipe was pin-tailed; Komito remained convinced that he wasn't sure. They retreated to the base and consulted an Asian field guide, which didn't offer enough new hints to change anyone's opinion.

Shortly after, though, there came news that could not be disputed.

A collector had shot and killed the bird. It was, conclusively, a pin-tailed snipe.

Komito was finally satisfied with the bird's identity. The identity of the killer, however, remained unknown.

Miller never thought he would admit this, but he was ready to get out of Attu. He missed the sun. He missed his privacy. He missed indoor plumbing.

He wanted fresh food. (His last Snickers bar for lunch had warned, "Use by 9/94.")

He wanted to spend time with Carol on her home turf. (She was a supermarket deli worker outside Boston.)

He wanted to call his father. He especially missed his father. This was the longest he had gone on his Big Year without phoning home. By now everyone on Attu was calling this the trip of the century. He had added forty-three life birds and fifty-four new ones for his Big Year list, which now stood at 555. He had seen Komito up close and decided maybe the Big Year record holder wasn't so invincible after all. Miller's father would have some ideas about that.

Miller wanted never to see another bicycle seat for as long as he lived.

On May 24 he squeezed his wet clothes into his duffel and marched one and a half miles with Carol past the wind sock to the runway. Miller's time on Attu was over. Komito was staying another two weeks with the next group. Let him have it.

They waited in the rain for an hour before a Coast Guard truck drove up with the news: fog was too thick for the pilot to land. The plane had turned around. Maybe tomorrow. Miller marched back to the base and found two more lifers, but he would have traded them for a break in the weather.

The next day, he got it.

Greg Miller and sixty weary birders shipped out.

Al Levantin and sixty fresh birders shipped in.

The only thing worse than missing one day of the trip of the century was missing that day and knowing full well that Sandy Komito was already there.

When Al Levantin finally walked off that Reeves Aleutian airliner, he was burning to make up for lost time. He ran like a man possessed. He covered twenty miles on foot and bike and scored four lifers and sixteen new birds for his Big Year. He returned to base exhausted but exhilarated. This was it. He had rocketed off to a terrific start before even getting to Alaska, and now Attu was serving up rarity after sensational rarity.

Then he noticed something strange indoors by the heating stove: Sandy Komito. Big Years were supposed to be about driving fast and hard. Levantin was giving it his all. Why was Komito already back at the base?

Levantin looked at the base's dry-erase board listing all

species that had been seen that season on Attu and realized: Komito wasn't running hard because he had already seen it all. The first two weeks on Attu were the trip of the century. The pressure was on Levantin to match it.

The one bird that got Komito moving was the yellow-throated bunting. It was the first sighting, ever, of this species in North America, and every birder on the island dropped everything to see it. (Even Macklin Smith had rousted himself from bed to chase it and was later evacuated on an emergency Coast Guard medical flight to Anchorage, where he spent four days in a hospital with a life-threatening case of pneumonia.) Levantin was thrilled to spot the bird. More astounding, though, was the way Komito saw it.

As soon as the rarity was discovered, an Attu guide followed island protocol and quickly retreated to radio in the bird and organize a sixty-person sweep. Because the bunting was up a canyon, he directed four birders to climb the ridge, two on each side, in case the bird tried to escape by outflanking the group. Komito was not one of the chosen four ridge runners, but he appointed himself the fifth member of the ridge patrol. Let the sheep in the valley take their chances with the shepherd's direction. The alpha wolf scrounged his way to the prime viewing position.

Komito stayed up top and saw the bird. Down low, Levantin did, too. A lesson was learned: If there was a good bird to get, Komito wouldn't take a chance. He would get it.

By the sixth day of the second trip, Levantin knew he was in trouble. The wind sock above base had shifted to the south, which meant the island got all the atrocious weather, but no

Asiatic birds with it. Every new species was a struggle. He spent days in the rain pointing his scope out on Murder Point, but it was just the same old, same old. He needed birds from Siberia, not the Bering Sea. Just when he thought birding couldn't get worse, the winds turned to the west, which blew everything rare back home to Asia. Komito stayed warm inside. Levantin withstood the rain and pounded the bush.

He lucked out and found a Mongolian plover on South Beach. (No art deco nightclubs on this one.) Buff-breasted with a black blindfold, the plover was one of the few Asiatic species that actually looked dramatically different from anything on North America. He called in the report and waited for other birders to descend.

His first visitor, however, had four legs. Up the beach strutted a blue fox, the same nonnative species brought to the island centuries ago by Russian fur traders. Levantin organized a line to keep the predator from the plover—grown men and women hooked their arms and called, "Go away, fox! Fox, get out of here!"—but the wild animal had no fear of man. The fox sauntered past. The plover flushed. Levantin retreated back to base, where Komito, who had seen the species during the first two weeks on Attu, was holding court again by the warm stove. Levantin was tired, wet, and succumbing to a nasty virus, but he had held out to help his fellow Attuvians see his rare plover. Komito was regaling yet another audience with some story of a long-ago bird chase. Levantin checked the dry-erase board. He was still behind by five Asiatic birds.

When the call went out for a Terek sandpiper on Alexai Point, both men peeled out for twelve miles of head-winds biking and hiking. With a half dozen others, they searched in vain until the radios crackled with another bird—a pin-tailed snipe was back at Massacre Valley. Komito smelled a problem. Attu was all about community birding—the more eyes searching for a rarity, the better the chances of finding it—and the community was about to leave him for another bird. Komito, who had already seen the pin-tailed snipe with James Huntington, was indignant that the others would consider leaving. The Terek was a new bird for Attu. The island needed it. Komito needed it. He pleaded with Levantin and the others to stay. They ditched him. Komito never saw the Terek sandpiper, but Levantin did get his snipe—and some satisfaction from a lesson in community birding.

Though the Terek was clearly a rare bird, it was rarer still on Attu because it was one of Komito's few misses. There was a good reason why Komito birded as he did. It worked. Toward the end of the tour, when Attu was buffeted with rain, sleet, and gales—but no new birds—Komito felt less compulsion to push himself outside for more misery. He had chased hard for weeks. Others muttered about a man paying so much money to spend so much time indoors. They were wet and exhausted. He had all the birds they did, but with only a fraction of the agony. It was the birding version of social Darwinism.

Komito logged more time back at the base telling more stories. Levantin started to listen. The rufous-capped warbler in Texas, Siberian accentor in Anchorage, Bahama mockingbird in the Florida Everglades—Komito had seen birds this year that Levantin hadn't even known were in North America. Some thought Komito was bragging, but Levantin figured it wasn't bragging if he could back it up. And Komito could. He was speaking broadly, expansively, and he was getting excited.

Finally Sandy Komito admitted it: he was doing another Big Year. He was spending $8,000 to $12,000 a month, but he was leaving Attu with 645 birds. Levantin was at 619 and spending half as much as Komito. Levantin still had a lot of easy birds to pick up back on the mainland, but he wouldn't be able to make up rarities that had come and gone before this trip, or the five extra birds that Komito had seen on the first two weeks on Attu.

At the start of the year, Levantin had thought he was running against Komito's 1987 record. Now he was running against the Master himself.

On his last day at Attu, Komito ventured outside. There were no rarities, but the winds were calm and the sun was shining. Terrible Mountain gleamed. Komito worried that the warm weather would bring fog and cancel the next day's flight. He had gone five full days on Attu without a single new bird for the year. He was ready to leave.

On his walk back to base, he looked up to check the wind direction. Something had changed. The wind sock was gone.

In its place was Mr. Pants.

When the plane came to end the birding trip of the century, Mr. Pants was left behind, purple and proud, sometimes flapping, sometimes stretching, but usually full of wind.

TWELVE

The B.O.D.

Greg Miller jammed his hand deep down his right pocket, then his left. Nothing. His coat pockets came up empty, too. He rifled his wallet one more time, but the result was the same—humiliation.

Miller was broke. Even in the dark of a June night in Minnesota, he could feel his birding guide, Dave Benson, eyeing him suspiciously. From 4:30 A.M. to 10:30 P.M. Benson had busted his tail to show Miller an amazing 111 species, one of the greatest birding days of both men's lives. Miller had gotten so caught up in the thrill of it all—nine new species for his Big Year, nineteen wood-warblers in a day—that he had forgotten about the guide's bill. Benson charged $15 an hour. Miller had enough cash to cover that, thank goodness, but he had promised to hire on Benson for another full day tomorrow. Miller had to break his promise. He didn't even have money for a tip. He thought about writing Benson a check that was sure to bounce. No, he thought, that would be mean.

He tried to look Benson in the eye. He was too embarrassed.

"I'm really sorry, Dave," Miller said, shuffling his shoes, "but I don't have the money to pay you for another day out. I feel really bad about it. I know it's high season for you. I feel terrible about canceling. But Attu left me all tapped out."

Benson was mad. Miller was ashamed. But neither man could do anything about it. Benson headed home. Miller headed for—well, he had nothing to head for. He really had told the truth. He was down to his last $50. He had maxed out four credit cards with $10,000 limits, and he wasn't sure how much wiggle room remained on the fifth. Maybe $550.

Miller decided to take a chance on a motel. While the front desk clerk processed his MasterCard, Miller tried to look calm, but he was betrayed by sweat beads on his forehead. He fidgeted. Why was it taking so long to clear his credit card? It was 11 P.M.—midnight in the headquarters of his credit card—and Miller was too exhausted to be humiliated again. Were bank card auditors raising holy hell? Or were the rural phone lines just that slow? Finally the motel clerk looked up. The MBNA gods had smiled upon Greg Miller. He pocketed the room key and didn't look back.

His stomach rose before the sun. His first instinct was to grab breakfast, but then he remembered: His wallet had only $50. His credit was murky. His flight home wasn't for another four days.

How could he do this to himself? Sure, Alaska and Minnesota had been fun, but all that fun had left him flat broke. He was forty and in the prime of his career. He wasn't supposed to feel like Evel Knievel every time a bill came due. He felt sad. He felt sorry. He felt stupid. Luckily, though, all this self-pity was quickly overcome by a more immediate urge. He felt hungry.

With no money for a real breakfast, he drove to the closest convenience store. He eyed the doughnuts—too splurgy; the bread—too boring; and the cookies—too sugary; then he finally settled on something that, in his mind, was both tasty and nutritious. He forked over his $5 and plopped himself back in the car. His breakfast of champions: Jif peanut butter and a bag of pretzels. He was surprised at how good it tasted, which was fortunate. Jif and Mr. Salty would be his companions for lunch and dinner, too.

Now he could concentrate. He had 595 birds for the year, an amazing start by anyone's standards, and he wasn't going to let an empty checking account stop him five species short of a major milestone. Maybe he could turn his four days into an opportunity instead of a problem. He really wanted to get five more birds. The question was, where?

He pulled out his trusty Rand McNally. He already had all the birds worth finding in Minnesota. His May days at High Island had taken care of most Eastern migrants; no need to chase them down now. The West, however, was an entirely different issue. The Rocky Mountains were home to the tough guys of the bird world, the species that lived over a mile high and laughed, or at least cackled, in the face of blizzards. They weren't fair-weather friends who fled on migration for friendlier climes. They were stickers. They wouldn't come to Miller. He would have to go to them.

Miller figured he had two mountain destinations that would meet his four-day out-and-back travel requirements. Rocky Mountain National Park in Colorado had lots of mountain birds, plus the continent's longest, and most spectacular, above-timberline road. Montana had Yellowstone, the same birds, and no highway speed limits.

For a boy who had grown up in the Amish land of horse-and-buggy, this choice was no contest. The speedometer on his Taurus promised 120 mph. He'd see about that.

First, however, he had some business in the flatlands.

The Baird's sparrow is an unremarkable bird. As tall as a can of Coke but with none of the fizz, it has a pale yellow face with a weak mustache and back streaked in three or four dull shades of brown. It often is confused with the much more common grasshopper sparrow, partly because the two species look a lot alike, but also because they both live secretively in deep, thick grass. The Baird's is one of those species that impatient birders dismiss as an LBJ—a Little Brown Jobbie too plain and confusing to merit the workup of a full field identification.

Baird's sparrow is also in deep trouble. It breeds only in the Northern Great Plains, preferably in native-grass prairies that have been grazed regularly by wandering herds of ungulates. For century after century in this part of the world, that meant buffalo. But now the buffalo were gone, replaced by wheat farmers who plowed the prairie fencerow-to-fencerow, and cattle, which had the appetite of the buffalo but didn't wander. The Baird's sparrow didn't like farm or cow. It was so sensitive to change that only five birds of a hundred ever returned to the same nesting area; the rest died or found another place with just the right grass and weather. Nesters usually ended up somewhere along the hundredth meridian, the climatic dividing line where the humidity of the East gave way to the aridity of the West. The bird's population, like its home, teetered on the edge. Since 1966, the number of the birds had dropped, on average, 1.6 percent a year. Biologists have considered protecting it as a federal endangered species, but heartland farmers, already reeling from plunging crop prices, have kicked up a political protest. So the Baird's sparrow continues its long, slow spiral down the drain of man-made extirpation.

Among birders, the Baird's separates the men from the boys. It winters in Mexico but migrates well west of the High Island hub. The best way to get the Baird's is to see it on its nesting turf, which is a long way from the nearest airport. As Miller drove five hundred miles across the headwaters of the Mississippi River, past the Land of 10,000 Lakes, through the green fields of the Dakotas, he realized that the only way to get this bird was to really want it.

He found two singing on a barbed-wire fence at the top of a hill near Crystal Springs. He watched them, and especially, he listened to them. They sounded like song sparrows without a rasp, a Lauren Bacall who had never taken up cigarettes. The most remarkable thing about Baird's sparrows was the effort required to see them.

Still, it was bird No. 596. That was something worth celebrating. He threw Mr. Salty into the backseat and splurged on a drivethrough dinner at McDonald's. Three hamburgers and a water set him back another $2.07. His credit card made it through another motel.

The kid behind the counter at the gas station in Livingston, Montana, was giving Miller the once-over twice. This must be a mistake, Miller told him. Try the MasterCard again. The kid did, but Miller's plastic had gone spastic. There was no way out. He had to pay cash.

Now Miller was down to $25, a half jar of Jif, and a quarter bag of Mr. Salty. He was 950 miles from Minneapolis. His Taurus had cracked 100 mph on Interstate 94, but he couldn't shake a nasty, lasting souvenir from Attu—a hacking cough. His lungs were full of lime Jell-O. His throat and his nose were erupting so often that he feared being mistaken for a two-legged Old Faithful.

If only he could see the famed geyser.

He had joined the line of bumper-to-bumper traffic outside

Yellowstone's Gardiner entrance when it struck him: How was he going to get in here? He had never counted on a park admissions fee. Of course, he had never counted on a malfunctioning credit card, either.

Twenty dollars, the park ranger said.

Miller's MasterCard didn't work again. He asked the ranger to try one more time. Through his rearview mirror, he saw heads poke out of windows in the cars idling behind him. Why the delay? His credit card was rejected again. Somebody in line honked. Miller fished out his wallet and paid cash. He was down to his last $5.

He pulled into the visitors' center and called MBNA— luckily, it had an 800 number—to straighten out the mess with his MasterCard.

Your problem, the MBNA woman told Miller, is that you're not making any payments. You missed two bills.

I'm really, really sorry, Miller said, but I've been away from home on a five-week vacation—I've been in Alaska and Minnesota and North Dakota—and I haven't been able to pay any bills.

You're on vacation in North Dakota?

Yes, Miller told her. I'm a birdwatcher.

MBNA silence.

I promise, I'll pay the $150 minimum as soon as I get home. Promise.

Silence again.

Finally MBNA spoke. Can you make the payment within a week?

Yes! Miller shouted, in a voice loud enough to set off another round of wet coughs.

He got his credit card back. His request for a beefed-up credit line, however, was met with more silence.

He had $400 left on his $10,000 MasterCard, and a big

rental car bill was due when he returned to Minneapolis. He could stop and figure out how he was going to pay for all this, or he could go birding. Not much choice there.

Miller got No. 600, a black rosy-finch, darting from scree to snow on Beartooth Pass. The highway sign said he was 10,947 feet above sea level.

He felt even higher.

Miller was so worried about his rental car bill that he drove seven hundred miles the next day, and three hundred miles the morning after that, just to turn in the Taurus a day early. This time, his credit card worked. He made two vows: Never again would he travel under such ridiculous money restrictions. And never again would he eat peanut butter and pretzels for six consecutive meals.

Those promises would have to be kept later. For now, he was stuck at the Minneapolis airport. His flight left tomorrow. No problem, Miller figured, he just picked up a courtesy phone and asked the Holiday Inn to pick him up in a courtesy van. But the Holiday Inn was full. So were the Best Western, Comfort Inn, and Radisson. He gulped and tried the Hyatt— that had to cost more than $100; how much more could his MasterCard take?—but that was booked solid, too. It was no use. Minneapolis was hosting some kind of health-care convention, and there wasn't an empty hotel room for fifty miles.

Miller slumped onto his luggage. He felt like crying.

Just as he dug back into the remains of his Jif and Mr. Salty, he was approached by a middle-aged man and woman. Call St. Paul, they told Miller. We've got to send someone off now, but we'll check on you later.

Miller called up and down the other Twin City, but found no room at anyone's inn. It was 4 p.m. He moved his duffel to the corner of the terminal and prepared to spend the night.

Then the couple returned.

This probably sounds a little odd to you, they told Miller, but we'd be happy to put you up tonight.

What? Miller was too tired for cruel jokes.

No, really, the man said. Minneapolis is a great city and we'd hate for you to think of it as the place where you couldn't get a room. Won't you stay with us tonight?

Miller snapped himself upright before the strangers had time to reconsider.

He treated them to dinner at Ruby Tuesday's—thank you, MasterCard—and slept that night on their living room sofa. The next morning, after buying him breakfast at the International House of Pancakes, they drove him back to the airport.

The woman's name was Laurie. The man's name, Miller never quite got. He was too embarrassed to ask.

Back at the nuclear power plant, the Jolt Guy had acquired a new nickname. He had become the Bird Guy.

Miller was the office novelty. There just weren't many people at Calvert Cliffs who ever took a five-week vacation, much less a five-week vacation to watch birds. He wasn't exactly hiding his obsession. On the side of his cubicle he put up one large sheet of paper with the number 611, which was his Big Year total by the time he finally returned from Minnesota via Attu.

A friend and fellow birder, Kyle Rambo, knew just how impressive that number was. But he was shocked when Miller announced he was done for the year. He was broke and buried with work and so run-down he couldn't shake his nasty cough from Alaska. Miller needed a break.

Rambo wasn't buying it.

Let me get this straight, Rambo said. You've got 611 species of birds and it's only June and you're not even going to try for 700?

Miller hacked again.

Rambo demanded: When are you ever going to get to 611 again? You're almost at 700 and you've got half a year left and you're going to quit? How can you just quit?

Miller shrugged. He had no scheduled time off. He didn't think he could get any more, either.

"You'll never know unless you ask," Rambo told him.

Rambo had a point there.

Miller walked into his boss's office the next day with two papers.

The first was the sheet with the number 611. The second was longer. It said:

ALL-TIME HIGHEST COUNT OF BIRDS:
721 Sandy Komito (1987)
714 William Rydell (1992)
712 B. Shiftlett (1993)
711 Benton Basham (1983)
699 Jim Vardaman (1979)

The bird thing, his boss couldn't understand. The prospect of a record, however, got him interested. To be only 110 short of the North American record, with half the year to go—that was something a boss could understand. He asked Miller to tell him a few birding stories. He liked the ones about Alaska.

Miller still had 250,000 lines of software code to debug for Y2K. But his boss agreed to judge him on output, not desk time. He could work four ten-hour shifts a week and get some extra time off down the line, as long as he got all his code done.

Now Miller had the time. He still needed the money.

He applied for and somehow received another MasterCard, this one with a $6,000 credit limit. How to pay for that—well, that was another problem. He logged eighty-six hours in his first two weeks back at work, which was enough to cover the rent and the minimum monthly payments on his five other credit cards. He was still short on cash. He didn't want to do it, but he had no other option.

Miller picked up the phone and called the Bank of Dad.

He felt squeamish asking his father for money. He was a grown man now, an alleged adult, with a good job and a car and a whole life outside of Holmes County, Ohio. But after his embarrassments with the birding guide in Duluth, the gas station kid in Livingston, and the park ranger at Yellowstone, Miller knew he needed the cash. It was worse groveling to strangers than parents.

When the phone was finally answered at his parent's home, Miller remembered one other complication: at the Bank of Dad, the chief loan officer was his mother.

"Hello, Mom," Miller started. He told her he had a problem and he needed help.

Miller's father picked up the other line. The son started his pitch. He was only halfway through the year but already had 611 birds and had a real shot at the all-time record—if only he had some money.

"How much?" his mother asked.

Five thousand dollars.

"Are you sure this is what you want to do?" his mother asked.

"It's absolutely what I want to do. I'm positive. I don't know when I'll ever have the opportunity again."

"It's an awful lot of money," she said.

Miller could feel his Big Year slipping away. His father interjected, "What's the money for? Where do you want to go?" As Miller told his father about the trogons in Arizona, the murrelets off California, and that weird hummingbird, a Xantus's, still divebombing feeders in British Columbia, his mother hung up her phone. Bird talk—she didn't get it.

When the father came back to the kitchen, the mother was waiting.

She just didn't understand this birding competition. Birding was supposed to be for fun, not for winning. It was you against the birds, not you against some stranger from another state. And what was with all these bills? How did birding ever get so expensive? It wasn't practical. What about Greg's job? This couldn't be good for his career. Greg was overspending his boundaries. Was he addicted to credit cards? He had gone way overboard on this one. He had to learn to control himself. He had to be reined in.

When she finished, she looked at her husband's face.

The son was living the father's dream. Who knew how much time the father had left for dreaming—or living.

The B.O.D. approved the loan.

Doubt

Al Levantin stared into the mountains from his home patio. He had returned from Attu a shaken man. He couldn't believe that Sandy Komito was so far ahead of him. Levantin wasn't used to finishing second in anything. It was frustrating. It was aggravating. It was . . . lonely.

Truth was, he missed his wife. In the first 180 days of the year, he had been away 120, including four straight weeks in Alaska. (While he was in Attu, she luxuriated in a villa in northern Italy.) Even as a road warrior in business, he hadn't traveled like that. But when he had gone away for work, he had usually fixed the problem. This was different. The Sandy Komito problem might not be fixable. Levantin wouldn't complain about that—he wasn't a whiner, never would be—but he still wasn't thrilled with the idea. There was only one person who could understand all this, and it was Ethel.

Al and Ethel loved to be together for the Aspen Music Festival, the two-month summer gala when eight hundred of the world's greatest classical-music students gathered down the road from their home and staged night after night of magnificent concerts. Though Al and Ethel had done the whole black-tie philharmonic thing in Manhattan and Philadelphia, there was something about this festival—the shirtsleeves informality, the wine with friends under the stars, the music that started in the meadows and soared to match the mountains—that was irresistible. Plus, Al's personal favorites were the same big, thumping compositions, the Mahlers and Beethovens, that so many students favored.

The Levantins had already donated $1,000 to the Aspen Music Festival. Every Friday night and Sunday afternoon of summer, they knew where they wanted to be.

Then Al's birds landed.

Ethel never said anything bad about birding. As a marriage counselor, she knew too many men who either lost their passion or let it burn only for business. She was thrilled her husband was chasing a dream. The last thing she wanted was for her husband to be halfhearted about it.

But after Attu, Al just didn't seem as crazy for birds. He liked Aspen. He liked the music. He liked staying home on the weekends with Ethel and their friends. He was sweet about it, actually. He wanted to have fun with his wife.

For forty years, he had dreamed of letting his birding obsession run wild. But now, for the first time, he wondered if this dream was worth it. The Big Year was for the birds, but was it still for him?

For six months, Greg Miller had thought only about birds. Now things were different. He was thinking about the bees, too.

Since Attu, Miller was swapping a lot of phone calls and e-mails with Carol Ralph. He really liked her. He even told his father about her.

His father accepted the news with some surprise. His son was freshly divorced, and emotionally raw and needy because of it. He worried about his son's ability to handle a new relationship so quickly, but was also thrilled that his son was even interested.

Miller really wanted to see Carol, but they could never quite get their schedules together. The more he pressed it, the more she talked about being such good friends. Miller figured a good friendship was the start of a great relationship, so he pursued a visit further. You don't meet a fun woman with a 667-bird life list—she'd added 41 in Attu—and just let her slip away.

Finally the right occasion presented itself—a little egret, the Old World cousin of North America's snowy egret, was being staked out in New Hampshire, just seventy miles north of Carol Ralph's home. To get the rarity, Miller would practically have to drive by her house. (Well, not really. She lived considerably west of the most direct airport-to-bird driving route, but Miller was not going to let an opportunity like this pass.) So Miller called her and landed an invitation to visit.

First things first, though. He drove to Newmarket, New Hampshire, and got the bird. Then he drove five hours to the rocky shores of Machias, Maine, and got four Atlantic seabirds on a pelagic trip.

Big Year birds under his belt, he drove 330 miles nonstop to Carol Ralph's home.

He showed her video from their trip to Attu. She showed him pictures of polar bears from her trip to Churchhill, Manitoba.

He was ready for romance.

She wasn't.

They were friends, good friends, she said, and they were going to stay that way.

Really? Miller asked.

Really, she replied.

Miller forgot about the bees and focused on the birds.

The Chiricahua Mountains were the Lower 48's version of Attu. They were out there. Historic hideout of the Apache chiefs Cochise and Geronimo, the Chiricahuas were a craggy island in the Arizona sky 170 miles east of Tucson, 400 miles south of Albuquerque, 210 miles west of El Paso, and north of nothing in particular. From the biggest town, Portal, you had to drive twenty minutes across the state line for gas. Children rode an hour by bus to school.

For Miller, the biggest problem here was crowds.

So many birders descended upon the Chiricahuas every summer that the U.S. government had to ban tape-recorded birdcalls. This was no small matter. The sycamore- and pine-shaded canyon of the South Fork of Cave Creek was the best one-stop shopping place on the continent for owls—elf owls, whiskered screech-owls, western screech-owls, and most importantly, flammulated owls.

The flamm owl drove birders crazy. It was six inches tall and weighed only as much as $2.50 in quarters. It slept by day in the darkest nooks of the woods and hunted bugs at night with charcoal eyes that, like the rest of its body, blended perfectly with surrounding tree trunks and limbs.

Birders found flamm owls only by being incredibly lucky, or by calling them in. Miller didn't have time for luck; he was due back at the office in two days. So he once again hired Stuart Healy, southern Arizona birding guide extraordinaire, to help call in the bird. But now it was a federal crime to play an owl tape in the Coronado National Forest.

So Miller and Healy stood in the dark and waited.

And waited.

And waited.

Four-day workweeks, followed by three-day Big Year sprints, were taking a toll on Miller. He was falling asleep on his feet. He shuddered himself awake. He couldn't afford to miss this bird. He hustled back to the car for his reserve of caffeine. Though the general store in Portal didn't sell Jolt, it did carry bottles of iced tea. Miller fought back a yawn and gulped.

Still no sign of any flamm owl. The tea wasn't making him more alert, just more full and uncomfortable. He really had to go. He couldn't take much more of this. He had to do something—quick.

He raised the bottle to his lips and blew. It didn't sound bad—deep, hollow toots. He blew again and again and waited, silently.

Poot. Poot. Poot. Poot. Poot.

Five times came the answer in the night. Miller froze. Healy froze.

That was the owl!

They waited on the edge of the woods for Mr. Flamm to show himself, but he never did. According to the rules of the American Birding Association, that made no difference. Miller had heard the distinct call of a flammulated owl. So had his expert birding guide.

Though Miller really wished he had seen the bird, rules were rules. Ethically and morally, Miller could count it. It was a fine victory. No one else on a Big Year had a flamm owl. But now Greg Miller did.

The only thing he felt strange about was using a twenty-ounce Lipton iced-tea bottle to get it.

Neither Miller nor Levantin knew it at the time—they didn't even know each other at the time—but that tea-bottle owl was important for another reason. For the first time in the Big Year contest, Greg Miller was ahead of Al Levantin.

He left Arizona on July 13 with 658 birds for the year.

Levantin ended the same day with 648.

Miller, however, had two major problems. Once again, he was perilously low on cash. He had underestimated the amount of money he needed for basics (rent, phone, gas, electric) and for birding (Alaska, Minnesota, Arizona, MBNA). Sandy Komito was spending as much as $12,000 a month on his Big Year, but Miller had only a $5,000 loan from the Bank of Dad to last him the rest of the year. The loan was running out. Miller had no idea what to do about that.

His other major problem involved birds. He had two big holes in his year's list. He needed California birds, and he needed seabirds. This was the kind of problem he enjoyed, because it had a solution, as long as his plastic held out.

Back home for another four-day workweek at the nuclear power plant, Miller picked up the phone and called Debi Shearwater, the California pelagic tour operator and High Queen of the High Seas. As soon as Miller identified himself, Shearwater cut him off.

I heard you're doing a Big Year, Shearwater told him.

Yes, I am.

Did you know that Sandy Komito is doing a Big Year, too?

I heard that.

Is there anything I can do to help you beat him?

Miller was stunned. He knew Komito had bothered some people over the years, but this was too much. Miller couldn't understand how Komito had put himself on the wrong side of Debi Shearwater, the last person any serious birder wanted to cross. She simply controlled too much—too many boat trips, too many guides, too much of birding's inside dope. Of course, that was Komito's problem now. Shearwater felt sorry for Miller's budget woes. Miller did not mind the sympathy.

He booked his California trip and went back to work.

On Thursday, July 16, while Miller cracked ten and a half hours of software code, Al Levantin was gliding in the field, doing comfortable trips for the easy summer birds.

Levantin saw a Mississippi kite, gray and graceful, soaring over Winkelman, Arizona.

It was Levantin's 663rd bird.

In his cubicle, as he battled another Y2K bug, Miller was squished back into third place.

Just because Sandy Komito was ahead didn't mean he was relaxing. He wasn't good at relaxing. When someone once suggested that golf was a relaxing pastime, Komito took it up and golfed one hundred days in a row. For four years in a row. (He wore rain suits.) Relaxing was not fun. Fun was, after five weeks in Alaska, flying to southern Arizona in the dead of summer for a crack at a bird in the desert.

The elf owl was the world's tiniest, one-quarter the size of your run-of-the-mill great horned owl and smaller still than a house sparrow. Its diminutive brain was still sharp enough, though, to let others do all the work when it came to nesting. The elf owl mooched off woodpecker holes. If birders drove slowly at dusk through the stovepipe cacti of the Saguaro National Monument near Tucson and carefully inspected hundreds of gila woodpecker holes, they might find a single elf owl.

Or they could just hang out below an old telephone pole at a $90-a-night lodge and look up.

The elf owls of the Santa Rita Lodge were the most famous in North America. Every evening during nesting season, dozens of birders gathered in a lodge parking lot one hour south of Tucson and stared at two fist-size holes about thirty feet up a phone pole. The routine: sun went down, owl heads popped up, birders cheered (in properly muted tones). Thousands of people had scored their life elf owls this way.

Joining a crowd of twenty below the telephone pole, Komito noticed a man acting strangely, wriggling a bit at first, then fully shaking his legs and slapping his ankles. Madera Canyon was an odd place for such a peculiar dance, especially a solo dance, and other birders gave the man a wide berth. Komito, however, knew exactly what was going on. Eleven years earlier, during his first Big Year, Komito had made the same mistake of standing atop a mound in Fort Lauderdale to get a better view of a black-faced grassquit. Without warning, Komito's legs had exploded with hurt, and he'd danced the same dance as the man now writhing before him. Komito knew this man's pain. He had felt it. He had suffered it.

"Let the ants out! Drop your pants!" Komito urged him. "Take off your pants and brush them off. That'll help!"

"*Aargh!*" cried the man, who was too modest to take Komito's advice.

Luckily, and most importantly, human yelps of anguish did not scare away the elf owl.

Halfway up a granite wall, Komito finally met his match.

He was chasing a MacGillivray's warbler through Yosemite National Park when, out of pure touristo awe, he glassed up the 3,000-foot face of El Capitan. He spotted three climbers somehow camping on sheer rock high above the valley. Komito, who never traveled anywhere without his own pillow and night shades, was amazed anyone could sleep in such a precarious place.

"Take a look at this," Komito told two nearby women. "There are people up there climbing up the wall."

"Yes, I know," a woman told Komito. "One of them is my boyfriend, Mark Wellman. He's a paraplegic."

Komito was dumbfounded.

Wellman, paralyzed below the waist, was the climber who had captivated the world in 1989 by taking seven days, four hours, and seven thousand pull-ups to conquer El Capitan. That had launched his career as a motivational speaker. Two years later he ascended the 2,200-foot Half Dome of Yosemite. Now he was on El Cap again.

Komito and the women watched the climbers pack their camp and start moving higher up the wall. Komito, who couldn't resist swapping one story for another, told the women about his own Big Year adventure.

For some reason, the women weren't overly impressed. Silly Komito: this wasn't Attu. For the first half of the year he had lived almost exclusively in the world of birders, where he was used to being the center of attention. In this other world, Komito earned only a shrug.

Now was his chance. Here he was an outsider, and he finally got to ask the exact question that had so often been thrown at him:

"Why is he doing it?" Komito asked.

"Why do you birdwatch?" the girlfriend countered. She didn't wait for an answer. "It's a rush. It's the same as when I skydive."

Skydiving? Paraplegic rock climbing? Komito was out of his league here. He excused himself and continued up the trail, where he got his thrills finding a red-breasted sapsucker.

After a four-day, 6,500-mile sweep of the Pacific Northwest, Komito returned home to a jarring phone call. Turn around right now and come back, the caller told him.

There's a Terek sandpiper working the surf in Anchorage.

For nine and a half hours in the air, Komito stewed. This return trip to Alaska shouldn't have been necessary. Six weeks earlier he had missed the Terek—a gangly Eurasian shorebird with stubby legs and a queerly upturned bill—after Levantin had ditched him on Attu to chase the pintailed snipe.

Retracing four thousand miles of contrails was not his idea of a good time, but he had no choice. Greg Miller probably wouldn't have the money to chase the Terek, Komito figured, but Al Levantin probably did. Komito was not about to grant Levantin a freebie, no matter the price.

Komito would need more than money to catch the Terek. He needed luck. The problem with chasing shorebirds in Anchorage was that the shore changed all the time. Tides in Cook Inlet averaged twenty-six feet. Most birds working the surf at low tide were well beyond the range of standard 60x telescopes. Only fools ventured out for a closer look; several times a year police raced out for dramatic rescues of people, mostly wading fishermen, who were stuck in thigh-deep mud and frantically trying to escape the rising 5 mph tide.

For Komito, the Terek would have to be a high-tide bird.

At 9 P.M., the asphalt path around Westchester Lagoon was filled with joggers, cyclists, and in-line skaters; anyone who survived an Alaskan winter was determined to stretch out every possible minute of Anchorage's nineteen daily hours of summer sunshine. Into this river of human Lycra waded Komito and Dave Sonneborn, the full-time Alaska cardiologist and part-time Attu guide who had phoned in the Terek tip to Komito. Reunited for the top of the tide, they were birdmen on a mission, snapping open their tripods and scoping the lagoon. Though hundreds of peeps and plovers and dowitchers followed the brine up the bay, there was no sign of any Terek. The two men finally packed up at midnight and agreed to meet ten hours later, in the same spot, for the same tide.

The Terek didn't come in for that tide, either. Now both men worried—Sonneborn that he had called Komito across the continent for nothing, Komito that the bird had gone someplace where Levantin could find it. (Where was Levantin, anyway? Did he get the bird before Komito had even arrived?) After three more hours of fruitless scoping, Sonneborn left to fix a broken garage door. Komito eyeballed on.

As the tide rolled out, weather rolled in. Temperatures dived into the fifties. Komito's scope fogged. His body shivered. He walked for warmth and scanned the growing mudflats for any bird that looked like an odd man out.

One hundred feet away, in a cluster of semipalmated plovers and semipalmated sandpipers, he saw it—an unpalmated Terek. He wanted to whoop for joy, but there was no one to whoop with. Sonneborn was still gone.

Komito locked the bird into his scope and followed its frantic feeding. Five minutes passed, then ten and twenty. Where was Sonneborn? This was not good. Searching two days for a bird that magically appeared as soon as his partner walked away—Komito feared his credibility might never recover.

The Terek took off. Komito's heart sank. Fortunately the bird landed another hundred yards out the mudflat, but then it fed farther and farther away. Komito had to do something.

He hustled up the trail and found Sonneborn glassing another length of the lagoon. Komito grabbed him.

When they returned to Komito's spot, the bird—the alleged bird—was gone. Komito was crestfallen. No matter what he said, he doubted Sonneborn would believe him. Komito didn't help himself when he mistakenly turned a distant spotted sandpiper into the Terek. Had Komito blown the original identification as well? He apologized, but even that sounded like desperation.

From behind a rocky point another bird emerged. It was the Terek—or at least what he thought was the Terek. He didn't bother telling Sonneborn where. He just muscled the doctor's eyeball into Komito's scope.

"Yes," Sonneborn said. "I do see your bird."

It was Komito's bird. Neither Levantin nor Miller had seen it. In fact, neither knew about it. The score was Komito 703, Levantin 663, Miller 658. Back when JFK was president, these numbers would have exceeded the life list of the immortal Roger Tory Peterson and all but one other North American birder. But now Komito, Levantin, and Miller each had bested those lifetime lists in less than seven months of a single year.

For this remarkable pace, ornithologists could credit El Niño, or easy jet travel, or the information revolution that allowed a guy in New Jersey to find out about a new shorebird in Alaska within four high tides at Cook Inlet. Komito, however, was in no mood for anything analytical. He remained eighteen birds short of his old record. He spent his plane ride home dreaming of ways to find them.

For Levantin, it was time for a gut check. This weekend he could stay home in Aspen at the peak of mountain wildflower season and enjoy Mahler and Mozart at the downtown music festival. Or he could fly two thousand miles to the Outer Banks of North Carolina and puke on another pelagic trip.

He packed his bags with Dramamine.

The music would be there when he returned, Levantin figured, but the seabirds wouldn't wait. There were four or five easy species waiting to be seen out over the Gulf Stream. His sea strategy, though shaky, remained intact. If he was going to make any run at Sandy Komito, he had to have those birds. His head knew it. His heart knew it. His stomach just had to survive it.

Dopey with seasickness medicine, Levantin staggered to the dock by 5:30 A.M. He didn't like what he saw. Winds ripped at a steady 20 mph, with gusts beyond thirty. Even the bay frothed with whitecaps. The seas on the Atlantic side of Oregon Inlet—the very thought made Levantin nibble another stoned-wheat thin.

This time, his fear had company. On the dock dozens of birders wondered aloud about wave size. Somebody's hat blew off. Levantin grabbed another cracker.

At 6:15 A.M. came the announcement: No pelagic today. The seas were too rough.

Never had a man traveled so far for so little and felt such relief.

He sat on a bench to box up the wheat thins and listen to others bellyache about the canceled trip. Somebody had driven six hours last night to get here by dawn. That guy was really babbling. He had been counting on this pelagic for months and really wanted to see just the basic offshore Atlantic birds—greater shearwater, Cory's shearwater, black-capped petrel, band-rumped storm-petrel.

Levantin commiserated. He'd like to see those birds, too.

The guy on the bench kept rambling. He didn't know what to do now. The whole reason he had come here was for pelagic birds. He had already seen everything else in this area this year.

He had?

He had. The guy on the bench was doing a Big Year.

Levantin's gut felt as if it were outside Oregon Inlet. Somebody else besides Sandy Komito was doing a Big Year?

Levantin had no clue. His mind raced. Who was this guy? Where did he come from? Levantin had never expected this. He looked back over at the guy on the bench and put on his best poker face.

"A Big Year? That must be something," Levantin bluffed. "How many birds have you seen?"

Six hundred sixty-six.

The guy's name was Greg Miller and he was from Lusby, Maryland, and he worked as a software engineer at a nuclear power plant and was due back at work Monday.

He was two birds behind Levantin.

Two birds.

The guy bubbled on. Now that the pelagic was canceled, maybe he would try to find a curlew sandpiper somewhere near here at Pea Island. Levantin tuned it all out. He congratulated the guy on his 666 birds and walked away.

For the first time Levantin confronted a dark fear. He might not finish in second place. He might finish third.

He still had time. He still had money. He still had tickets to the Aspen Music Festival, but they would be of no use now.

FOURTEEN

Forked

Fear is a powerful motivator. Al Levantin most assuredly did not want to finish his Big Year in third place, so he blasted off on a birding bender. He got warblers in West Virginia; Atlantic seabirds off Cape Hatteras (he threw up); Pacific seabirds off Monterey (he threw up again); the continent's smallest bird (the three-inch calliope hummingbird) on a 14,000-foot mountain in Colorado; and a Eurasian tree sparrow in the hometown of Abraham Lincoln.

But no bird gave him greater pleasure than the fork-tailed flycatcher.

When the tropical vagrant was first reported on Plum Island, a coastal spit north of Boston, Levantin dropped everything. This species was notorious for its one- or two-day visits, and he had to catch it fast. No concert that weekend; he was a birding fiend. Though a line of cars idled at the entrance, Levantin didn't worry. Those vacationers were destined for Plum Island's white-sand beaches. He was headed for Hellcat Swamp.

At the parking lot he chanced upon three local birders, who took him straight to the flycatcher. There was no mistaking this bird: it was black-and-white with a freakishly split tail twice as long as its body—and it was perched on a post in the middle of a pond.

Levantin was so pleased with his sudden victory that he did something unusual. He told the other three birders about his Big Year. The other guys were fascinated. The more Levantin told them, the more they wanted to hear. At first it felt odd telling other birders about his grand adventure—this was the first time he had ever done it with strangers—but it also felt exhilarating. He was out in the open now, talking up his obsession with the people who understood it. He had to admit: this was pretty fun.

Just a few weeks before he had sat side by side on a bench with a rival and Levantin never even identified himself. Now he was blabbing all about his Big Year to total strangers. What had changed?

What had changed was that Sandy Komito didn't have the fork-tailed flycatcher.

Greg Miller didn't have the fork-tailed flycatcher.

Al Levantin did have the fork-tailed flycatcher, and he had it first. That felt good.

Greg Miller was sick. Ever since Attu, he had hacked a wet cough during the day and shaken with chills at night. He felt lousy all the time, but there was medicine for that. His main concern was a more consuming malady.

For the past three days he had been paralyzed with flycatcher fever. He wanted to cure it—oh, how he longed for a cure—but he remained stuck in his cubicle. It wasn't easy to work when a real rarity was just a short plane flight away in Massachusetts. But Miller had two more days and a few thousand lines of code before he could do anything about it.

In the meantime, he checked. He called the Massachusetts Rare Bird Alert hot line to make sure the bird was still there. It was. He scrolled down the Massachusetts Rare Bird Alert

Web page to see the exact locations of the latest sightings. Somebody had found the bird near the parking lot, someone else had found it along the dike, and another person had found it on a pole in a pond.

A short line at the end of that report really made Miller's temperature rise.

On the day the flycatcher was found on the pole, it was seen by a stranger who had traveled thousands of miles just for this bird.

This stranger was from somewhere out West. He was doing a Big Year.

A North American Big Year.

The amazing thing, this Web poster said, was that this Big Year birder already had seen 675 species this year.

Miller didn't need Jolt to understand that number.

There was someone else out there doing a Big Year, and it wasn't Sandy Komito.

Who was it?

Miller clicked his Netscape Navigator back over to www. travelocity.com. Whoever this third Big Year birder was, Miller wasn't going to fall behind him by a fork-tailed flycatcher.

The only thing worse than messing with Sandy Komito's sleep was messing with his sleep after he'd missed a bird.

After a failed search for the fork-tailed flycatcher, Komito had retreated to his motel room and rested up for a repeat assault in the morning. At 2 A.M., he was jolted awake by a loud voice in the next room on the telephone. Komito managed to fall asleep again, but was awakened at 2:30 A.M. by the same voice on another call. The voice returned at 3 A.M., then a half hour later.

Komito seethed.

When Komito rose the next morning at six, he decided to get even. He picked up the phone and called the now-silent room next to him.

"Hello, Charlie?" Komito boomed into the phone.

A groggy voice replied, "What?"

"Hi, Charlie!" Komito yelled.

"This isn't Charlie and you woke me up!" replied the voice, now angry.

"Oh, I'm so sorry," Komito said, then hung up.

That was wimpy. He could do better than that.

After breakfast Komito picked up the phone in the motel lobby and rang the room again.

"Good morning!" he boomed again. "This is your neighbor. It seems you called everyone last night but me. How come?"

"Who is this?"

"I told you, it's your neighbor from across the hall. I heard you call all night in a loud voice and you kept all of us up."

The voice replied that he was using a speakerphone and he did not care one whit about Komito's beloved slumber. His curse words grew louder and more frequent just before he slammed down the phone.

Komito scrambled to his car and raced back out to Plum Island, where he found the fork-tailed flycatcher on top of a sign. He snapped a few pictures of the bird's tail, but decided the guy back in the motel room still deserved to be forked.

By 9 a.m., Komito was back in the motel lobby, posing as a guest and asking the desk clerk to ring his room—it was actually Charlie the voice's room—with a wake-up call in another hour. When she agreed, Komito walked over to the lobby phone, punched in a number, and walked away while the phone in the voice's room was ringing and ringing.

He had his bird, and he had his revenge. The revenge was more fun.

Miller's fever subsided. His binoculars caught the flycatcher. Bird No. 682 was such a thrill—and such a relief—that Miller couldn't resist telling everyone in Hellcat Swamp about it.

One birder took particular interest. He did a double take on Miller's name and asked him to repeat it. He asked if Miller was the guy doing the Big Year. When Miller confirmed it, the other birder said he had a special message to deliver:

"Sandy Komito says hi."

Five hundred miles from home in the middle of a swamp and Miller was receiving a social nicety from, of all people, Sandy Komito? What was up with that? How did Komito know he'd be here? Did Komito have people watching him? Had Komito been here? Did he have this bird?

Did Komito have 682, too?

FIFTEEN

Conquest

Greg Miller knew he was close to Sandy Komito. He could feel it. His first five days here in California couldn't have been better. Even the disappointments were turning into triumphs. When monster waves canceled that Monterey Bay pelagic, Debi Shearwater personally chaperoned Miller deep into the foothills for a Lawrence's goldfinch. (The High Queen of the High Seas hardly ever went inland; she must really have a thing about Sandy Komito.) Now Miller was knocking them off again—a mountain quail and white-headed woodpecker (No. 692 and No. 693) in the San Gabriel Mountains above Los Angeles, a hermit warbler (No. 694) just off the 8,800-foot summit of Mount Pinos north of Santa Barbara.

He had found every West Coast mountain species that he needed. But under the pines of the McGill Campground he was confronted with something completely unexpected—a van of birders from New Jersey.

One of the van guys relayed a message: "Sandy Komito says hi."

It was the third time Komito had planted the same head-game time bomb for Miller. (Besides the fork-tailed flycatcher in Massachusetts, Komito had made sure Miller was also greeted during his failed chase for a whiskered tern in Cape

May, New Jersey.) Miller would not let the opportunity pass again. He asked about Komito's Big Year.

Last time anyone in the van had heard, Komito was at 712, 713, something like that.

Seven hundred twelve! Miller was close to Sandy Komito. If a Monterey Bay pelagic ever got off, and if he could pick up a few Rocky Mountain birds, and if his money held out. Miller might actually be able to take him. For the first time in weeks, his sinuses cleared.

The Jersey birders wished him luck. Miller sat alone in his rental. Sandy Komito says hi. How nice of Sandy Komito to consider Greg Miller. Maybe Greg Miller could give Sandy Komito something to think about.

The second Miller walked on the boat at Monterey, Debi Shearwater buttonholed him. She was ready. He was ready. They had company. The New Jersey birders were on board, too, carrying along the usual salutation from Komito.

Not far offshore the buzz on the deck was about the sheer weirdness of this trip. Sandwiched on the water between two dense bands of fog was a raft of hundreds of black-vented shearwaters, a fairly common species, but unusual in these numbers. Hurricane Isis had slammed Mexico just two days earlier. Though Isis was brutal—10 dead, 2,300 homeless— these powerful Pacific storms did push birds up the coast. Miller hoped they weren't all commoners.

Off the bow someone shouted, "Two o'clock," and two divers with dusky underwings, Craveri's murrelets, zoomed by. They were No. 697. A few minutes later the stern was crossed by the hunchbacked pirate of Antarctica, the south polar skua, the very bird on the license plate of Komito's Town Car. If that wasn't a sign, what was? It also was

No. 698. Miller was in the zone. He was feeling it.

Miller milled about the boat. They were a few miles offshore, and the Pacific was strangely warm and calm. Back toward shore, the fog had lifted. Views were longer now.

Pumping low over the ocean was a flesh-footed shearwater. That bird nested in New Zealand. What was it doing here? That was No. 699, his third new bird in two hours. This was no ordinary pelagic. Beyond the bow a blue whale spouted twenty feet above the water. While Miller and the Jersey boys jockeyed for the best cetacean views, somebody cried, "White bird on the water!"

One hundred tons of whale was forgotten like yesterday's newspaper. Miller ran with all his might to the starboard side of the bow. Oh, the curse of a short person on a pelagic— everyone in front was a full four inches taller than Miller. "Down in front!" he roared. No one moved. Frantically he muscled bellies, shoulders, arms, heads—anything—out of the way. Still no clear view. From up top Shearwater cried, "Red-billed tropicbird!"

Desperation.

Where?

Panic.

Needed it. Wanted it. Had to have it.

Got it.

Shearwater hurtled out and crushed Miller with a hug that would cost good money from a chiropractor.

"That's not seven hundred for a life list!" Shearwater bellowed to the boat. "That's seven hundred for this year!"

After all the hugs and high fives, handshakes and hoorahs, Miller sauntered over to the Jersey birders with a message of his own:

"You tell Sandy Komito that Greg Miller says hi."

Where he was, Sandy Komito wasn't saying hi to anyone.

With a death grip on the handlebars of his Honda ATV, Komito blasted through the horizontal rain on a treeless island in the Bering Sea. Even the Eskimos were staying home this morning. Komito was forty miles from Siberia, four thousand miles from home, and searching for lost Asiatics. He was finding more than he bargained for.

The weather, for one, was brutal. Something about the arctic circle made rain feel like flying forks. Back home in Jersey it was ninety degrees. Here the wind tears in his eyes were freezing.

At least there was no danger of becoming mired in mud. There was barely dirt here. Saint Lawrence Island was a hundred-mile pile of dark pea gravel that rolled like ball bearings every time Komito stepped. He nearly fell a million times. He'd shelled out to rent the ATV, which was fun if you didn't mind whiplash. It blew a flat. He offered an Eskimo teen $5 to fix the tire, but groused that the kid pumped air slower than a girl. The teen—surprise, surprise—ditched Komito, who then blew two hours running down the guy who'd rented him the ATV. The renter took his time fixing the flat. Even in a 30 mph wind, locals could smell desperation.

The population center here was a subsistence village of 660 called Gambell. In a good year the Eskimo Yupiks killed a bowhead whale. In a bad one they lived off seal and seabirds. The only significant outside income came from visitors who wanted to see the same wild animals that Eskimos ate.

There was no eerier place in North America to find birds. The premier locations for songbirds were the three centuries-old boneyards, where arctic warblers perched on bowhead ribs and wheatears waited on seal spines. Every day by 10 A.M. or so, Eskimo men trekked from Gambell to dig trenches in the boneyards; a three-hundred-year-old walrus tusk was a prized source of ivory that could be carved and sold for the price of three months of ATV gas.

Another sweet spot was the town dump. Komito was a landfill connoisseur, but the one on Gambell was truly memorable—thirty feet high, two hundred feet long, and smoldering from a fire that burned all summer. The smoke was fueled by a daily parade of locals dumping five-gallon honey buckets filled the night before. The place smelled worse than fried walrus liver. Wagtails liked it, though.

Looming above it all was 614-foot Sevuokuk Mountain. Sea cliffs of this mountain provided nests for unbelievable numbers of seabirds, hundreds of thousands of auklets, puffins, and murres that blackened the sky off the end of the island's western point. Yet Komito kept finding himself drawn to a more ghoulish sight. Because of permafrost, Gambell residents did not bury their dead. Jutting from the slopes of the mountain were dozens of plain wood caskets, some intact, others not, with generations of the dead. It gave Komito the creeps.

For six days at Gambell, Komito was rained on and blown on and sleeted on. He was tired. He picked up only one new bird, a gray-tailed tattler, but felt good about that one. It was found by a tour group whose members paid $3,000 each to be led around Gambell. Komito walked up to the tour leader's scope, peered inside, and tallied his tattler—at a mere fraction of the tour group price. Komito may have been grossed out by boneyards, sewage dumps, and rotting coffins, but he could still not resist the lure of a cut-rate rarity.

Other trips were more productive. In three weeks that taught him the first names of half the gate attendants at

Continental Airlines, Komito scored a south polar skua off Cape Hatteras, a razor-bill outside Nova Scotia, more seabirds on a Monterey pelagic, and a whiskered auklet in the Aleutians.

The best, however, was a land bird.

Tough and aggressive, it had few natural enemies. It was gaudy enough to be recognized by anyone who cared. It was bold enough to mooch the work of others. It was resourceful enough to stash a private reserve of food for days. It was loud enough to force neighbors to shut their windows at night.

A yellow-billed magpie, found by Komito on a tree branch in central California, near Solvang, was the bird that broke his 1987 record.

SIXTEEN

Cape Hatteras Clincher

If a Big Year were a contest that most people understood—a football game, say, or even something more important, like the baseball play-offs—then Greg Miller would know how to describe his situation. The two-minute warning had sounded. His back was to the wall. It was the bottom of the ninth in the seventh game of the World Series, and his Cleveland Indians were down to their one last hope.

He had to catch Komito.

He had to see birds no one had seen.

He had to go to sea.

The sad truth was that Miller could spend weeks wandering the bush for some lost migrant and still come back empty-handed. It was October. There just weren't that many land birds left to find. Besides, he had little money to search for them. He had already returned to the Bank of Dad for a second loan of $3,000. A third loan was out of the question.

But even this pelagic trip, from Cape Hatteras on the Outer Banks of North Carolina, was a long shot. Fall migration had run its course. Most birders were nesting at home. Though Miller had signed up for two offshore trips, on Saturday and Sunday, the tour operator had canceled the Sunday trip for lack of interest.

Miller was determined to make this one count—so determined, in fact, that he got to the dock at 5:40 A.M. For the first time all year, he was twenty minutes early for something. Desperation had a way of waking up a man before the alarm clock sounded.

He boarded the seventy-two-foot *Miss Hatteras* and bolted straight for the bow. For once, he had secured the prime viewing spot. It may have been the first time he ever moved quickly for the best spot instead of the last. Binoculars around his neck, he was ready. He waited. He fidgeted. Nothing was happening here. What did early people do with all their extra time, anyway?

He walked back to the cabin to find something to do. Other birders were arriving. Miller overheard one, a distinguished-looking man with graying hair, talking about the fork-tailed flycatcher in Massachusetts. Miller had chased that same bird. He eavesdropped a little closer. Something seemed strangely familiar about this man. Could this be the guy, the mysterious third man on a Big Year? Miller couldn't stand it any longer.

"Excuse me," Miller interrupted. "I'm Greg Miller and I'm doing a Big Year. You sound like the person who got the fork-tailed flycatcher for your 675th bird. Are you on a Big Year, too?"

The other guy looked at Miller and beamed.

"Well, yes, I am," said Al Levantin.

It had taken ten months, but finally they had met. (The earlier sit-down on the other Outer Banks dock didn't count; Levantin had never fessed up to Miller that he was a foe.) Both men felt an overwhelming urge to start comparing notes—how often do you meet a complete stranger who has surrendered to the same obsession?—but first they boiled down ten months of their lives to a simple question.

"What have you got?" Miller asked.

"Six hundred ninety-one," Levantin said.

"I'm at seven hundred and five," Miller replied.

The roses in Levantin's cheeks turned white. He started to talk, but words wouldn't come. He had spent so much time worrying about second place. Now he faced the possibility of third.

What he thought was: Third place? Third place? All this for third place?

What he said was: "I've still got some easy ones left." This claim was true—he needed a storm-petrel on this trip, and some sparrows and that damn spotted owl still out in Arizona.

Boy, was Miller smiling.

Third place. Third place. Levantin couldn't stop thinking about it. He had to change the subject.

"What's Komito got?"

"Last I heard, seven hundred thirty-one or thirty-two. That was about a month ago," Miller said. Now the smile fell off Miller's face, too. With two and a half months to go, Komito was at least two and a half dozen birds ahead. Miller felt cold. Was there a draft in this cabin, or had someone just opened a door?

Suddenly the boat cabin rocked with a voice—that deep foghorn voice. Miller and Levantin snapped around.

It was Sandy Komito.

The Three Musketeers, together at last.

"Al," Komito said. "Where you at?"

Levantin eyed his tormentor and cracked a sly grin.

"Hatteras," he said.

Miller laughed. Levantin didn't flinch. Komito turned to Miller.

"How about you, Greg? Where are you at for the year?"

"Doing very well, Sandy. I'm at seven hundred and five," Miller said.

"Congratulations on breaking seven hundred, Greg," Komito said in the kind of tone that uncles reserve for nephews. "Only a handful of people have ever achieved that goal."

Komito smiled, then turned back to Levantin.

"So, Al, really. How many birds do you have for the year?"

Levantin looked Komito in the eye. "I'm at seven hundred thirty-seven."

"*Wow!*" Komito blurted.

Komito fell back a step. The shout had burst from his mouth before his brain could control it. He was always loud, but this time people were looking at him. Seven hundred thirty-seven? My God, how did Al Levantin get 737? Komito's eyebrows hit the top of his ears and tried to blast off even higher. Komito struggled to compose himself.

"Well, Al," Komito stammered, "I'm at seven hundred thirty-six."

Komito eyed Levantin, hurt.

Levantin eyed Komito, strong.

Miller eyed both men, amazed. Levantin had just told a baldfaced lie, and his heart hadn't even skipped a beat.

Komito, however, was wobbly. His eyes were so wide they had more white than blue. He looked ready to faint.

Levantin stared back with a face of stone.

With Komito swooning and Levantin locked in his imitation of Mount Rushmore, Miller couldn't hold it any longer. His belly exploded with a laugh so loud, so ribald, that the rest of the boat took notice.

"He got you good, Sandy," Miller wheezed to Komito.

First Levantin, then Komito, keeled with laughter.

The gamer had been gamed.

The two-hour motor to the Gulf Stream passed quickly. The waves were tall but the tales even taller, and the three birders bantered like schoolboys on the playground. Levantin and Miller wanted to know how Komito had pulled so far ahead. But when they asked, they inevitably became stuck in yet another twisting and turning Sandy story. Could they learn anything from the leader without putting up with all the blarney? Fat chance.

Besides, some of Komito's tales were pretty wild. He had even chartered a helicopter this summer in Nevada to see a Himalayan snowcock. Levantin and Miller had already written off that species as an unattainable freak.

Komito was wise enough to play to his audience. Misery loved company, and at this point no one understood the agony of a missed bird better Levantin and Miller.

So Komito told about his fruitless trips for the great gray owl.

Miller told about his fruitless trips for Swainson's warbler.

Levantin told about his fruitless trips for the spotted owl.

And so on. And so on.

The bull session was so much fun that Levantin suggested they all meet for dinner that night. Miller jumped right in, but Komito begged off, mumbling something about some previous (but unspecified) plans.

Komito and Miller moved to a bench on the starboard side of the bow.

Levantin slipped back to the stern, where he vomited overboard.

Over dinner that night, Levantin and Miller swapped the obligatory snide remarks about Komito—*He's thirty birds ahead and doesn't have time for a restaurant with us!*—and compared notes.

Levantin was the only one to add any birds during that day's eight-hour boat trip (black-capped petrel, over the warm Gulf Stream, No. 692 for the year). Though there still were some gettable pelagic birds, he was sick of being seasick. Fortunately, most of his remaining easy birds were in the Arizona desert.

Miller's targets were mostly in Florida. Levantin had already scored those tropical birds back in February and was happy to offer Miller some advice. When searching for flamingos in the Everglades, he told Miller, beware the mosquitoes.

They laughed and joked and teased. Inevitably, though, the conversation came back to Komito.

At this point, there was little doubt that Komito's list was solid. Too many people had spotted him chasing too many birds. No fraud there. It was his attitude that grated. He wasn't just beating them—he was rubbing their noses in it. There was nothing like traipsing far into the backcountry only to have some well-meaning innocent inform them, "Sandy Komito says hi." But this morning on the boat, when Komito had finally got a chance to say hi in person, he didn't bother. He asked only about their numbers. In a sport sugared with niceties and politeness, Sandy Komito had been a birding machine—an unstoppable tank plowing a loud path through the avifauna of North America. It would be up to Levantin and Miller, and only Levantin and Miller, to chink Komito's armor. The lead was big, but it might not be insurmountable.

Before they chose their main courses at the restaurant that night, Al Levantin and Greg Miller agreed that they faced a common foe.

They decided to go out and catch him—together.

SEVENTEEN

Two in the Bush

Maybe this was Sandy Komito's revenge. Komito, after all, had told everybody at Cape Hatteras that this trip was a cinch. Following the leader's advice, Levantin and Miller had joined in the no-man's-land of the Nevada desert to charter a helicopter for, of all things, a Himalayan snowcock. Everyone knew Komito loved to make things sound more miserable than they actually were. If he said the snowcock was easy, then it must be easy, right?

But all last night, snow had pounded the Ruby Mountains. When Levantin and Miller had woken, the peaks weren't even visible; the top fifteen hundred feet of the entire range— the place where the birds lived—was engulfed in clouds.

The two birders stood side by side on the tarmac while their pilot scanned what was left of the Rubies. Levantin and Miller could only guess where the clouds ended and the mountains began. Frustration sank in: the snowcocks were up there, but the birders were down here. They'd have been just as close to their goal if they'd stayed home in bed and ripped up $100 bills. Another wasted trip.

Just as the birders braced for the inevitable trip cancellation, a wavy dollop of blue sky, a little doughnut hole, cracked the gloom.

265

"I think we should go," the pilot announced.

Both birders did a double take. Go where? The tops of the mountains were missing.

"I'm an experienced pilot," he told them. "I've flown plenty of trips up there."

The pilot began wheeling his Bell 206 Jet Ranger out of the hangar with a hand-pull dolly. He really meant it. Weather or not, he was going to fly.

Was this safe?

Was this insane?

Was this Komito's idea of a cruel joke?

Levantin didn't say anything, so Miller stayed mum.

Miller didn't say anything, so Levantin stayed mum.

The pilot fired up the rotors.

Both men knew this trip was borderline crazy. Before agreeing to this joint expedition, Levantin and Miller had spent a grand total of five hours together. (It would have been longer, but Levantin had excused himself on the boat to get seasick.) Now the two men, strangers but fierce competitors, were stuck with each other in the lonely sagebrush of Elko, Nevada. Neither Levantin nor Miller had ever attempted anything like that before.

Levantin had qualms about relying on another birder for help.

Miller had qualms about all the money involved.

As helicopter blades twirled faster overhead, discomfort turned to fear. Flying a helicopter in the mountains during a snowstorm to see a Himalayan snowcock—that was not what either man had ever envisioned for his newspaper obituary.

The pilot motioned both birders to climb in the helicopter.

Each spied the other for an awkward pause, a hesitation, a sideways glance that betrayed a second thought. Would one let the other win?

Levantin and Miller both boarded the chopper.
It was too late for doubt: they were airborne.

If the prospect of chasing a bird in a helicopter seemed
strange, then the story of how the bird got there in the first
place was even stranger.

In the late 1950s, Nevada state fish and game com-
missioners worried about a nagging problem: they had
thousands of square miles of open space, but nothing to kill in
it. Nevada was simply too dry for most game animals. Most of
the state received less than nine inches of precipitation a
year—it takes thirty-six inches to grow a basic bluegrass
lawn—and the only shootable bird tough enough for those
conditions was the sage grouse. Sage grouse tasted like sagebrush. Nobody wanted to hunt something that tasted like a
gnarled bush.

Enter the great white hunter. In 1961, after filling his
trophy room with the heads of the Grand Slam of North
American sheep—the bighorn, desert, Dall, and Stone—a
Lincoln-Mercury dealer from Reno, Ham McCaughey, turned
his rifle sights beyond his home continent. His target: the
world's largest wild sheep, the Marco Polo of mountainous
Central Asia. The Marco Polo, it turned out, shared its home
at the top of the world with another outsize creature, the
Himalayan snowcock. While playing Marco Polo high in
the Himalayas for his next stuffed head, McCaughey hired
local trappers to net him six live Himalayan snowcocks. He
meant it as a goodwill gesture for the game wardens back
home. But when he tried to fly the birds to Reno, U.S.
agricultural officials feared the exotic wildlife would spread
exotic diseases throughout North America. McCaughey had
to quarantine his six snowcocks for thirty days in Honolulu.

Living in a tropical paradise for the first time in their lives, five Himalayan snowcocks died. But the one survivor was so magnificent—bigger and stronger than a grouse, but with the rich white meat of a pheasant—that Nevada wildlife officials were smitten. They ordered Glen Christensen, a state biologist, to open negotiations immediately with the governing mir in the Hunza region of the Himalayas to bring more birds to Nevada.

In 1964, during a spring intermission in warfare among Pakistan, India, and China, Christensen flew to Hunza, in present-day Kashmir. The most spectacular place he had ever visited, Hunza is a long box canyon rimmed by snowcapped, 23,000-foot mountains. Everywhere he walked, Christensen was trailed by Indian and Pakistani agents, who suspected that the pale interloper was a spy. When Christensen told his tailers that he was only interested in a local bird, they grew convinced he was a spy—and redoubled their stakeouts.

Despite all the security, Christensen was able to capture ninety-five snowcocks. The big challenge was getting them back home. The only regular flight out of Hunza was an old Fokker warplane that accepted both people and livestock. So he loaded the ninety-five snowcocks in cages and crammed them in the aisles around the goats and chickens and other Hunzans also flying to Rawalpindi, Pakistan. (This was one use of a Fokker that Der Führer had never considered.) This time the snowcocks were quarantined in New York, and forty-eight survived. With the help of a biologist from the University of California and a wildlife nutritionist from Purina, Christensen built an air-conditioned pen for the foreign birds in Yerington, Nevada. He started breeding them. By 1970, when India and Pakistan finished one awful war over Kashmir and girded for the next. Christensen realized it was too dangerous for him to catch any more wild birds in the

Himalayas. He started releasing his progeny into the American wild. By 1979, a total of 1,569 Himalayan snowcocks were freed into the Ruby Mountains of northeastern Nevada.

The transplant program, which cost taxpayers $750,000, barely succeeded. Today no more than eight hundred snow-cock survive in North America, and in some bad-weather years the population plummets to just two hundred. Though game-and-fish officials had dreamed the bird would become a major attraction for sportsmen, only about a hundred hunters a year bother trying to shoot a snowcock; the birds are just too high, and on peaks too treacherous, for most people. Only about ten snowcocks are killed each hunting season, a dismal return on a $750,000 investment.

While the Himalayan snowcock flopped with hunters, it soared with birders. Because the Ruby Mountains had none of the recurring wars of the bird's native home in Kashmir and Pakistan, eastern Nevada quickly became the number one place in the world to see a snowcock. By 1998, hundreds of birders, including dozens of Europeans, were converging on Elko. There was only one helicopter charter in town, El Aero, and it was caught unaware by snowcock fever. The first time pilot Ted McBride hovered up to a snowcock, he worried that his customer, a retired physician, was suffering a seizure. No worries; it was just pure ecstasy. "I've never had a woman who got me half that excited," McBride said. He also never had a woman who would pay $550 for a one-hour ride. Thanks to the snowcock, birders were giving McBride, and his partner Dale Coleman, a fat wallet.

Ooomph!
Miller's ribs slammed against his chest straps. Levantin braced in his seat with all his might. Out the helicopter

windshield, their horizon had turned crooked.

Both men silently mouthed the same wish: I hope this helicopter pilot knows what he's doing.

The Rubies were twenty miles to the southeast, and Dale Coleman, the pilot, knew the route well. Just because he was flying another bird run didn't mean that he couldn't have some fun. So he banked his turns hard and let the rotors rip. When birders paid by the hour to find a snowcock in the mountains, the pilot wouldn't waste time dillydallying over the low sage.

All three men were connected in the cockpit with headsets. Over the whir of the blades, the pilot laid out the tricks of this treasure hunt: After last night's storm, the snow line in the Rubies was at forty-five hundred feet. The clouds began at ten thousand feet. With any luck, the snowcocks would be either at the bottoms of the cliffs or the tops of the peaks.

Neither Levantin nor Miller said anything about it, but they both knew full well that the highest peaks still were in the clouds. If the snowcocks rode out the storm up there, this trip would be a $550 bust.

Miller tried to take his mind off any chance of failure by video-taping the cattle a half mile below. His hands fumbled with the camera. Something wasn't right. Nothing would focus. Was the camera broken? The pilot saw his predicament and grinned. Miller was so nervous that he had steamed up his entire side of the helicopter bubble. A flip of the aircraft defroster cleared up his fog, but the camera still wouldn't see straight. Miller checked his LEDs. There would be no tape today. He had forgotten to recharge the camera batteries last night.

In the back, Levantin wore his stiffest poker face. He said nothing. On the outside he looked calm, but inside was another story. Levantin wanted, desperately, to keep from getting sick. He had lost his breakfast on eight boat trips this year and didn't want to suffer the same mess in the confines of a helicopter cockpit. He had successfully survived one earlier helicopter trip, though that was on a cushy business-trip glide over the streets of Paris. Maybe, just maybe, his stomach did better on air than water. He kept his eyes fixed on the horizon. The chopper blasted over miles of sage and range cattle. The speedometer read ninety knots. Levantin hoped the pilot was done with those banked turns.

The closer the helicopter came to the Rubies, the bigger they looked. Sheer, jagged, and brawny—these weren't the Appalachians. Clouds lifted, and the morning sun spotlighted the mouth of a tight canyon. The chopper sliced inside.

Miller wanted to say something about the raw beauty of it all—snow below, cliffs to the side, clouds streaming above—but the reverberating *thwomps* of the rotor off both rock walls made conversation impossible. The chopper slowed to gain altitude.

They whirred closer to a ridgeline and picked up speed and suddenly—whoosh!—the earth fell away. What a chasm. Forget about butterflies: Miller felt a live bat skittering in his stomach. In the backseat, Levantin wasn't talking.

Beyond the ridge the pilot dropped down and banked right, trailing the cliff face and scanning for snowcocks. Down low, a white mountain goat struggled through a neck-high drift of last night's snow. Would the goat survive? This trip was single-mindedly focused on another quarry. Their chopper cut hard again into another canyon.

"There goes one!"

Levantin, alive after all, was shouting into his headset.

"Over there! Over there!"

Below and just behind the helicopter a rusty brown bird furiously thumped its wings.

"Snowcock! It's a snowcock!"

The canyon was tight. Could the chopper spin backward for a better look? It didn't matter. Though the speedometer read sixty knots, or roughly seventy miles per hour, the Himalayan snowcock was overtaking them. This race was never in doubt: bird was faster than whirlybird—faster and stronger even than its primary predator, the golden eagle. When the five-pound creature rocketed over the next ridge, the helicopter had to lag behind momentarily to gain altitude. The bird was out of sight. The helicopter was finally high enough to make the ridge. It zoomed forward.

"If we don't keep up, we'll lose that bird!" shouted the pilot.

Whoosh! The helicopter cleared another sheer drop and continued the chase. The bird was a quarter mile ahead. The chopper raced forward along the edge of the cliff. Levantin and Miller were terrified. A 70 mph helicopter race along a rock wall for a bird? This was insane. The rotor echoes were deafening, but Miller, in the front seat, was too afraid to check how much space was between the wall and the spinning blades.

One hundred feet below them, the snowcock dropped into a cliffside scree field. The chopper hovered. No luck. Half a world from its Himalayan home, the bird wore the exact same colors as the rust-and-gray talus of the Ruby Mountains.

The bird had vanished.

Miller whooped out loud, partly from joy and partly from relief. A forty-five-second look at a lifer! He made the helicopter bubble fog over again.

In the backseat, a grin finally cracked Levantin's poker face. He wasn't celebrating aloud, but he clearly was the happiest man aboard. His breakfast remained intact.

Back on the ground in Elko, Levantin and Miller settled up their charter bill and thanked the pilot profusely. "I'm glad you were as good a pilot as you said you were," Miller told him.

The Himalayan snowcock was Miller's 708th bird. For Levantin, though, it was No. 700—cause for celebration. Only a handful in history ever had reached that milestone. Levantin wanted to call his wife, but he knew she wasn't home.

Levantin and Miller eyed each other. Two men, together in the desert, eight birds apart, eight weeks left in their competition. What next?

Levantin broke the silence. "You know, I don't have a gray partridge yet."

Miller did. But his flight home wasn't until tomorrow—he had set aside two days in Elko for the snowcock, just in case dicey weather canceled the helicopter trip—and he had to rely on Levantin for the two-and-a-half-hour ride back to the Salt Lake City airport. Miller knew where the gray partridge lived. He had been there three months ago.

"Want to go to Boise?" Miller asked.

Four hours, 220 miles, and six golden eagles later, Levantin and Miller were in Boise and turning into a subdivision of McMansions on HolliLynn Drive. The big boxes cast long shadows; the sun offered only another half hour of light.

Miller hoped they had arrived early enough. Levantin started glassing the neighborhood for a grayish brown chicken with a rusty face.

Between the third and fourth house down the street, Levantin's Leicas found something moving.

They were the yard birds of HolliLynn Drive, eleven gray partridges, No. 701 for Levantin's year.

The next day, as they road-tripped back to the Salt Lake City airport, both men started thinking.

Miller was driving Levantin's car, a Lexus SUV with heated leather seats. The car alone was worth more than anything Miller owned. Miller realized he had no idea what Levantin did for a living. It would feel rude to ask. With a car this plush, though, Levantin must have some money. He never talked about it. Al Levantin was humble, but he was a sly dog, too. After the gray partridge in Boise, Miller was only seven birds ahead. Miller knew he should focus on the leader, Sandy Komito, but somehow he couldn't. He was only a handful of birds ahead of a chaser whose reserves exceeded the Bank of Dad.

Third place, Miller fretted. Third place.

In the passenger seat, Levantin realized he didn't know much about the man at the steering wheel. Good birder, terrific ear, all enthusiasm, but could Miller really work that many hours in the office and expect to find more birds? Levantin was only seven birds behind. He still had easy ones left, and he had the time to get them.

Second place, Levantin thought. Second place.

Miller was home in Maryland sometime after midnight, and back at his desk in the nuclear power plant by 9 a.m. He logged nine and a half hours that day. Y2K was coming. There were still birds for him to chase in Florida. He was already down $8,000 at the B.O.D. He really wanted to go to Florida. He put in seventy-six hours the rest of the week. He was saving his money for Florida.

Levantin drove back to Colorado to an empty house. While

he'd been chasing the Himalayan snowcock in Nevada, his wife was adventuring in Bhutan and Nepal, riding elephants, trailing white rhinoceroses, and luxuriating on safari at the famed Tiger Tops Jungle Lodge. She might not be spending as much as Al on his Big Year, but she was making a run at it. She would be out of the country for four weeks with two girl-friends. Levantin really missed her. All that talk about keeping a marriage fresh by going off to do your own thing sounded good, but it could be lonely, too. Levantin wanted to celebrate his 700th bird. He wished his wife was home to help him do it.

He called eight friends and invited them over for steaks, which Levantin cooked himself. They laughed. They drank. They toasted the Himalayan snowcock. Levantin missed his wife even more.

When Ethel finally returned home, Levantin told her all about his 700th bird. She was thrilled that he had reached the Big Year milestone, but she was impressed he had staged his own dinner party.

EIGHTEEN

Nemesis

When Al Levantin had started his Big Year, he vowed he wouldn't do it. He didn't want to do it. He worked mightily to avoid it. This was all supposed to be a grand personal adventure, and adventure meant that you didn't lean on anyone else for help.

So much for idealism. Levantin needed one bird, bad, and he didn't have much time for it. He stared at the phone. It was now or never. He didn't feel good, but he had to do it. He had to hire a guide to find him a bird.

By now Levantin had memorized every branch on every tree up Scheelite Canyon. The geologic wrinkle in Arizona's Fort Huachuca Army Base was supposed to be the world's easiest place to spot a spotted owl. He had spent five hours searching there in February and five more in July. The hikers' journal at the trailhead kept insisting the owls were up there. All the birding books said the same thing, too. Experts estimated that 80 percent of all people who had ever seen a spotted owl in the wild had seen it in Scheelite. These experts had never talked to Al Levantin.

He knew all their advice. Spotted owls roost within twenty feet of the ground. In live oaks, they stay on branches far from the trunk. On pines they favor closer boughs. Either way, the owls can be tough to see—three or four shades of brown flecked with white spots that turn the eighteen-inch bird into a vanishing piece of sun-dappled background.

Levantin even carried maps with dots on the specific roosts favored by the owls. This whole backpack of information ultimately was useless and made Levantin feel as if he were the high school freshman being sold an elaborately printed elevator pass. Were spotted owls really in Scheelite? Maybe they were just a prank.

By the time Levantin finally caught on, it was too late. The one man who could have guaranteed him his spotted owl was dead.

Robert T. Smith—Smitty, to legions of birders—was an army draftsman in the 1960s who, on a whim, bushwhacked his way up a little-used corner of the 73,000-acre military base. Scheelite Canyon's mix of massive boulders, cool rock walls, and towering pines took his breath away. So did the 20 percent grade.

A half mile up the canyon, at an elevation of six thousand feet, Smitty spotted the owls for his first time. He stood transfixed. Until this hike, he had never thought much about birds, but something about these birds—their beauty, serenity, rarity—inspired him. When he retired from the army in 1973, the thin, flinty man started hiking up Scheelite five times a week to check on the owls, keeping detailed records of each visit. He knew where they perched and when they perched. He even named most of their roosting trees. These owls, joked the lifelong bachelor, had become his grandchildren.

Smitty almost single-handedly scratched out a trail up Scheelite and, like the precise army man he was, posted it in one-eighth-mile increments. Over the years he personally led more than six thousand birders on hikes to see the spotted owls.

Oh, how Levantin now wished he had been one of the six thousand. But two months ago, Smitty had died at the age of seventy-nine.

Luckily, Smitty did not take his owling maps to his grave. Before he died, Smitty met a diminutive man at a Huachuca Audubon meeting whom he deemed worthy to receive his owl knowledge. The two made an unlikely duo—Smitty the army veteran who had served in the jungles of Southeast Asia, his new friend a native of Manchester, England, who owned one of America's foremost music and video collections of the martyred Tejano singer Selena. Thanks to Smitty, the repository of spotted-owl wisdom now rested with Stuart Healy, the very birding guide who had spent so much time earlier in the year with Greg Miller.

In the Big Year battle, Healy wasn't choosing sides. He was, however, accepting paying customers.

Levantin arranged to meet Healy at 7 A.M. at the eastern security gate of Fort Huachuca. By now, Levantin knew the directions by heart. Like so many places along the Mexican border, the base had a two-hundred-foot blimp tethered two miles above the desert, an eye in the sky that was supposedly searching for airborne drug runners. If only Big Brother could find him his owl.

He couldn't complain too much, though. The military was the whole reason why the owls were here. Founded in 1877 as an outpost to hunt down Geronimo and the Apaches, Fort Huachuca today was home to more than eleven thousand army intelligence workers. The base was one of the few Southwestern mountain forests off-limits to most logging.

The spotted owl was famous for its dislike of chain saws. The northern race of the same species was responsible for one of the nastiest environmental fights of twentieth century: the logger vs. conservationist blowup in the Pacific Northwest.

Though humans never quite resolved whether old trees were best viewed as habitat or jobs, the spotted owl clearly preferred its timber uncut. Scheelite had that and more—no roads, few humans, and a steady smorgasbord of voles, mice, and bats.

Levantin had to admit, it felt strange to be at the Scheelite trailhead with another person. But if Healy could finally put Levantin onto a spotted owl, his company would be worth it. Levantin wondered how much his $10-an-hour guide was going to cost him.

As it turned out, Levantin didn't even need Healy. A spotted owl was perched on a live oak branch directly above the trail. If Levantin had kept walking, he would have slammed it with his forehead. Levantin and guide were in and out of the canyon in less than an hour.

Technically speaking, Levantin got Bird No. 704 for the price of a single Alexander Hamilton. There was no estimate on the psychic cost.

Two hours from the Everglades Marina, paddling a canoe for the first time since high school 4-H, Greg Miller choked back his panic. He was lost in a sea of saw grass. His strokes were wobbly and his neck seared without sunscreen. While the wind blew from the north, a vast thunderhead barreled in from the south. He was stranded in an alligator-infested swamp. A lightning storm was coming and his only cover was an aluminum boat.

This was all the flamingos' fault. Miller should have nailed those birds months ago. But his springtime trip to Florida had come up empty, so he'd ditched his family on Thanksgiving Day for a jet trip to Miami and a so-called holiday feast alone in a Bennigan's where English was a second language.

He should have stuck with the Snake Bight Trail. That was
how everybody got their flamingos. Just park the rental car
past the Everglades National Park gates and look for the
brown trailhead sign and start walking. Off the end of
the point set up a 60× spotting scope and start looking for
pink. No big deal.

Actually, there was one complication. Miller hated the
Snake Bight Trail. Not because of snakes—had he never seen
one there, though he did worry about them a lot. No, the
problem with Snake Bight was insect bites.

After a year of chasing birds through the Great Dismal
Swamp of Virginia, the spring marshes of Alaska, and the Ten
Thousand Lakes country of Minnesota, Miller fancied himself
an expert on mosquitoes. The mosquitoes fancied him, too.
He slathered on Off!, Cutter, and Muskol; the mosquitoes
thought it was marinade. Pure Deet? Bug treat. Those Avon
wetnaps may have worked for some, but on Miller they
created a new aroma that turned mosquitoes into winged
wolves.

Snake Bight was the worst. The last time he'd hiked it, he'd
wrapped himself like a sheikh. He came back with more
welts— but no flamingo. Never again, he said at the time, and
he really meant it.

For this trip he did some planning. Just beyond the Snake
Bight trailhead was a bayside shop that rented boats. He didn't
feel comfortable with a motorized skiff, but how much trouble
could he get in with a canoe? Best of all was the promise from
the guy behind the counter: once you get off the shoreline, he
told Miller, the mosquitoes are gone. The half-day rental was
$22. He was supposed to be back by 2:30 P.M. There was no
way Miller needed all four hours. Snake Bight only took an
hour and a half. So he bought a 1.5-liter bottle of water and a
bag of pretzels and hit the dock. He was smug.

But a canoe as an idea is different from a canoe as a mode of transportation. When Miller lowered himself into the boat, the boat lurched left. To balance himself he jerked right— and the boat jerked, too. Ouch! He skinned his shin on the aluminum gunwale.

Steady, steady, he told himself. A mosquito landed on his knee and reflexively he crushed it. The boat moved, but didn't rock. He laughed with relief. He paddled his first few strokes. So far, so good. He cleared the marina and paddled a little harder and moved a little faster. The water was the color of tea, but transparent enough to reveal crabs on the bottom. A broad-winged hawk soared overhead.

His hands finally relaxed on the paddle. He was amazed at how quickly this canoe traveled. It even kept tracking when he swapped his paddle for binoculars. He was a natural-born canoer.

When he saw the Snake Bight Trail, he got really excited. He wondered how many poor saps were being eaten alive as he floated on with ease, with joy, and, yes, with burgeoning amounts of grace. Confidently, he set down his paddle and lifted his trusty Zeiss 10×42s. In the distance, he saw the color of his dreams.

Pink was in Florida Bay.

The birds still were too far off for Miller to make a positive identification. No problem. Paddling was fun. Let the others sacrifice blood for flamingos on the Snake Bight Trail. Miller had outsmarted them. He was Huck Finn.

Around a saw-grass point opened a passageway toward the pink. He paddled through and the surface erupted with silvery fish. Mullet were stacked in this water. Hundreds of snowy egrets flecked the shoals. An osprey soared. Pelicans dive-bombed. And a reddish egret canopy fed just fifty feet off Miller's bow. Unbelievable.

Gradually, though, Miller noticed something different. What had started out as four-foot water had become eighteen-inch water and was now turning closer to a foot. Good thing canoes drew so little water. Good thing, too, that the breeze was blowing toward the pink. He pulled out the bag of pretzels and let the wind do his work for a while.

Finally he had drawn close enough to see pink flecks instead of a pink blob. He raised his binoculars again.

Whitish head . . . gray bill . . . body more pink than orange . . .

He wasn't chasing flamingos. He was chasing roseate spoonbills. Oh, no! He had scored the spoonbill months ago.

It was 1 P.M., and his trip was a bust. He had to hustle back.

He turned around but the head wind was unforgiving. One bad paddle stroke and the boat spun like the second hand on his watch. Grace gave way to zigzag. He pulled hard to return to the saw-grass passageway.

Was this the right passageway? It seemed a lot shallower than he remembered; every stroke pulled up as much muck as water. Maybe the marina really was around the tip of that other shoal.

He turned. He hit bottom. He turned again and bottomed out again. Now he knew why it had been so easy to paddle to the pink—he was running with an outgoing tide. No more. He was fighting the flow, and down to just four inches of water. He dug hard and the canoe moved up two feet. When he pulled the paddle out, though, the boat slipped back a foot. He dug again. Up two feet, back one.

His eyebrows dripped with sweat. He tried to rub it off with his T-shirt, but that was soaked, too. He swallowed a long slug from his water bottle and felt grateful to be in the shade.

Shade?

In the Everglades?

Miller looked up and saw the thunderhead looming.

Deep in his stomach, Bennigan's turkey fluttered.

Don't panic, don't panic, don't panic, he told himself. This was a national park. Surely someone would come to help.

Nobody did.

What used to be the bay was now an expansive mudflat. On the far shore, two hundred yards away, a pair of teenage fishermen grinned. "You might as well head back in this way," one called.

Was this a joke? The bay in front of the teenagers still looked more like mud than water.

But Miller was too desperate to be cynical. So what if the teens were mocking him? If he could just get his canoe back to shore, he could walk it back to the marina. Was that thunderhead growing?

For the first time, he stood up in the canoe. It wasn't so tippy in four inches of water. He bent over and grabbed the gunwales. Then, slowly, he hoisted his feet over the side, to the Everglades, which swallowed him. He was thigh-deep in trouble—skanky, oozing, slimy trouble.

The fishermen laughed so hard that Miller could hear their wheezes above the pounding of his heart. His T-shirt and his jeans were caked with the brown badge of stupidity.

He trudged on, relying on the canoe as both a balance beam and a rest stop. In the swamp mud, every footstep sounded like a busy bathroom plunger. His leg wormed deeper. He tripped. He threw his arm over the boat and grabbed the far gunwale for support. The canoe jerked ahead. He stopped it with his other arm. He was down to his crotch in muck and scared to death that he might sink farther.

With a burst of adrenaline, he hauled his filthy body back into the canoe. This time, he was not getting out. He speared his paddle back into the muck and turned the boat into an aluminum inchworm. "You're making progress," a fisherman called. Miller laughed, surprised that he still could.

Arms trembling, he paddled back to the marina and arrived at 2:40 P.M., or ten minutes after the rental return time. The marina attendant took one look at Miller and waived the $8 late fee.

With every step on the dock, Miller left behind a foul trail of sulfurous grime. He felt bad about the mess, so he hosed away his footprints. Then he turned the hose on himself.

Blasting the tap water down his jeans, up his armpits, around his back—anywhere and everywhere the Everglades had penetrated—Miller attracted a crowd of tourists. The creature from the black lagoon was showering in public.

The next day, Miller returned. He parked his rental car beyond the national park gates and hiked the Snake Bight Trail. He was eaten alive.

Off the end of the point he searched for pink. This time, the bird had a black-tipped bill.

Miller got his flamingo.

He would not come back to Florida anytime soon.

'Twas the night before Christmas, and all through Duluth, not a creature was stirring—except Sandy Komito. He was wrapped in frustration. From an hour before dawn to an hour after sunset, he had driven every road and glassed every tree in the Sax-Zim Bog, but he still couldn't find his great gray owl. It was the only breeding bird of North America that still eluded him. Wile E. Coyote and the roadrunner had nothing on Komito and his great gray owl. He had chased it on nine different trips this year—Minnesota in March, June,

November, and two tries in December, Wisconsin in November and December, California in June, and Oregon in December. Today he had called three different guides to help him find the bird, but all were staying home with family for the holiday. Komito was not a religious man, but a full day of finding nothing when the thermometer topped out at five degrees left him wondering about the plight of Job.

His immediate problem was finding someplace open for dinner on Christmas Eve. On his first drive through Duluth, he couldn't find an open restaurant—no Bennigan's, no Ponderosa, no TGIF. On his second drive he noticed that even McDonald's, Burger King, and Wendy's were all closed. After such a lousy day afield he didn't want to go to bed hungry. He had to find something. On his third drive he found a Chinese restaurant in a strip mall. The only thing he disliked more than ethnic food was ethnic food in a place without a major ethnic population. Duluth was full of broad-shouldered Lutherans who should have been happy to serve him his prime rib, medium well. But all those Lutherans were in church tonight. Komito wasn't about to stoop to a hot dog at 7-Eleven for dinner, so he took a chance on the Chinese restaurant.

Just one other table was occupied. They looked like outsiders, too. Komito ordered his food as bland as he could—egg drop soup with pork-fried rice. A thousand miles away in New Jersey, his daughter was preparing to celebrate Christmas with her husband. Komito wanted to be back home for that. His son-in-law's mother had died two Christmas seasons ago, and the Komito family tried to do what it could to bring some happiness to the holidays. Komito would be a lot happier on his flight home tomorrow if he had got his bird.

Usually when he dined alone, Komito spent his time filling a notebook with the day's events. Today there wasn't much to report. He couldn't help thinking about the past. At one point, on his November trip to Aitkin County, Minnesota, Komito thought he might have had his bird. From a road he saw a large owl—was it a barred, great horned, or great gray?—take wing in the distance over the spruces and fly not far from him. But as the bird landed, Komito heard four gunshots. It was hunting season. Komito would have chased the owl into the woods but he didn't want to be mistaken for a deer.

Though the egg drop soup was palatable, the fried rice was awash in oil. He drained a few forkfuls and dumped the rest. For the first time in a long, long year, Komito wondered what the hell he was doing chasing a bird so far from home. The other customers left. He was alone in the restaurant. Ever since his yellow-billed magpie in California, every bird for Komito had been a recordbreaker. But he wanted to break it even worse. He wanted a record no one else could break. He tried to think of anyone who would want a bird so much that he would eat alone in a Chinese restaurant in Duluth on Christmas Eve. The whole thought was too depressing. He wouldn't let himself dwell on failure. He was still birding tomorrow.

Komito was back out at dawn on Christmas Day. He saw two bald eagles but had no interest. In his entire Big Year, Sandy Komito had not been defeated by a human. He was beaten by an owl.

NINETEEN

Honorbound

From his perch on a ridge high up the Colorado Rockies, Al Levantin soaked in a view that reached forever. On his right and left jutted four of the continent's ninety-two peaks over fourteen thousand feet. At his feet stretched the neatly restored mining town, Georgetown, that once was the world's greatest producer of silver. Behind his back, though, was a view more difficult to understand.

Greg Miller lagged hundreds of feet below on the ridge. He clearly wasn't used to mountains, snow, or exercise two miles above sea level. His face was a shade of red not often seen in nature. He looked about halfway to a heart attack. Levantin hoped Miller was okay. He still couldn't see how he was losing to this guy.

There were only fourteen days left in the year, and Levantin trailed Miller by three birds. If this were an ordinary competition, Levantin would be going all-out right now to crush his opponent. But there was a code of honor among top birders: if one asked for help, the other provided it. Greg Miller had asked Al Levantin for help. He still needed a white-tailed ptarmigan, a bird that Levantin had seen in his own home state ten months ago. To show Miller a ptarmigan, Levantin would have to drive two and a half hours from his house at Snowmass, spend even more time climbing mountains just beyond the Continental Divide, then drive two and a half hours back. Of course, Miller had already guided Levantin to a gray partridge in that neighborhood in Boise. But a partridge was a drive-by bird. Ptarmigans were work.

Levantin checked again down the slope. Miller really was struggling. When they'd started trekking from the saddle of 11,600-foot Guanella Pass, the snow had been packed tight. That had changed higher up. Here, the top layer was strong enough to support Levantin but not all 225 pounds of Miller, whose feet kept crashing through the crust into the soft powder below. Postholing, they called it—walking gingerly on a wind-packed snow crust until you suddenly blasted through, like a stake being rammed in for a rancher's fence. It made for a brutal contrast: there was Levantin, scampering like a goat high up the ridgeline, and Miller, gasping and heaving through snow up to his thighs. Postholing meant Miller expended twice the energy to go half the distance. He was still sick from Attu. Wheezing, grunting, stumbling—the noise was tremendous. Levantin could do nothing to help. He pressed on ahead.

Besides, he had company. At the trailhead they'd met another birder who had just seen the ptarmigan. After picking up his camera in the car, the stranger had agreed to show the birds to Levantin and Miller. Levantin did not want to offend the helper with a slow pace up the mountain. As a general rule, Levantin tried not to offend large men with few teeth.

So Levantin and the gap-grinned stranger played the engine to Miller's caboose. If a Big Year were won on physical fitness, this would be no contest. Levantin could outrun, outhike, and outjump both Miller and Komito. But in the car ride up the mountain this morning, Levantin had learned there was one thing Miller outdid him at—boat trips. Miller had scored five extra seabirds this year, more than enough to erase Levantin's land-species advantage. Levantin couldn't believe it. He was supposed to win at sea. He had kept getting sick again and again because it was his ticket to the biggest list. Now it turned out that Miller had outsailed him. The mere realization turned Levantin queasy again.

Halfway up the ridge, Miller felt iffy, too. The air here was thinner than his hair; he sucked so hard that he swore he could taste his lungs. Was this bird really worth it? Twice in the 1970s he had tried for ptarmigan on Guanella Pass and failed, but those attempts were in summer and involved no hiking. This felt as if he were back on his bike at Attu.

"Greg! Up here!"

A hundred yards up the ridge, Levantin was yelling. Miller's first reaction: How did he have enough oxygen to be so loud? Second reaction: Run!

Miller blasted through the snow. He was no Prancer, but he wasn't going to come this far for one bird and miss it. He made it ten feet up the slope before running out of air. Slow down, Levantin urged him. The birds weren't going anywhere. Miller calmed down. It was fatherly advice, which Levantin certainly was old and wise enough to be dispensing.

Levantin doubled back down the slope to help Miller with the final ascent. Miller was grateful for the hand, but even more grateful for the news. At least ten ptarmigan huddled at the top of the rise.

Miller's adrenaline took over. Eighty more yards and he would be there. He postholed two steps, rested, then postholed two more. His head swirled with altitude. Two steps, rest. Two steps, rest. This, he had heard, was how climbers conquered Mount Everest. Except Everest didn't have life birds on top.

This Colorado mountain did. With Levantin at his side,

Miller finally reached the crest and was rewarded with a forty-foot view of his first white-tailed ptarmigan—a pigeon-size bird that lived its whole life in the rarefied atmosphere above timberline. Seeing a ptarmigan in winter plumage is one of the most lusted-after prizes in birding. Ivory white, with just the tiniest black dot of an eye and beak, the ptarmigan has such perfect winter camouflage that the best way to find a bird is to look for the shadow beneath it in the snow. Miller found one gray shadow, then another, and another. All ten ptarmigan were here, just as Levantin had promised. Miller wished he could enjoy an even closer look. But every time he raised his binoculars, body heat fogged over the glass. Steam swirled off his scalp.

On the hike back down the mountain, Miller learned a new lesson about postholing: it's a lot easier when you're euphoric.

As for Levantin, he wasn't saying much. He had just given away the bird that would almost certainly cement him in third place. Levantin was now four birds behind Miller, 710 to 714. He had no chance of victory. But his honor was intact.

TWENTY

December 31, 1998

On the last day of the Big Year, Greg Miller was so spent he couldn't roust himself from bed. His head and nose were exploding. Both ears were infected. He had a weeks-old hundred-degree fever. For all this, he blamed Attu. He wanted to chase a snowy owl, the one bird he could have had and should have had, but he was lucky to reach the bathroom. Just after he'd split up with Al Levantin in Colorado, Miller had found a brown-capped rosy-finch, his 715th bird for the year. It was the third-highest total in the history of Big Years. He had flown eighty-seven thousand miles and driven another thirty-six thousand. He had spent $31,000. All six credit cards were maxed out. He remained in hock to his parents, but his father was too proud to care. Miller sat up in bed and celebrated with two Tylenol and antibiotics.

Al Levantin skied that day, but without binoculars. Snowmass had a thirty-eight-inch base of snow, with a half inch of fresh powder. The sun was brilliant. Like Miller, Levantin had taken off for one more bird—in his case, a black-tailed gull on the Chesapeake Bay Bridge, No. 711 for the year—but he returned on December 23 tired of it all. The year had been fun. He had had his adventures. He'd survived 135,000 United Airlines miles, plus thousands on smaller carriers. But more than $60,000 later, he didn't want to travel any more. He was home with his wife. He felt free.

Sandy Komito, however, did not. On December 29, he left for Delray Beach, Florida. He wanted this trip so badly that he agreed to sit in the main cabin—he had flown first-class for almost every other trip of his Big Year—and in a middle seat. Sitting in the center wasn't so bad, Komito thought, until he saw his seatmate board the plane. It was a woman, large, very large, so large that when she sat, Komito swore he was being smothered by an avalanche of polyester. He was horrified, but too scared to say anything, for fear that she might talk back. Her body touched his the entire two-and-half hour flight. When she rose, she left behind a sweat stain on the shoulder of Komito's golf shirt. There were two days left in the Big Year. The lady had not sung yet.

He had 744 birds. He hadn't just broken the record. He had destroyed it. Mark McGwire and Sammy Sosa had crushed a record, too, that summer, but each guy always had the other to goad him on. Komito competed mainly with himself. Sure, he made little comments about Levantin and Miller from time to time, but they had never come close to catching him, much less passing him. Komito had been in uncharted birding territory for his entire year. No one had ever seen so many birds so quickly. No one had ever built a record so dominant. So why did he care so much about one more bird in Florida?

He couldn't answer that. He just wanted it. Even if he hadn't missed that great gray owl, he'd be out here today. One year on the road and he was in his groove. He was chasing.

This time, it wasn't even much of a chase. He found the bird, a white-cheeked pintail that should have been down in the Caribbean, nibbling in wetlands fed by a sewage plant just up the road from one of south Florida's biggest retirement condo complexes. The only excitement came when Komito spotted the bird and others didn't. He wanted to make sure he had witnesses, so he stuck around until everyone had seen his No. 745.

Two days later, on New Year's Eve, Komito waited at home by the phone. It didn't ring. The hot lines were silent. No bird was being seen in North America that he hadn't already seen.

He spent a quiet night at home with his wife. He didn't try to stay up until midnight.

On December 31, 1998, Sandy Komito, owner of the new Big Year record, set his alarm for 5 A.M. The next morning would be a new year, and he was rising before dawn to go birding.

Epilogue

When the American Birding Association published Sandy Komito's Big Year total of 745 birds, competitive birders gasped. His number was almost beyond belief. Though some called it the birding equivalent of the moon shot, that wasn't fair. People had walked on the moon after Neil Armstrong, but no one would manage to see even seven hundred Big Year species in the years after Komito, Greg Miller, and Al Levantin. Komito hit the magic combination of the strongest El Niño on record and the trip of the century on Attu. He also accomplished all his travel in a different, friendlier world; it would not be easy to log 270,000 last-minute miles through the increased security of today's borders and airports. For all these reasons, many top birders say Komito set a record that may never be broken.

Five months after the Big Year, Komito's wife earned her degree from a community college. To celebrate, Komito took her on an around-the-world trip. While she went sight-seeing in a city, he'd bird the backcountry. They would met at the end of the day for dinner. They had a wonderful time. Back home, his dawns remained reserved for birding. He found no great gray owls.

Al Levantin stayed retired for twenty-two months in

Colorado before succumbing again to business. When another executive resigned, he filled in as acting president and chief executive officer of CDI Corporation, the world's largest search and recruitment organization, with $1.6 billion of business from 1,325 offices in eighteen countries. He ran the company for a year before announcing another retirement, his fourth. He said this one was his last. He summoned the courage for another offshore birding trip in Monterey Bay, where, with the help of a Scopolamine patch applied behind his ear six hours before dock time, he saw birds without seasickness.

Greg Miller's father died of congestive heart failure in November 2000. Six months later, Miller himself was diagnosed with acute lymphocytic leukemia, a form of cancer that usually strikes children. He was hospitalized for forty-five days. From the window of his seventh-floor hospital room, he spotted twenty-six bird species, including a peregrine falcon. He celebrated his release from the hospital by completing a 2002 Big Year inside his home state of Ohio. He finished in third place, with 285 birds. He followed that with an Ohio Big Month in January 2003, but finished second, with 130 birds. He is trying to pay off bills from his 1998 North American Big Year through his fledgling business as a birding guide. On his first trip he took two college students six thousand miles in a car on spring break and showed them 311 species in nine days.

After a long Aleutian winter, Larry Balch returned to Attu in the spring of 1999 to find Mr. Pants still flying on the wind-sock pole above main base. The next year, regulations and letters from the U.S. Coast Guard, Federal Aviation Administration, and Fish and Wildlife Service made it clear to Balch that his birding tours on Attu were over. When Balch left the island for the last time in the fall of 2000, Mr.

Pants still flapped proudly in the wind, testament to the durability of Sandy Komito's Big Year record—and the power of polyester.

ACKNOWLEDGMENTS

Full disclosure: I did not personally witness a single day of the 1998 Big Year. This account is based on hundreds of hours of interviews with participants and witnesses, plus fieldwork in many of the places they visited. My biggest thank-you goes to the three contestants themselves, who supplied me with their personal journals, receipts, and notes to help re-create this description of their grand adventure. I end this project in awe of their stamina both traveling the continent—and answering my questions. Sandy Komito repeatedly performed the amazing feat of making me laugh at 5 A.M. before coffee. Al Levantin's enthusiasm is remarkable and inspiring. Greg Miller has the most indestructible sense of optimism I have ever found. I am grateful to each of them.

While reporting this book I relied on the old credo of trust but verify. If a contestant recalled that he saw a bird a half hour before dawn with a half-moon still in the sky, I checked out government records for that day's sunrise and moonset. Much corroborating evidence also came from eyewitnesses. I learned much about the men from the women who know them best, Bobbye Komito, Ethel Levantin, and Greg's mother, Charlene Miller. I was also greatly helped with advice and stories from Michael Austin, Larry Balch, Benton

Basham, Bob Berman, Glen Christensen, Dale Coleman, Dave DeLap, Ted Floyd, Bob Funston, Dan Gibson, Larry Gilbertson, Stuart Healy, Leroy Jensen, Jennifer Jolis, Kenn Kaufman, Stuart Keith, Geoff LeBaron, Cindy Lippincott, Ted McBride, Harold Morrin, Floyd Murdoch, Marion Paton, Gerrie and Lloyd Patterson, Carol Ralph, Craig Roberts, Scott Robinson, Bill Rydell, Debi Shearwater, Macklin Smith, Dave Sonneborn, Joe Swertinski, and Jim Vardaman.

The formulation and completion of this book required valuable adult supervision. I thank my agent, Jody Rein, a perfectionist with a wonderful sense of humor, and my editor, Leslie Meredith, who can say "red-bellied woodpecker" and "dangling participle" in the same sentence—and magically make writing better.

Nobody put up with more difficult conditions during this project than my family. My parents, John and Alice Obmascik, flew to the rescue when I needed help the most. My sons, Cass and Max, have the brawn to blast down ski runs, the finesse to tell a mountain from black-capped chickadee, and the heart to give big hugs on my worst days. My wife, Merrill, gave me patience and inspiration exceeded only by love. This book is dedicated to her.

Birding is the most literate of outdoor pastimes; few birders would ever consider going into the woods without a trusty field guide. While researching this book, I learned most birders are picky about their field guides and the ways they use them. To identify species, beginners and intermediate birders rely mainly on bird pictures; experts depend heavily on text descriptions, which offer more detailed information. The field guide most popular with top competitive birders is the *National Geographic Field Guide to the Birds of North America*. It has excellent maps, outstanding descriptions, and more rarities than any other top guide. The drawback: it's complicated to use. Putting so many species in one book means you have to thumb through many pages to find the more common birds typically encountered afield. For ease of use, especially by novice or intermediate birders, it's hard to beat the time-honored *Peterson* field guides, which use arrows on paintings to highlight key identification marks, or Kenn Kaufman's newer *Birds of North America*, which combines *Peterson*-like ID arrows and an excellent indexing system. In recent years, *The Sibley Guide to Birds* has become the reference standard for many birders. Though it contains few exotics—many species that figure prominently in *The Big Year* aren't even mentioned in *Sibley*—it does offer terrific paintings of most North American birds in several plumages and positions. The problem with *Sibley* is its bulk; I find it too clunky to lug 545 fullsize pages into the field. David Allen Sibley tried to solve this weight problem with separate, smaller guides for Eastern and Western species, but these new books are still too big to cram into my back pocket. Maybe I'm the one who needs to lose the weight.

Here are other books and publications I used for research:

Able, Kenneth P., editor. *Gatherings of Angels: Migrating Birds and Their Ecology.* Ithaca, New York: Comstock Books, Cornell University Press, 1999.

Audubon, John James. *John James Audubon, Writings and Drawings.* New York: Library of America, 1999.

Audubon, Maria. *Audubon and His Journals.* New York: Dover Publications, 1960.

The Birds of North America series. American Ornithologists' Union, Cornell Lab of Ornithology, and the Academy of Natural Sciences of Philadelphia.

Blaugrund, Annette. *The Essential John James Audubon.* New York: Harry N. Abrams, 1999.

Devlin, John C., and Grace Naismith. *The World of Roger Tory Peterson: An Authorized Biography.* New York: New York Times Books, 1977.

Durant, Mary, and Michael Harwood. *On the Road with John James Audubon.* New York: Dodd, Mead & Co., 1980.

Kaufman, Kenn. *Birds of North America.* New York: Houghton Mifflin, 2000.

———. *Kingbird Highway.* Boston: Houghton Mifflin, 1997.

———. *Lives of North American Birds.* Boston: Houghton Mifflin, 1996.

Komito, Sanford. *Birding's Indiana Jones.* Self-published, 1990.

———. *I Came, I Saw, I Counted.* Fair Lawn, N.J.: Bergen Publishing Co., 1999.

Lane, James A. *A Birder's Guide to Southwestern Arizona*. Denver: L&P Photography, 1974.

————., and Harold R. Holt. *A Birder's Guide to Denver and Eastern Colorado*. Sacramento, California: L&P Photography, 1973.

Migration of Birds. Revised by John L. Zimmerman, U.S. Fish and Wildlife Service, 1998.

National Geographic Field Guide to the Birds of North America, 1st ed., Washington, D.C.: National Geographic Society, 1983.

Pettingill, Olin. *A Guide to Bird Finding East of the Mississippi*. New York: Oxford University Press, 1951.

————. *A Guide to Bird Finding West of the Mississippi*. New York: Oxford University Press, 1953.

Peterson, Roger Tory. *Birds Over America*. New York: Dodd, Mead & Co., 1948.

————. *A Field Guide to the Birds*. Boston: Houghton Mifflin, 1934.

————., and James Fisher. *Wild America*. Boston: Houghton Mifflin, 1955.

Rydell, William B., Jr. *A Year for the Birds*. Minneapolis: Bullfinch Press, 1995.

Sibley, David Allen. *The Sibley Guide to Birds*. New York: Alfred A. Knopf, 2000.

The Sibley Guide to Bird Life & Behavior. Illustrated by David Allen Sibley and edited by Chris Elphick, John B. Dunning Jr., and David Allen Sibley. New York: Alfred A. Knopf, 2001.

Vardaman, James A. *Call Collect, Ask for Birdman*. New York: St. Martin's Press, 1980.

Weidensaul, Scott. *Living on the Wind: Across the Hemisphere with Migratory Birds*. New York: North Point Press, 1999.

INDEX

How did you find this story?
I got lucky. I was a *Denver Post* reporter going from one set of depressing stories (Columbine High School massacre, Texas Seven manhunt, Environmental Protection Agency negligence at toxic waste sites) to another (U.S. Senate campaign). I needed a break. I wanted to write something my kids could read. So I called the American Birding Association, which is based in my home state of Colorado, and asked for the names of some of the most accomplished birders in North America. I ended up on the phone with a New Jersey industrial contractor who had a voice that started about three floors below the basement. From him I learned for the first time that some people are so obsessed with birds that they actually compete to see them. Competitive birdwatching – what a wild concept! Sandy Komito was so much fun – and so unlike the Miss Jane Hathaway stereotype of birders – that I had to find out more about the 1998 Big Year competition. After talking with Al Levantin and Greg Miller about their Big Year adventures, I was hooked.

How did you pick Sandy Komito, Al Levantin, and Greg Miller to write about?
They picked themselves. This was the only time in history that three people saw at least 700 species in one year. Though others attempted a Big Year in 1998, Komito, Levantin, and Miller were so far ahead of everyone else that they only worried about one another. The more I found out about these

men and their life stories, the more I liked them, both as people and characters.

How many birders do a Big Year?

Every year dozens of birders manage to see more than 500 species, but only a handful have the time, money, and drive to attempt to break the Big Year record for North America. Because the logistics of a North American Big Year are so formidable, many more birders scale back their dreams and compete in a smaller landscape. Hundreds do Big Years in their home states; thousands chase birds in their home counties. Even more common is a Big Day, a 24-hour marathon that, in big states like Texas and California, sometimes includes rides on chartered planes and helicopters. For some, the urge to compete is irrepressible. At age eighty-one, Leroy Jensen of California grew too infirm to chase many birds afield. So he did his Big Year on television, taping and watching 1,800 shows and listing 1,136 species worldwide. For him, the Discovery Channel produced even more rarities than Attu. He feared competitors with satellite dishes.

Are you a birder?

When I began this project, I was more interested in writing about obsession. Most people live their lives with the brakes on. What happens when someone spends a year surrendering to the one thing he always wanted to do? But the more time I spent in the field with Sandy Komito, Al Levantin, and Greg Miller, the more their enthusiasm for birds rubbed off on me. The three men in *The Big Year* were so refreshing. They carried an infectious zest for life, an indestructible sense of optimism that was too seductive for me to resist. I surrendered. I went native. I am a birder.

Why birds? What is it about this one animal that inspires such incredible devotion?
I tried asking that question of these three guys a million different ways. Finally one cut me off and asked, "Why did you fall in love with your wife?" I came to conclude that obsession, passion, is something you can't put into words. You just feel it. Birds are beautiful creatures with amazing life stories. Stalking them is fun. Birding exercises your brains and your legs, and it's one of the few outdoor activities that can be simultaneously enjoyed by children, grandparents, and other alleged adults.

What about cheating? How does anyone really know that Sandy Komito, Al Levantin, and Greg Miller really saw all those birds?
Much of my newspaper career was spent covering politicians which made me naturally skeptical about any claim offered by someone in the throes of competition. So I gave the men of *The Big Year* the once-over twice. Whenever possible, I called witnesses to verify claims of birds seen in the field. (Because of the popularity of Web-based rare bird alerts, many tough species are descended upon by dozens of birders.) When the Big Year competitors in their field journals listed weather conditions and times of sunrise, sunset, and moonrise, I checked their reports against National Weather Service records. I checked hotel and restaurant receipts. I also asked each competitor about the others' Big Year lists. After all this work, I could not find a single case of fraud. I did, however, find some awe-inspiring cases of honesty. In a September trip to the northernmost reaches of North America, Sandy Komito thought he might have seen a Ross's gull in the fog of the Arctic Sea off Barrow, Alaska. But he couldn't be sure. So a few weeks later he retraced his contrails from New Jersey back

to Alaska to definitively record this bird. Would a cheater do that? As Al Levantin once told me, "Why do you do a Big Year? There's no cash prize, no trophy, no trip to Disneyland for the winner. If you cheat in a Big Year, who are you cheating?" I ended up concluding that, for these three men, the Big Year contest was as much about honor and integrity as it was about winning. I wish I could cover a political campaign like that!

What's it like to be with these guys in the field?
Thrilling and exhausting. It's thrilling because they always seem to identify birds before I spot or hear anything; they make me feel like a kid in the audience at a magic show. Birding with them is also exhausting, because they never, ever give up. There's always one more bush, one more tree, one more cattail that just might hold one more bird. When I was driving with Greg Miller across southeastern Arizona, he started compiling a new list of species every time we crossed into a new county – or turned onto a new road.

Do these guys really appreciate nature or is birding for them little more than a game?
Big Year birding is not typical birding. It's a game of beat-the-clock in the bush. Though all three men loved the challenge of competitive birding, they also grew weary of the mad scramble. I think each man ended the year proud of what he had accomplished, but grateful to be done with it. Like all avid birders, they longed for a leisurely day in the field. I've seen Sandy Komito, Al Levantin, and Greg Miller bask in very long looks at very common species. They love birds, and they love the outdoors.